MACDONALD GUIDE TO

BUYING ANTIQUE

POTTERY & PORCELAIN

MACDONALD GUIDE TO

BUYING ANTIQUE

POTTERY & PORCELAIN

Rachael Feild

Wallace-Homestead Book Company
Radnor, Pennsylvania

A Macdonald Book

© Rachael Feild 1987

First published in Great Britain in 1987
by Macdonald & Co (Publishers) Ltd
London & Sydney

Published in United States of America by
Wallace-Homestead Book Company, Radnor, Pennsylvania
19089

Library of Congress Cataloging-in-Publication Data

Feild, Rachael
   Macdonald guide to buying antique pottery & porcelain /
Rachael Feild.
         p.   cm.
   Bibliography: p. 171
   Includes index.
   ISBN 0-87069-539-8
   1. Pottery, English. 2. Pottery—Collectors and collecting.
 3. Porcelain, English. 4. Porcelain—Collectors and collecting.
 I. Title. II. Title: Buying antique pottery & porcelain.
 III. Title: Buying antique pottery and porcelain.
 NK4085.F45   1989
 738'.0942'075—dc20   89-5742
                                                      CIP

Filmset by MS Filmsetting Limited, Frome, Somerset

Printed and bound in Great Britain by
BPCC Paulton Books Limited

Editor: Catherine Rubinstein
Designer: Nancy Chase

Macdonald & Co (Publishers) Ltd
66-73 Shoe Lane
London EC4P 4AB

Contents

Acknowledgments

Grateful thanks are due to the following for their considerable generosity in helping the author and providing illustrations and photographs:

Sotheby's, New Bond Street, London. European Ceramics Department.
Sotheby's, Summers Place, Billingshurst.
Sotheby's, Chester.
Woolley & Wallis, Castle Street, Salisbury.
Christie, Manson & Woods Ltd, King Street, London.
The Fitzwilliam Museum, Cambridge.
The City Museum and Art Gallery, Stoke-on-Trent.
The Antique Dealer & Collectors Guide photographic library.
Trevor Lawrence, for line drawings.

The author is particularly grateful to Ann Morris for her time, trouble, encouragement, helpful research and correction in the compiling of this book.

An introduction to collecting

When people in England first began to collect china, there was no question of anyone collecting such a base and lowly material as pottery, unless it were a collection of archaeological bits and pieces – sherds and fragments of pots from classical antiquity. In the seventeenth and eighteenth centuries – and most of the nineteenth as well – china was porcelain of one sort or another, made in the Far East, or on the Continent and, eventually, in England. The enormous amount of other materials was lumped together under the heading 'pottery' and for generations was considered to be crude stuff, not worthy of attention, much less of study. And so the two fields have grown apart, with specialists and collectors gradually investigating the many and varied products of Staffordshire as well as the strictly limited and rarefied porcelain objects which were mainly made in the eighteenth century. The development of pottery and porcelain is therefore a perplexing story, and one very important category, that of stoneware and its many variations, is often left out entirely, although it forms some of the most important links between the two fields.

There are, however, many landmarks in the development of bodies, pastes, glazes and designs which are familiar to almost everyone with the smallest interest in the subject. Just where they fit into the general picture is often difficult to discover, for this is the world of the specialist collector, and all too often one narrow field is studied in isolation, unrelated to the broad sweep of history.

Here, then, is a review of all the key developments from early delft to creamware, through the jumbled maze of stonewares and later nineteenth-century ironstones to bone china. The parallel developments at every stage are laid out, showing how the ultimate aim of all English pottery and porcelain factories was eventually achieved. That aim was to produce some kind of 'china' which, in appearance at least, was as close to Chinese porcelain as possible.

In order to demonstrate all the potteries' endeavours in the development of bodies, pastes, glazes and decoration, the Oriental theme is used as a guiding thread through the chapters covering the progression from early blue and white delftware in the seventeenth century to the brightly coloured Japan patterns of the nineteenth century. The story that emerges is a repetitive one, returning over and over again to the ultimate aim of reproducing the coveted, delicate translucency of Chinese porcelain. Once the sequence of development has been firmly grasped, other important periods in style and decoration can be understood with much less difficulty. Recognizable shapes and patterns emerge, as fashion influenced the makers of pottery, stoneware and porcelain – the delicate wares of Meissen and Dresden, the deep blues and formal patterns of Vincennes and Sèvres, the recurring motifs of flowers and birds, figures and landscapes, culminating in the development of blue and white transfer-printing, which brought blue and white tableware to every home in Britain and was exported all over the world.

Once identified, each 'family' of pottery, stoneware or porcelain is set in its historical context, with a summary of the variations which look similar and may confuse an enthusiastic beginner who has a shape or pattern firmly in the mind's eye and not enough knowledge to be warned by other vital clues to authenticity.

The great delight in collecting English pottery and porcelain lies in its complexity. On the Continent, where hard paste porcelain was made from the beginning of the eighteenth century, collecting is largely a matter of recognizing the marks and periods of the various factories, and being prepared to dig deep into the pocket. In England, geologically deprived of deposits of china clay and china stone – the vital ingredients of porcelain, which are only found in one remote corner of the British Isles – inventiveness and skill produced an enormous variety of wares, many of which have been largely ignored until recently. Pottery and porcelain were made to be used and admired – every day, from some dining room cupboard or kitchen dresser, unrecorded pieces of pottery, porcelain and, most particularly, fine stonewares find their way on to the market. Discoveries can still be made – prices need not be too high to start a collection. Armed with a real general knowledge of the whole wide spectrum, it will be easier to identify lesser-known pieces, and to appreciate those outside the reach of all but the wealthy few. Above all, a basic knowledge will set you on the right path, and enable you to ask the right questions and choose the right specialist books which will deepen and enrich your knowledge of English pottery, stoneware and porcelain.

English pottery and porcelain

It is tea-time. The Queen Anne table is laid and round it sits an elegant family, drinking tea from delicate Oriental tea bowls. It is obvious that the tea is extremely hot by the way they hold their tea bowls – they nip the foot-rim with their fingers, or hold the bowl gingerly between finger and thumb on rim and base. The date is about 1730, the artist probably Richard Collins. On the table is a silver teapot on a stand, a hot water jug, a tea canister and a sugar bowl – all in finest Queen Anne silver, because at that time there was no porcelain being made in England and, it has been said, the English could not make teapots which would withstand the heat of boiling water, except in silver.

There are few pictorial records of tea-drinking in England before the reign of Queen Anne, but tea was certainly being consumed, though in small quantities, from the time the East India Company was founded in 1600. Silver teapots were used by fashionable and aristocratic households, while in the families of much-travelled merchants and sea captains, small red stoneware teapots imported from China were probably more common. But since in those days a

Left *Straight-sided early 18th-century London tin glazed earthenware mug or tankard decorated with birds, flowers and insects. 6¾ in (17 cm) high.*

Above *Round-bellied jug with simple decoration, London c.1650–75, decorated in blue and brown. Earthenware jugs seldom had lips until the 18th century.*

pound of tea cost more than a year's wages for an artisan, and the price of a teapot equalled a farm labourer's annual family subsidy, the demand for either was small and the price too high for 95 per cent of England's population.

In 1730, however, there were over 2,000 chocolate and coffee houses in London and at least 64 pleasure gardens where the populace could sit and watch the passing parade of fashionable society, drinking tea

Ring-handled jug or vase with boldly painted bird in blue and brown from the late 16th century.

Above *Lambeth fuddling cup with decoration in blue, brown and yellow, c.1680.*

Right *Drab-coloured Fulham stoneware mug with the ribbed neck dipped in thick brown slip before firing, c.1685. 4 in (10 cm) high.*

Rare Bristol puzzle jug c.1760 with neck pierced with concentric rings. Most puzzle jugs were made in Liverpool.

and listening to music in the open air. Neither the public tea gardens nor the rowdier coffee houses would have been prepared to outlay a great deal of money buying expensive Oriental porcelain, only to have it cracked and broken by their customers. It would seem that perhaps too little attention has been paid to the activities of English potteries in the long years before fashionable porcelain makers began to supply the wealthy with delicate chinaware towards the middle of the eighteenth century.

The Early Years: a backward nation

The story behind English pottery and porcelain is one of intrigue and rivalry, of secrecy and industrial espionage – of men whose knowledge of chemistry and physics was surprisingly great, and whose paranoia over each successive invention was such that they would go to any lengths to protect themselves from their competitors. They had no guild to regulate the flow of knowledge inside their trade, or to protect them from having their secrets stolen. So they took out patents on their discoveries, and fought lengthy legal battles in defence of their validity, mainly to no avail.

In essence, pottery- and porcelain-making are sciences, and endless difficulties were encountered in arriving at a suitable substance which would withstand the required heat in the kilns so that the glaze could fuse to the body. Different glazes vitrify, or become glassy, at different temperatures, and obviously the clay body must be compatible in order that this change can take place. The fuels used for firing kilns and furnaces burn at varying heats: charcoal only reaches a relatively low temperature, coal achieves a greater heat, and coke the greatest. Most potteries, glass-houses and metal-workers in the southern part of England used charcoal, at least until the end of the seventeenth century. It has been said that the technique of firing kilns with coal only reached England in about 1752, yet in Staffordshire the potteries had been using coal for centuries, and English ironmasters were firing their furnaces with coke as early as 1709.

Until the great canal-building revolution of the second half of the eighteenth century, England was an island of islands – small pockets of industry and manufacturing which were more or less self-contained, and about which the rest of the country knew little or nothing. The wealthiest part of England lay within a triangle marked out by London, Bristol and Norwich. Roads were few, and virtually impassable for heavy waggons for most of the year. It took 10 days to travel from London to Newcastle by road, and 6 days to Chester. If loads could not be carried by pack animals, they had to be sent by sea round the coast, or travel by barge up and down the few rivers that were navigable. The countryside consisted largely of undrained swampy land and huge tracts of scrubby forest. Where there was coal there were colonies of miners – often lawless, rough communities, isolated and for the most part living in conditions of appalling hardship. The exception was Newcastle, where the citizens grew rich on coal, which went by sea to London. The port of London was always jammed with fleets of colliers and, south of the river, tar was used in the shipyards and rope factories. In the Pennines, lead miners worked in atrocious conditions, with the added hazard of dying of lead poisoning, a danger which was well known by the seventeenth century. Where there was good clay there were brick kilns, and in and around the brick fields there were often potteries too. But the brick fields were also rough havens for vagrants and out-of-work labourers, where law-abiding citizens seldom ventured.

Up and down the country, where the clay was suitable and there was sufficient fuel, local potteries made mugs, jugs, dishes, bowls, crocks and pots for preserving, salting and soaking meat, fish, hams and bacon. The most common glaze used for making earthenware non-porous was made from lead, and the disadvantages of lead glaze were also well known: pickling liquids made from vinegar or acid fruit juices could dissolve the lead oxide in the glaze and make a deadly solution.

Spouted Lambeth posset pot with serpent handles dated 1687.

Teapots and Butter Pots

Mr Simeon Shaw, writing in 1829 about the origins of the Staffordshire potteries, remarked that 'we cannot help indulging in conjecture, that the Kindling of Fires, the Baking of Bread, the Formation of Butter and Cheese, the Working of Metals and the Burning of Clay into Bricks were practices coeval with the want of these articles by the human family.' He added that 'Man would soon feel the necessity of possessing Vessels to use for food, drink or occasional refreshment. . . . Indeed, unless we admit that they possessed vessels

Lambeth posset pot or loving cup with a turned base, decorated with crowns and fleur de lys.

Two Liverpool moulded wall-pockets, c.1750 with a rather stilted shape and c.1760 showing curving rococo influence.

Liverpool flower brick c.1760. Those made in Bristol usually had straight bases with four small feet.

of different kinds by which they could convey liquor to the mouth, we cannot readily account for the prevalent intemperance of the Ancients.' He might have added 'the Drinking of Tea' to his list of necessities, for many developments in pottery and porcelain have hinged on the discovery of suitable clays, glazes and colour pigments with which to manufacture and decorate all the paraphernalia which went with the custom of tea-drinking.

In England, the earliest teapots made were in red stoneware, in imitation of the little Chinese teapots that were shipped into the country by the East India Company. The first recorded attempts at making red stoneware were by John Dwight, a potter in Fulham, who took out a patent in 1684 for making 'red porcelayne' and other stonewares, firing his furnaces with coal, which was readily available to his pottery on the banks of the River Thames. Whether he ever succeeded in making 'red porcelayne' is in some doubt, but within a few years his secret was stolen by the Elers brothers. Originally from Nuremburg, where metals were smelted with coal, the Elers brothers had a good knowledge of pottery and silversmithing, and soon after they arrived in England in 1685 they travelled to Staffordshire. By 1690 they were making both 'red porcelayne' and 'black porcelayne' by adding manganese to the clay body. John Dwight later sued them for infringement of his patent but, as several other Staffordshire potteries had been making variations of stoneware for a considerable time, he was unsuccessful.

The Elers brothers in turn had their secret pirated by John Astbury, one of Staffordshire's most talented and inventive potters, in spite of all the precautions they took. They installed themselves in an isolated spot at Bradwell, near Burslem, and employed 'only the most stupid and ignorant persons' as workmen, who were locked in during working hours and searched every time they left the premises. John Astbury duly presented himself, suitably dressed 'with all proper vacancy of countenance' and was taken on at the pottery. He kept up his disguise for about 18 months, during which time he made notes, sketches and models of all the machinery, including an 'engine lathe' operated by foot treadle. When he felt there was no more to be learned, he 'threw a fit of sickness' and returned home. A short time later he began making red stoneware teapots, which, at between 12 and 24 shillings apiece, represented a very profitable line. Later he brought white pipeclay from Bideford in Devon to Staffordshire, loaded on pack horses, and decorated his red stoneware in white applied relief.

Elsewhere in Staffordshire, and in Derbyshire, Kent, Sussex and Devon, local potters made basic domestic articles in reddish-brown clay decorated with white slip, or dipped in white slip to give the earthenware a cream-coloured coating, over which thick dark brown slip was trailed in intricate patterns raised in relief. This slipware was glazed with a very basic lead glaze which discoloured the white slip, turning it a streaky yellow when fired. Most local potteries also made quantities of unglazed or 'unleaded' butter pots in various sizes to contain anything from 1 pound to 14 pounds of butter to be sent to market. The unglazed pots were not ideal containers, but the dangers of lead in the glaze had been recognized, and clearly there was a need to develop some other glaze which was less lethal.

Tin Glazed Earthenware: functional and decorative

The tin mines of Cornwall were one of the few known sources for tin in the whole of Europe, and a thriving trade had existed with most of the Mediterranean countries since earliest times. The Phoenicians used to trade Irish gold for tin, to make bronze as well as tin glazed earthenware – using a technique that had originated in the Near East and had been developed by the Italians into a fine art to produce ware known as 'maiolica'. Yet the English themselves had made very little use of tin, nor was any tin glazed earthenware made in England before two Flemish potters, Andries and Jansen, came to England from Antwerp in 1567 and set up a pottery in Norwich, where there were colonies of emigré Flemish weavers and craftsmen. Using clays from Norfolk and Suffolk, Andries and Jansen began to supply apothecaries with drug jars, ointment pots, pill slabs and syrup jars, glazed with a brilliant white glaze in which the lead was fixed and would not dissolve with the action of acids and potions.

In 1571 Jansen and Andries moved to Aldgate, and other galley-ware potteries established themselves up and down the banks of the Thames, among them Lambeth and Southwark. Their main stock in trade remained apothecaries' ware, but by the end of the century they were making decorative chargers and plates, mugs, jugs and flasks for wine. Similar potteries were set up at Brislington and in and around Bristol soon after the East India Company began trading in 1600. There was good clay in the neighbourhood, tin came by sea from Cornwall, and there was lead in the Mendips for the basis of the glaze.

Without exception, all tin glazed earthenware made in England until the end of the seventeenth century was decorated with blue, using cobalt pigment. Cobalt pigment was discovered in Saxony in about 1545, and was imported ready-prepared, to decorate the brilliant white tin glazed earthenware. It is no accident that almost every stage in the development of Oriental porcelain, as well as English pottery and English porcelain, began with a range of blue and white wares. Most colour pigments behave unpredictably when subjected to the heat of the kilns. Some change colour completely, while others darken or lighten out of all recognition. Cobalt pigment, however, behaves in a completely consistent manner, changing from its natural brownish state to a brilliant blue when fired.

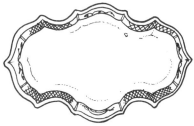

Trinket or spoon tray with silver shape and diaper border, Liverpool c.1750.

Slowly, and with experience, as the potteries discovered that other metallic oxides could be used to produce colour pigments, more colours were brought in to decorate delftware. Yellow from antimony was used, though sparsely, on apothecaries' ware, followed by reds from iron oxides, a range of pinks, purples and black from manganese oxide, and a more difficult green from copper oxide. The growing range of colours was gradually introduced for an increasing range of decorative and commemorative plates, dishes and chargers in most of the galleyware potteries from about 1620 onwards. Tin glazed earthenware was very colourful and attractive, but it was not strong enough for everyday use. The glaze was soft and easily damaged, and the earthenware itself chipped and cracked. Nor, since it was unable to withstand the heat of boiling water, was it suitable for teapots and coffee pots. Examples of delftware teapots have survived, mainly decorated in Chinese-type patterns, but it is likely that these were more decorative than functional.

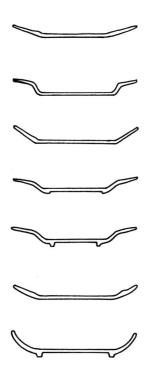

Early pottery plate and dish shapes. Top to bottom *With no foot rim c.1650–90, Lambeth c.1690–1780, Bristol and Liverpool 1710–70, standard pattern c.1730 onwards, Lambeth and Bristol dish c.1710–50, standard dish pattern c.1730 onwards, standard saucer pattern c.1730 onwards.*

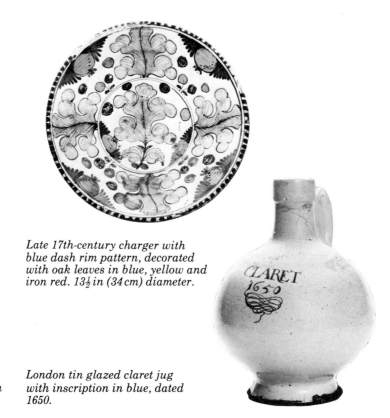

Late 17th-century charger with blue dash rim pattern, decorated with oak leaves in blue, yellow and iron red. 13½ in (34 cm) diameter.

London tin glazed claret jug with inscription in blue, dated 1650.

Bankrupt for Blue and White

Oriental porcelain, mainly Ming blue and white, had been coming into England even since the East India Company began trading. By the time William and Mary succeeded to the English throne in 1689, collecting Chinese blue and white porcelain had become such a passion that at least one great aristocratic family was virtually bankrupted by the huge cost of financing trading ships to bring back cargoes of Oriental porcelain. William's queen had an entire room set aside at Hampton Court to display her vast collection of Chinese blue and white and Dutch delft, and great English families displayed their smaller collections with more pride than silver on the high corner chimneypieces and on shelves of elaborate buffets and court cupboards.

English potteries began to copy the distinctive designs on Oriental porcelain in blue and white. If the earthenware body was coarse and heavy, with little resemblance to the delicate translucency of Chinese porcelain, at least it could deceive the eye. In Bristol, where cargoes of porcelain were unloaded from ships of the East India

Rare Lowestoft blue and white soft paste porcelain tea bowl decorated with flying cranes and insects, c.1758–9. 8½ in (21.5 cm) in diameter.

Large blue and white dish in Chinese porcelain decorated with a bird, flowering plants and peonies, surrounded with panels of diaper patterns and flowering peaches on the rim. Ming period c.1640. 18½ in (47 cm) diameter.

Company's fleets, decorators of tin glazed earthenware studied the curious images of rocks and peonies, weeping willows and prunus blossom, and reproduced them with increasing skill on the difficult powdery surface of the unfired white glaze. In Staffordshire, where no tin was available, the potteries began their long search for a white-bodied clay which would withstand the heat of boiling water, and for a glaze which would not discolour when fired, nor release its lethal lead content as a result of chemical changes.

In about 1690, Staffordshire potteries discovered that common salt would vaporize and fuse to the surface of stoneware when the kilns reached their greatest heat. Vitrified salt glazed stoneware in drab greyish or brownish colours, similar to John Dwight's Fulham stoneware, was made in considerable quantities for domestic crocks and pots, wine flasks, jugs and mugs. Further experiments with purifying the clay body and using refined calcined flint eventually led to a near-white salt glazed stoneware which could withstand the heat

White salt glazed stoneware coffee pot decorated with chinoiserie scenes, with a dragon spout.

Beautifully decorated inside of a rare Lowestoft blue and white tea bowl, c.1758–9. 8½ in (21.5 cm) diameter.

of boiling water. It was an enormous leap forward technically, but there was one major drawback: because the firing and glazing took place in one operation, it was not possible to produce blue and white wares. If cobalt pigment was applied to the once-fired body at the 'biscuit' stage, at the high temperatures necessary for salt glazing the cobalt pigment 'flew' or dispersed in the fumes of the kiln. Some pieces of salt glazed stoneware were decorated in blue with the ancient 'sgraffito' technique, known as 'scratch blue', but on the whole this technique was not a great success. It was not until the K'ang Hsi polychrome enamels of 'famille rose' and 'famille verte' became fashionable in about 1720 that English salt glazed teapots were made and used in any quantities.

Precious blue and white Oriental porcelain mug mounted in silver with a fruitwood handle, c.1675–1700.

English Porcelain: the missing ingredients

If the countryside of England was backward and undeveloped, the same could not be said of the people. Staffordshire potters could name and recognize hundreds of different clays to be found all over the country, in much the same way as a wine taster knows a vineyard and a vintage. 'Manganesian or steatitic Clay ... stains the fingers ... when laid on the tongue it dissolves in a smooth pulp.' 'Pipe clay is of a greyish or yellowish white colour ... it adheres to the tongue; it is very plastic and tenacious.' But, as their searches seemed to prove, the two vital ingredients for making porcelain – china clay and china stone – were not present in the geological strata of the British Isles. Both these elusive substances were allied to granite, and were obviously found in plentiful supply in Germany, for in about 1710 a German factory at Meissen began to produce a porcelain that was very similar to Chinese and Oriental wares, apparently without much difficulty. Although this was a calamity at the time, it was precisely because England lacked these vital ingredients that English pottery and porcelain are so rich in alternatives which were discovered,

Lattice-rimmed Meissen dessert plate painted with lovers in a landscape. Mid-18th century. 9½ in (24 cm) diameter.

developed, used and eventually discarded in favour of 'bone china' – a purely English invention which, incidentally, was developed by the potteries and not by the porcelain makers at all.

Once Meissen porcelain began to be imported, the fashion for blue and white 'china' gave way to the latest 'famille rose' and 'famille verte' K'ang Hsi porcelain and the delicately painted and enamelled flowers and sprigs from Meissen. Merchant houses grew rich on shiploads of Meissen and Dresden and soon, adding insult to injury, on French porcelain from Vincennes. Staffordshire potteries re-doubled their efforts to develop a white body and a glaze apart from salt which would not discolour with heat. The first breakthrough came with a colourless lead glaze which was developed in about 1740 by Enoch Booth. It could be used over white-bodied earthenwares and stonewares without causing them to discolour and, moreover, could be applied after a first firing at high temperatures, at the biscuit stage.

Fine slip-moulded salt glazed stoneware dessert basket in rococo style.

The next advance was the discovery that colour pigment could be mixed with this colourless glaze compound and applied over the glaze. The piece was then fired again at a lower temperature, when the coloured glazes fused to the body glaze – a technique known as enamelling. Inevitably, it was not without its problems. Reds and purples made from iron and manganese oxides changed colour radically at different temperatures: at low temperatures, manganese turned a delicate rose pink, but as the heat increased, it darkened through shades of purple, fading to pale violet at even higher temperatures, and vanishing completely when the heat rose to 1000°C (538°F). When enamels were used over a salt glaze, the surface proved delicate and crazed easily, and the body itself became brittle after more than one firing.

Worcester basket-moulded junket dish decorated with sprigs and panels of flowers, c.1770. 9 in (23 cm) diameter.

Two figures from the famous Meissen 'Monkey Band' first made in 1747 and copied by Derby and other English porcelain factories. 5¾ in (14.5 cm) and 4¾ in (12 cm) high.

The white stoneware body was very strong and malleable in its unfired state, however, and could be twisted, shaped and pierced in wonderfully delicate shapes, particularly for such things as dessert baskets, chestnut warmers, food warmers, and plates and dishes with pierced and latticed rims. A whole range of white salt glazed stoneware was made in moulds and casts with surface decoration of quite remarkable quality and crispness, much of it following the lines of contemporary silver. The one exception to the rule was the shape of teapots, which developed in a distinctive and traditional manner, with a round body, crabstock handle and angular spout – a design that hardly changed over a period of fifty years or more.

White salt glazed stoneware teapot with moulded relief decoration of vines and leaves.

The next two decades saw an incredible surge forward in refining earthenware bodies and developing clear and coloured glazes, but in Staffordshire at least there was still no sign of those elusive elements needed for making 'true' porcelain – china clay and china stone. Since both these substances were geologically related to granite, research had begun to centre on the remoter parts of the West of England and Cornwall. Other interests outside the potteries – chemists, scientists and entrepreneurs – had become involved, and many of the hopeful contenders were connected with trade in Bristol, whose sea links with Cornwall had been established over the centuries through the brass industry, the metal-workers and the ironmasters based around the Severn estuary.

The only power available to these early pioneers of industry was water power, with wheels driven by rivers and streams, horse power, windmills, or laborious processes carried out by hand. Most of this work was extremely bad for the health, if not deadly. The men who ground calcined flint to powder risked ruining their lungs; lead was lethal; and fumes from salt glazing shrivelled the leaves on trees and plants, killed insects and put the entire community at risk. Enoch Booth, in developing his colourless lead glaze, was motivated as much by the health of his workers as by commercial necessity. Gradually, grinding and crushing mills were installed, and flint and lead were ground in water to reduce the risks of inhaling the fine powder. Larger kilns were built, and techniques were devised for stacking wares inside them so that a greater quantity could be fired at one time. But still the stoneware was not sufficiently white, and the new colourless glaze could not be fired at the same high temperature as the stoneware itself. What was needed was either an opaque white glaze which did not use tin as an ingredient and which would cover the greyish body, or a white-coloured stoneware body.

Red stoneware teapot of traditional Staffordshire shape, with applied sprigged decoration and crabstock handle.

Many potteries began experimenting with bodies composed of mixtures of different clays, as well as with glazes coloured with various metallic oxides. Stoneware was fired once at a high temperature to vitrify the body, dipped in glaze and fired again at a lower temperature. In sophisticated potteries that were decorating tea ware with enamelled colours, the wares were fired three times or more to control the colour pigments, adding considerably to the expense. Thomas Whieldon and John Astbury were among those inventive potters who experimented with mingling different-coloured clays, and in about 1740 both Whieldon and Astbury made 'solid agate' ware. One of the first uses for this strangely marbled body was for knife handles for the cutlery trade in Sheffield. Later it was used for tea ware, mugs, jugs and decorative plates.

Derby soft paste porcelain figure of 'Falstaff' with sprigged waistcoat and turquoise breeches, on swirling rococo stand, c.1765–70. 13 in (33 cm) high.

Pottery and Porcelain: the great divide 1740–50

The expanding market for tableware of all sorts continued to be monopolized by Continental factories, which were producing an increasing range of porcelain, no longer limited to richly decorated exclusive wares for the rich and noble houses, but also including great quantities of plainer, less costly wares to export to England and abroad. It was galling to the pride of the English and bad for the pockets of the potteries that the profits from all these imports went to the merchants and middlemen because there was still no home-grown porcelain industry in England. Rich markets in the colonies, too, were still not supplied with chinaware from England, and a vast export trade was not being exploited.

Chelsea leaf dish with dark green border painted with sprays of flowers and insects. Gold Anchor period, c.1756–60.

In 1745 a Plymouth chemist, William Cookworthy, at last discovered both china clay and china stone on Carloggas Moor in Cornwall. Richard Champion, a successful merchant and member of the family that had founded the Bristol Brassworks, at once expressed an interest, convinced of the commercial potential. But in order to obtain a licence to quarry these two precious substances, Cookworthy first had to take out a patent for making porcelain – an endeavour which took him over 20 years. Meanwhile, other interested parties were at work, attempting to find a substitute for china clay and china stone. Among them was another Bristol brass and copper merchant, Benjamin Lund. In 1748 or 1749 Lund, almost certainly the proprietor of 'Lodn's Glass House or China House', obtained a licence to quarry soapstone at Gew Graze near the Lizard. Shortly after he obtained his licence, he was making 'blue and white wares' at the Bristol China Works. It is also known that Edward Heylin of Bow in London was in touch with Benjamin Lund, and Heylin, too, was a brass and copper merchant.

English soft paste porcelain was composed of refined white clay

Early Derby coffee pot painted in 'famille rose' enamels with chinoiserie scenes, c.1758–60, 9 in (23 cm) high, and coffee cup with wishbone handle.

mixed with a pulverized glassy substance which gave it translucency. In about 1745, Edward Heylin had devised a formula of paste by grinding together a mixture of sand, gypsum, soda, alum, salt and nitre, melting them and fusing them into a glassy mass, which was then pulverized and mixed with a fine-bodied white clay. Bow soft paste was unable to withstand boiling water in its early stages, but it was admirably suited for making Dresden-like figures and ornamental wares. In 1749 the paste was improved by the addition of bone ash, which gave it more strength, whiteness and resistance to sudden temperature changes. By this time the Chelsea China Factory had opened in direct competition, making a series of extremely fine ornamental figures as well as a considerable range of decorative tableware after the style of Meissen.

White salt glazed stoneware slip-moulded sauce boat in a silver shape, c.1745.

In 1750 Dr Pococke of Bristol reported that he had found 'soapy rock' with 'white patches in it, which is mostly valued for making porcelane and they get five pounds a ton for it, for the manufacture of porcelane now carrying on at Bristol'. Dr Pococke also noted that the Bristol China Works 'make very beautiful white sauce boats adorned with reliefs of festoons which sell for 16 shillings a pair'. At this point, another chemist, Dr Wall from Worcester, began to see the commercial possibilities of this venture, and promptly gathered together 14 partners to form the Worcester Porcelain Company. In 1752 an advertisement announced that the Bristol China Works had amalgamated with the Worcester Porcelain Company, and they were in business, making porcelain 'in imitation of Dresden ware'. Dr Wall's formula for 'soft paste porcelain' contained soapstone and was resistant to sudden changes of heat, thus making it suitable for making teapots and coffee pots. It was an instant success commercially, and the Worcester Porcelain Company produced by far the largest output of useful wares of all the English porcelain manufactories throughout the eighteenth century.

Chelsea porcelain leaf-shaped butter boat with open scroll handle, c.1756.

All these activities in the south and west of England were in no way connected with the manufacture of 'earthenware', nor, it seems, had any of the protagonists greatly interested themselves in the laborious experiments with glazes and bodies that had been taking place in Staffordshire. The English porcelain makers established themselves in the old, traditional power-bases of commerce and wealth: Bristol, London and, soon after, Lowestoft, where there were merchants dealing in Oriental porcelain coming from the Netherlands. Only one Staffordshire pottery, under the management of William Littler, began to make soft paste porcelain, at Longton Hall in about 1749.

Leaf-shaped cream jug with twig handle made by both Chelsea and Derby, c.1750.

Unhampered by the isolation and lack of transport still holding Staffordshire back, the Worcester Porcelain Factory went from strength to strength. Well placed on the River Severn to transport raw materials from Bristol, and to carry finished goods to the growing towns and cities of the Midlands, the Worcester porcelain factory, under its shrewd management, made slow inroads into the rich market for porcelain tableware – less expensive than the costly

Continental wares, and more than acceptable in its quality, patterns and designs.

Wedgwood and Creamware: pottery rivals porcelain 1760–70

Unlike European countries, where the division between rich and poor continued to widen, England had a solid layer of middle class – merchants and professional men who grew rich in the entrepreneurial atmosphere of Georgian England. They had both the money and the desire to live in a similar manner to those at the top of the social tree, and represented a huge market for luxuries of all kinds. Nor were the earls and dukes of the realm averse to making money from trade in England. The first canal to be built by James Brindley was for Francis Egerton, the young Duke of Bridgewater, to link his coalfields directly to the growing industries of Manchester. He financed the whole operation, which was completed and opened in 1761. Shortly afterwards, with the enthusiastic encouragement of Josiah Wedgwood, the Grand Trunk Canal was built, linking the two great rivers of the Severn and the Trent, and running through the potteries.

Typical pottery handles: crabstock, scrolled, and double intertwined with leaf terminals.

Josiah Wedgwood, one of the greatest names in England's commercial history, was born into a Staffordshire family with a long tradition of pottery. Apprenticed to his brother at the age of 14, he joined Thomas Whieldon in 1754, working on experiments to improve clay bodies and making coloured glazes. In 1758 Wedgwood succeeded in producing a rich translucent green glaze, and began making a range of leaf dishes, dessert baskets and dessert plates which have been made almost continuously ever since. Three years later he succeeded in developing an opaque, richly cream-coloured glaze and, making use of an earlier discovery that light-bodied stoneware fired at lower temperatures turned almost white, produced his celebrated 'Creamware'. The glaze was too soft in its early stages, and not strong enough to stand up to daily punishment from knives and forks, but he continued to make improvements to the body and the glaze until by 1764 creamware was not only tough enough for everyday use, but of a good enough quality for grand dinner services and tableware.

Wedgwood 'Creamware' serving dish with black line and printed border pattern in sepia, with flower finial, c.1770.

Following European fashions, the English porcelain factories had been making wonderfully decorative dishes in leaf shapes, translucent and sparkling with clear bright enamelled colours, as well as tureens and serving dishes in the shape of melons, lettuces, pineapples and other exotic fruits, and basket-moulded and latticed game dishes, often with a partridge modelled in high relief on the lid. Wedgwood's range of green glazed leaf dishes did not really compete with their porcelain equivalents, but a hint of the coming clash came with his 'cauliflower ware', for which he used his two coloured glazes, the cream and the green, in spectacular shapes of fruit and vegetables in creamware.

In 1769 Wedgwood went into partnership with Thomas Bentley, and their new factory at Burslem began to make creamware in large quantities, simply decorated with border patterns which were hand-painted in enamels and extremely attractive. Queen Charlotte, George III's wife, commissioned an entire dinner service from Wedgwood and, delighted with the accolade, he promptly renamed his creamware 'Queen's Ware' in her honour. Queen Charlotte was a homely person and cared very little for court ceremony: it is said that she liked nothing better than a quiet evening at home with George toasting muffins while she fried the sprats. So it was much in character that she should have preferred an honest English creamware to fashionable, highly decorated foreign porcelain.

Pale cream-coloured creamware jug with mask spout and pierced neckband, decorated with stripes of green under the glaze, Leeds, c.1775. 3 in (7.5 cm) high.

The period between 1750 and 1770 saw every fashionable design made in English porcelain from moulded silver shapes to bright 'Japan' patterns and the rich 'gros bleu' of Sèvres. Financially secure, well managed, and with a formula of paste that was consistent and reliable, the Worcester Porcelain Factory had captured the bulk of the market for tableware. The Chelsea China Works was less fortunate – there was trouble with the ingredients of their soft paste and production was halted for two years between 1756 and 1758. When it was resumed, the formula for the paste was changed to include a certain amount of bone ash – an ingredient used at Bow

Below right *Creamware teapot and cover with beaded borders, printed and painted in enamels and signed 'Greatbach', c.1775. 5¼ in (13.5 cm) high.*

since 1750. But during the two-year stoppage, Chelsea lost some of its skilled workers to Bow, who reaped the benefit of Chelsea's troubles. In spite of financial difficulties, Chelsea porcelain made between 1758 and 1769 was undoubtedly some of the finest ever made in England. The colours in particular were unequalled by any other English manufacturer of the time, the modelling of ornaments and figures was quite exceptional, and the quality of the paste was harder, denser and more translucent. But the factory never fully recovered from its financial setbacks, and its troubles continued throughout the 1760s. In 1769 the Chelsea China Works finally closed down, having lost more of its workers, this time to Worcester, during its last years.

Early painted version of willow pattern on a tin glazed blue and white marriage plate dated 1754.

Davenport stoneware version with two birds swimming in the foreground.

The Narrowing Gap 1770–80

In the mid-eighteenth century, the traditional centres of manufacture and commerce were still hidebound by ancient guilds and restrictions, but the towns which grew into cities from the 1750s onwards had no such fetters on their progress. Bristol now began to lose its position as one of England's major shipping ports to Liverpool, which had been quietly growing in importance since the beginning of the century. A delftware pottery had been established in Liverpool in about 1710 to make tin glazed earthenware for the local population, and in 1756 Richard Chaffers of Liverpool advertised a range of soapstone porcelain. Soft paste porcelain was also made in Liverpool at about that time, but it was not of tremendously high quality and had a dull, greyish appearance. High-quality tin glazed wares, however, were still being made in Liverpool in the 1760s, and once the port began to flourish, the pottery specialized in huge great punchbowls decorated with ships in full sail.

Leeds transfer-printed blue and white willow pattern.

In 1772 the Grand Union Canal was completed, joining the Severn

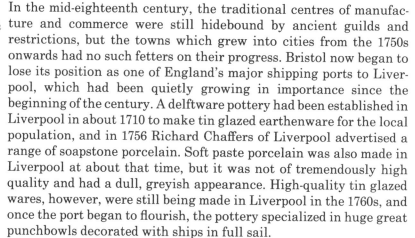

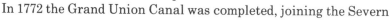

with the Mersey, and the last link was forged in the chain of raw materials, manufacturers and markets. Competing ranges of Worcester porcelain and creamware from the potteries were unleashed on a population for so long and so incredibly deprived of ordinary 'china plates'. Newspapers and journals packed with advertisements were printed in every neighbourhood, and news travelled fast. A lady in Newcastle-upon-Tyne ordered a dinner service with 'an arabesque border' direct from Wedgwood's factory, impatient with her local retailer who had not heard of this latest fashion from London. The cost of transport fell dramatically. It was four times cheaper to send goods down the inland waterways than overland by road, and a great deal safer for breakable loads of pottery and porcelain.

At last it was possible for thousands of ordinary households in

One of a set of Chinese export tea and sugar vases decorated with Oriental versions of armorials, with Korean lion finials.

Transfer-printed border patterns from (top to bottom) *Ralph Stevenson & Williams, Cobridge; J. & J. Jackson, Burslem; and J. & W. Ridgway, Hanley.*

England to replace their pewter plates and horn mugs with china tableware. The demand for tea ware soared, the size of teapots increased, and a great number of potteries were engaged in making teacups with handles instead of tea bowls. In Staffordshire, where tea was taken in a curious fashion, cups and saucers were sold with 'cup plates' so that genteel provincial ladies could 'saucer their tay' and put the cup down on a plate to prevent it marking the table while they sipped tea from their saucers.

Transfer-Printing: inexpensive decoration

Josiah Wedgwood was an irascible employer, a hard taskmaster and an extremely astute businessman. He installed the first 'clocking in' device in his factories, bemoaned the fact that his workers needed to take time off for meals, and carried out regular inspections of his products. Any pieces he deemed defective he would smash with his walking stick in front of the offending worker. He walked with a limp all his life, and some say it was his wooden leg that he used like a club in later life to reduce substandard pieces to smithereens. At an early stage in the development of his creamware, he was extremely concerned with the cost of decoration. He kept the number of colours down to a bare minimum but, although the artists became extremely skilled and incredibly fast at their work, it soon became impossible to keep up with demand unless he hired dozens more artists, which would have greatly increased the cost of creamware.

At the Worcester Porcelain factory, where the management was equally efficient but the decoration far more lavish, the problem was much more acute. Not only were the artists themselves extremely expensive, but each enamel had to be fired at different temperatures, adding considerably to the cost. Both Worcester and Wedgwood saw the possibilities of printing on the surface of glazed ware, a technique which had already been used successfully on enamels, and in due course both manufactories instigated enquiries into the process.

There is conflicting evidence as to the origins of this technique. One body of evidence has it that an Irish engraver named John Brooks took out a patent for a transfer-printing process to be used at the Birmingham enamel factory in 1753. Alternatively, it is said that the technique of using engraved copper plates originated at the Battersea enamel factory, where it was introduced, again by John

A set of six Derby coffee cans painted with landscapes, within gilt line panels, c.1796–1806.

Brooks, in 1753. It was also said that this process had been used at Bow for printing on porcelain. What is certain is that Robert Hancock, maker of engraved copper plates for book illustrations, perfected the technique in 1754, when the first of his engravings appeared on Bow porcelain, on Battersea enamel ware, and on some trial pieces of Worcester porcelain.

Quite independently, as they later swore on oath, two Liverpool men, Sadler and Green, were making transfer-printed tiles in about 1756. Josiah Wedgwood had certainly heard of their transfer-printing process, and as soon as he had perfected the body and glaze of his creamware, he began sending cartloads of undecorated wares to them in Liverpool to be decorated with printed border patterns. In the first years of production between 1761 and 1764 it seems that he sent crates of creamware to Mrs Astbury to be hand-painted in rather simple unsophisticated border patterns, more typical of traditional Staffordshire ware. As soon as Wedgwood and Bentley opened their new premises at Burslem in 1769, Sadler and Green were taken on to the permanent staff, to work exclusively for Wedgwood. Among the many fine transfer-printed designs produced after this date were some very passable imitations of the fabulous birds from the atelier of James Giles, which Chelsea and Worcester had used to decorate their porcelain only a few years earlier.

Creamware was not just a success in England. Exports boomed, and cargoes of creamware were shipped from Liverpool to the colonies, and from the eastern seaports across to Europe, where there was no 'china' for the middle market, only expensive hard paste porcelain for the rich, and tin glazed faience and maiolica were the only alternatives. Canals carried raw materials and coal to the potteries and took crates of finished goods to the ports for export, and

Blue and white transfer-printed plate borders. Top to bottom *Floral by Ridgway; Oriental birds and animals, Spode; columbine and honeysuckle, Clews; and country garden, Heath.*

Above left *Creamware sauce tureen from a Wedgwood 'Queen's Ware' dinner service decorated with sepia printed outlines and green painted leaves, with a flower finial, c.1770.*

to the big merchants' warehouses the length and breadth of England. Dozens of Staffordshire potteries were making creamware, and by 1770 the production of white salt glazed stoneware and cream-coloured earthenware had virtually ceased. And yet, for all its commercial success, creamware was not considered to be close enough to 'true' porcelain, and many people, including Josiah Wedgwood, believed that their products could be wonderfully impro-ved by the addition of those two elusive ingredients, china clay and china stone.

Hard Paste Porcelain: brief success and swift demise

At about the same time as Josiah Wedgwood was perfecting the body and glaze of his creamware, William Cookworthy finally succeeded in taking out a patent for making hard paste porcelain, and thus obtained a licence to quarry the two minerals from Lord Camelford's land on Carloggas Moor in Cornwall. That licence effectively de-barred anyone else from access to the only deposits of the two substances in the whole of the British Isles – ironically, at a time when the first strands in the network of canals would have made it possible for china clay and china stone to be carried by waterborne transport to the potteries in Staffordshire.

In 1768 Cookworthy established the 'Plymouth New Invented Porcelain Company' and began to make the first 'true' porcelain in England. But hard paste porcelain, the unattainable translucent paste from which Oriental 'china' was made, was not easy to manufacture. The paste had to mature for a considerable length of time in order to allow certain chemical changes to occur. Then it had to be fired at extremely high temperatures so that the glaze, which contained pulverized china stone, could fuse to the body and acquire the necessary translucency. William Cookworthy, a skilled chemist, did succeed in making a small quantity of hard paste porcelain at Plymouth – mainly figures and ornamental wares – for a very brief period between 1768 and 1771. But there were too many problems with the paste, the glaze and, above all, the financial position of the Plymouth factory; although he clung on for a few more years, in 1774 Cookworthy finally succumbed to Richard Champion's offer to take over both patent and licence, which still had eight years to run. Champion had waited patiently for a long time to get his hands on the precious ingredients. As soon as the deal was complete, he transfer-red the Plymouth manufactory to Bristol, where he still confidently expected to make his fortune.

Swirl-moulded Worcester tea service from the Flight & Barr period, c.1792–1807.

Instead of the long-awaited success, Champion met with nothing but trouble. Many of the wares collapsed in on themselves, or cracked and shattered in the kilns. The paste itself was only left to mature for six months – the Chinese left theirs for decades, during which certain elements decayed and fused together, resulting in exquisite translu-cency combined with extraordinary strength. But unlike Cookworthy,

Champion was no chemist – and he was in a hurry to make his fortune. It seems that his workmen compounded his problems by attempting to follow the 'Chinese sequence' of firing, instead of the traditional English sequence. The Chinese sequence entailed firing the paste at a very low temperature, then coating it with glaze and firing it again at a very high temperature. Since Champion's paste had a tendency to soften at some stage during the second firing, the wares collapsed and subsequently shattered in the kiln.

Concerned by his slow progress, and still determined to succeed in spite of his worsening financial state, Richard Champion applied to have his patent extended in 1774. It was due to expire in 1782, and after a bitter battle in the courts he succeeded in getting it extended for a further 14 years. But he met with considerable opposition, notably from Josiah Wedgwood, on the grounds that natural raw materials were being denied to the potteries. The final terms granted to Champion were that china stone and china clay should be prohibited to all makers of translucent porcelain, but that they could be used by any pottery making non-translucent wares. And so it was that Josiah Wedgwood and John Turner, another extremely talented potter, were free to buy supplies of china clay and china stone. They travelled to Cornwall, fully expecting to be met with violence by the tin miners, who were up in arms against the potteries for replacing pewter with 'china' and thus causing the price of tin to drop disastrously. But in the event they were met with great civility, and arranged for regular supplies of both ingredients to be sent up to Staffordshire.

Swansea cabaret tray painted in colours with 'Billingsley roses', c.1814–17.

Sucrier and saucer from a Worcester tea service decorated with sprigs of flowers in puce, green and gilt. Flight & Barr period, c.1792–1807.

Five years later, in 1780, Richard Champion was in such dire straits that he offered, cap in hand, to sell Wedgwood his lease, patent and 'the secret of making China', but was curtly turned down. In the intervening years, Wedgwood had produced a much-improved body for creamware, incorporating both china clay and china stone, which he called 'pearlware'. His heart was not entirely made of stone, for although he turned poor Richard Champion down, he gave him the names of other Staffordshire potters who might be interested in buying him out.

A small group of brave men took over Champion's patent in 1781, with 15 years to run. They opened the New Hall Porcelain Company and made a small success out of their venture, producing a fine range of tea ware for a select market. The main reason why they succeeded where Champion had failed was their adoption of the traditional English sequence of firing instead of the disastrous Chinese sequence. Wares were fired to biscuit at very high temperatures, when the paste became translucent. The glaze was then applied and the wares were fired again at a lower temperature, when the glaze fused to the body. But New Hall came on the market too late to compete with the enormous popularity of creamware, and in 1810 they abandoned the manufacture of hard paste porcelain. By 1812, along with many other manufactories, they had switched production to bone china.

Porcelain: expansion, setback and takeover 1770–90

At the beginning of the 1770s, soft paste porcelain was being made by Bow, Chelsea, Derby, Lowestoft and Liverpool, while Worcester had by far the largest share of the market for useful wares. But Chelsea, which had been in trouble all through the 1760s, was finally taken over by William Duesbury of the Derby Porcelain Company, a name which had not figured greatly up to this time. It had been established by a Frenchman, André Planché, and, financed by a Derby banker, had been making competent but rather unexciting 'Darby figars', standing a little apart from the general development of English porcelain. Derby figures were sent 'in the white' to London to be decorated by William Duesbury from 1749 to 1755; in 1756 Duesbury took over the entire Derby factory, and there was a noticeable improvement in quality. But although the modelling of Duesbury's Derby wares is extremely fine and the paste of good quality, the colours were poor and washed-out, and lacked brilliance.

In 1770 Duesbury acquired the ailing Chelsea Porcelain Company, and the change was almost immediately noticeable. Enamels were brighter, more brilliant, in exceptional and original colours – among them a rare apple green, a bright orange and subtle shades of violets and reds, from pale lilac to coral, crushed strawberry to deep claret. Up to this date, although dessert services had been included in their advertisements, the paste was not resistant to boiling water, and the glaze was too soft for tableware. Glass lining plates were used at this time to protect the delicately enamelled decoration of dessert services. From about 1770, the paste was improved with the addition of bone ash, an ingredient pioneered by the Bow Porcelain Factory some 20 years earlier. This manufactory was also in difficulties from

Lobed serving jug in silver shape, on three small ball feet. First Period Worcester, c.1755.

about 1765 onwards, when there were troubles in obtaining some of the vital ingredients for the paste, and this long-established company too was eventually bought out by William Duesbury in 1776.

One new venture was opened during the 1770s, to make soft paste porcelain: Thomas Turner moved from Staffordshire to Shropshire and opened the Caughley 'Salopian' porcelain works. The Turners, like the Wedgwoods, were a well-known family in the potteries, and both men had followed the same lines of research and development of bodies and stonewares. Turner had in fact produced a body which was distinctly porcellanous and had a degree of translucency, following a line of experimental formulae which eventually led to the development of ironstone. This unique body was taken up and developed by David Dunderdale towards the end of the century at his Castleford pottery. It may well have been this near-porcelain stoneware that prompted Thomas Turner to transfer his interests to porcelain with a soapstone base, very similar to Worcester.

By the middle of the 1770s, the Caughley works were turning out near-copies of all Worcester's early designs, from cabbage-leaf jugs with mask spouts and openwork baskets to tea and coffee wares, many of them in blue and white patterns which seem to have been lifted straight from early Worcester chinoiserie decoration. Turner seems to have been less single-minded than Wedgwood, and less far-sighted: although he timed the reintroduction of blue and white wares to a nicety, he became a victim of his own experimental work in fine stonewares, which were taken up and exploited by other, shrewder men.

In 1796 Champion's patent, now held by New Hall, finally ran out, although china stone and china clay had been freely available to the potteries from 1776 onwards and had been incorporated into refined earthenware bodies by many Staffordshire potteries. It might seem

Elaborate design for Davenport bone china serving jug, c.1840.

Three Pratt-type jugs with moulded decoration and typical colouring, c.1800. Left to right Heart-shaped panels enclosing scenes of 'Sportive Innocence', 7½ in (19 cm) high; miser with his money-bags within a zig-zag frame 7¼ in (18.5 cm) high; and with a continuous hunting scene and bands of leaves, 6 in (15 cm) high.

that there were no longer any problems to prevent late-eighteenth-century entrepreneurs from catching the rising tide of profit in domestic ware and tableware at home and abroad. But international politics and economics hit the potteries just at the point when the future seemed to be at its brightest. The American Wars of Independence caused a swift and sudden slump in the trans-Atlantic export trade. The price of tea escalated when the Government imposed a prohibitive duty of 119 per cent. Duty on silver was also reintroduced and silver teapots went up from around 6 shillings to 10 shillings or more. The great British public retaliated swiftly against these punitive measures, and well-organized bands of smugglers took over the 'import and distribution' of tea to such an extent that over half the prodigious quantity consumed came into the country illegally, and in 1784 the ineffective levy was lifted.

That was not all, however. Europe raised trade barriers against English imports in tardy retaliation for English restrictions on Continental porcelain. Workers were laid off and there were riots in the potteries in 1783. Competition for the home market increased in ferocity and only the giants in the industry seem to have remained undisturbed by these calamitous upheavals.

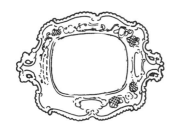

Over-elaborate shape of 19th-century dish from a dessert service, decorated with landscapes in panels and gilt diaper decoration over dark blue ground.

Elegant leaf-moulded early 19th-century Davenport dinner service with hand-painted botanical specimen flowers, c.1800–10.

Bone China: the final merging 1790–1810

The flow of workers, artists and decorators between pottery and porcelain factories was fast becoming a two-way tide. Erstwhile makers of earthenware and pottery shifted into the field of porcelain. Changes in management took place in the porcelain factories, and workers deserted them for the more financially rewarding world of fine stoneware and creamware. Two men from Turner's Caughley factory left him in 1781 to work for Josiah Spode, a one-time apprentice to Thomas Whieldon, contemporary of Josiah Wedgwood but three years younger. Spode had managed Turner and Banks' pottery at Stoke-on-Trent from the age of 27, making a range of stoneware with relief decoration and unexciting domestic ware. In 1770, Spode acquired the premises he was managing and expanded production to include creamware. Armed with the evidence of Caughley's successful blue and white range, Spode introduced a limited range of transfer-printed tea ware in blue and white with designs copied straight from Oriental porcelain, in about 1781. It was an instant success. The body and glaze were still too creamy for genuine blue and white, however, and Spode continued to refine his formula, adding a minute quantity of cobalt blue to the white glaze as a 'blue whitener'. Eventually he produced a fine white pearlware, transfer-printed under the glaze with a particularly rich deep blue, in an increasing number of Oriental and Chinese designs, among them the illustrious willow pattern.

The New Hall Porcelain Factory still held the patent on Champion's original translucent porcelain, but by the 1790s anyone attempting to disentangle 'earthenware' from 'porcelain' must have been hard put to tell the difference. By 1795 Spode, like the soft paste porcelain manufacturers before him, was adding bone ash to his pearlware formula and so, it has been claimed, was the definitive inventor of 'bone china'. There was still a year for the New Hall licence to run, and there was already another contender in the field – Thomas Minton.

In the closed and competitive world of the potteries, the web of connections between one family or one factory and another is dense and complicated. Thomas Minton had originally been apprenticed at Thomas Turner's Caughley factory, where he worked as an engraver. After that he worked in London for a time, and then with Josiah Spode before setting up on his own in 1793. For the first few years, he bided his time and contented himself with making transfer-printed creamware and pearlware. But as soon as the New Hall licence ran out in 1796 he began to make bone china. The following year he founded the Hendra Company at St Dennis in Cornwall to mine and purify china clay, a highly successful venture in which both Josiah Wedgwood and the New Hall Porcelain Company were partners, and which continued to prosper until 1854.

Wedgwood's fortunes were untouched by the dramatic events of the 1770s and the 1780s. Secure in the steady growth of profits in creamware, he cemented his relationships with both the Adam Brothers and Matthew Boulton, eighteenth-century moguls of inter-ior decoration, metalware, ormolu and silver. For them he developed a marbled body which could be used like stone for making classical urns and vases at his new factory at Etruria, as well as the 'Adam' or 'Wedgwood blue' jasper ware for plaques, cameos, urns and vases.

Simple shapes of early 19th-century teapots.

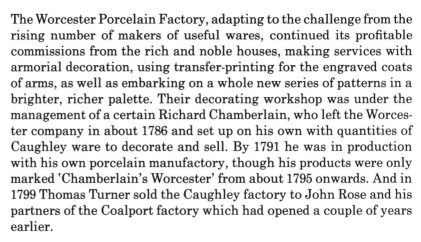

The Worcester Porcelain Factory, adapting to the challenge from the rising number of makers of useful wares, continued its profitable commissions from the rich and noble houses, making services with armorial decoration, using transfer-printing for the engraved coats of arms, as well as embarking on a whole new series of patterns in a brighter, richer palette. Their decorating workshop was under the management of a certain Richard Chamberlain, who left the Worcester company in about 1786 and set up on his own with quantities of Caughley ware to decorate and sell. By 1791 he was in production with his own porcelain manufactory, though his products were only marked 'Chamberlain's Worcester' from about 1795 onwards. And in 1799 Thomas Turner sold the Caughley factory to John Rose and his partners of the Coalport factory which had opened a couple of years earlier.

Repetition is the Mother of Invention 1800–50

The last great flowering of creative design came, yet again, from Wedgwood, at a time when Thomas Hope was designing Regency interiors with designs inspired by ancient Egypt. The range of black basaltes and 'Etruscan' wares from Wedgwood's Etruria works crowned the success of this truly remarkable man, who once wrote to his partner Thomas Bentley, 'I Shall Astonish the World all at Once,' and lived to see his own prophecy come true.

After his death in 1795 came the rise of glorious ostentation, overblown decadence and decline. Of all the porcelain factories which flourished at the beginning of the nineteenth century, the one that was synonymous with the ultimate, the unattainable, the most exclusive, was Rockingham. From humble beginnings as partners in the Swinton pottery of the eighteenth century, the Brameld family ambitiously began to make a range of particularly fine bone china in about 1826. It was remarkably dense and white and extremely lavishly decorated. It was also quite impossible to produce profitably, and the family was on the verge of bankruptcy when the elderly Earl of Fitzwilliam came to its rescue. The Bramelds used the Earl's griffin crest as their mark and, after receiving the patronage of William IV in 1830, used a mark as flamboyant as their china: 'Brameld. Royal Rockingham Works. Manufacturers to the King'. The next seven years saw enormous table services from Rockingham, heavily gilded, with velvety blue grounds, dark claret reds, a unique opaque apple green and a deep yellow, all in Georgian silver patterns and destined for the greatest houses in England. Unhappily for the Rockingham fortunes, William IV died in 1837 and Rockingham ceased production in terrible financial trouble a brief five years later – a short but glorious career.

Increasingly elaborate shapes of mid-19th-century bone china teapots, including a swooping half-melon shape.

Meanwhile, the swathe of middle-class households bought bright blue and white transfer-printed wares from Spode, Minton and a score of other Staffordshire factories, and the ubiquitous Turner family began to experiment with a new and more durable earthen-

Brown salt glazed stoneware harvest jug from the Mortlake factory, the top half dipped in brown slip and decorated with portraits of George III and Queen Charlotte and a continuous hunting scene below, c.1800. $10\frac{1}{4}$ in (26 cm) high.

Large Minton majolica conservatory plant stand decorated in vivid colours. 18½ in (47 cm) high.

Ironstone teapot in bright 'Japan' pattern from a tea service by A. J. & W. Ridgway, c.1825.

ware, made with felspathic rock found on land belonging to the Marquis of Stafford. This promising new development was stifled in its infancy by the Marquis's refusal to allow the Turners to make good use of the stone. The Turners went bankrupt in 1806 and some of their moulds were acquired by Spode, which had recently added 'stone china' to its repertoire. Many other potteries made versions of this hard-wearing, long-lasting body, but it was Mason's Patent Ironstone that captured the market.

The Mason brothers began to produce a brightly coloured, extremely durable range of useful wares in heavy, faintly translucent 'china' in 1813. Part of their success must be attributed to their choice of patterns, which aped the expensive Japan pattern wares of the porcelain factories of the eighteenth century. As with furniture and fashions in general, the time lag between London and the provinces could be as much as fifty years, and while nineteenth-century London

Belleek biscuit barrel and thistle-headed vase with mother-of-pearl lustre glaze, c.1860.

Staffordshire teapot commemorating the Anti-Slavery Movement bat-printed in sepia with a negro kneeling with his wrists in chains, c.1820–30.

flung itself headlong into Frenchified styles heavy with ormolu and gilding, in the provinces good 'Chippendale' mahogany furniture was selling as fast as the furniture manufacturers could turn it out. Mason's Patent Ironstone complemented the solid worthiness of provincial furniture to perfection.

Other, older traditions were very much alive too. Liverpool was still making tin glazed delft punch bowls and dishes, while in the country districts, slip-glazed pie plates were made and used until well into the middle of the nineteenth century. Like dishes stacked on top of one another, every layer of pottery and porcelain was being made and used in the first decade of the nineteenth century.

Artist Potters: the great revival

Scarcely had traditional wares ceased to be made than the Arts and Crafts Movement revived them. Salt glazed stoneware, which for a considerable time had quite literally gone underground, and had been used for making land drains in the great plumbing revolution, was revived by Henry Doulton. The prosperous firm of Minton produced a more durable version of Italian maiolica and Doulton followed swiftly with a range of 'Faience'. Terra cotta plaques, ewers, garden troughs and jardinières were perfect for Victorian conservatories and indoor aspidistras until Minton began to make gigantic, highly coloured ornamental plant stands, conservatory seats, and suitable ornaments for garden ponds and lawns.

There was a quirky taste for grotesques, inspired by medieval gargoyles, which the Martin Brothers exploited with great success, making weird Grimm-like jugs of human heads, and grotesque birds, as well as an excellent range of stoneware tankards, jugs and vases. The Martin Brothers were protégés of the Doulton Lambeth factory, as too were the famous Barlow sisters who decorated vases with poignant sgraffito Highland cattle and shaggy ponies and who – unlike the Martins, who moved to Southall – remained attached to the Doulton factory for the rest of their lives.

Some of the most beautiful pieces made towards the end of the nineteenth century were tiles inspired by Turkish and Persian ceramics of the fifteenth century, but decorated with pure Art Nouveau designs with swirling patterns of flowers and arabesques. The most gifted and original designer of much of this work was a pupil of William Morris, William de Morgan, whose work can be seen in all its glory covering the walls of the forecourt at Leighton House in Holland Park, home of the Pre-Raphaelite painter Holman Hunt.

In many districts, regional pottery was revived by small family concerns. At Bideford in Devon, George Fishley made traditional harvest jugs and simple slipware decorated with time-honoured designs. In Manchester the Pinkington Pottery, established in 1802, revived 'Nottingham ware' and attracted some famous artists to design for the owners, William and Joseph Burton.

At the turn of the century, English potters turned to Japan and the

Belleek figure in statuary parian, introduced to the factory in 1863.

East for inspiration. Bernard Moore is less well known for his wonderful 'sang de boeuf' vases and bowls than Bernard Leach who, together with a young Japanese potter, Shoji Hamada, founded the St Ives school of pottery. A quieter, more self-effacing figure was William Staite Murray, who produced some remarkable pottery and who, in the 1920s, succeeded in having some of his work shown in art galleries with works of contemporary artists, underlining his belief in pottery as an art form, and becoming a seminal influence in the Studio Potters movement.

Among the most shining examples of true Studio Pottery are the works of Lucy Rie, who produced commercial tableware for the Kardomah Café to fund her quite extraordinary talents before achieving the recognition she deserves for her pure and indescribably beautiful work. It is hard to understand an age which puts the nursery-bright crockery decorated by Clarice Cliff into the same price-range.

Miniatures in bright 'Japan' pattern from the Royal Worcester Porcelain Company, c.1920.

A typical shape developed by Lucy Rie: slightly waisted porcelain bottle vase with flaring neck, covered in rich dark brown-bronze glaze with bands of russet on the rim and shoulder. Impressed with **RL** *seal. 9 in (23 cm) high.*

Techniques and terms

There are three separate elements involved in all but the simplest pottery, all of which must be compatible.

Body or paste The raw material of pottery (body) or porcelain (paste), with all its variations, mixtures, additional ingredients and methods of manufacture.

Glaze The glass-like coating over the body or paste which renders it non-porous and adds a transparent, translucent or opaque surface.

Decoration Colour pigments, enamels, gilding and other ornament which increase the decorative appearance of the finished article.

Body and Paste

The earliest method of making **hollow ware** – pots, bowls, jugs and mugs – was on a potter's wheel. A lump of malleable clay was spun on a wheel powered by a foot treadle and raised by hand to the required shape and size. This method of **'throwing'** pots was not suitable for **flatware**, and plates and dishes were made by pressing a flat disc of clay known as a **bat** into a wooden **mould**. Handles for jugs and mugs were made separately and **applied** to finished pots while the clay was still wet, using **slip** (diluted clay) as an adhesive. **Spouts** were made separately and married to a circular hole cut in the vessel, often with additional **applied** decoration to strengthen the join. **Vitreous stoneware** does not need to be glazed – when it is fired at a higher temperature than earthenware, the vitreous ingredients fuse with the clay, resulting in a hard, non-porous substance. **Red stoneware** in its unfired state is very hard and was **turned** and finished on a lathe. Vessels and flatware could be accurately trimmed and foot-rims were neatly finished before firing. Methods of **moulding** were devised for making spouts and handles, and by the time **white salt glazed stoneware** teapots were being made in the early eighteenth century, small piecework potteries specialized in making spouts and handles. Small teapots were not very easy to **throw** on a wheel, and by about 1720 most Staffordshire potteries had changed to **moulding and casting.**

Master moulds were carved in Derbyshire alabaster or made in cast brass. **Working moulds** were taken from the master moulds in clay and fired to make them hard and firm. Soft clay was pressed into the two halves of the earthenware mould, the edges joined with **slip**, the mould bound together and left to dry. The mould was then opened, the **cast** trimmed by hand and the piece was fired. Finer detail and more elaborate shapes were made by **slip casting**: slip was poured into finely carved or modelled **casts** made from earthenware, taken from master moulds. As the earthenware mould absorbed water from the slip, a layer of solid clay was deposited, particle by particle, on the inner surface of the mould. When a suitable thickness had built up, the surplus liquid slip was poured off and the cast allowed to dry, shrinking in the process. It was then removed from the mould and fired. In about 1740 **plaster of Paris** was used to make the moulds, producing even finer, crisper detail and modelling. Casting and moulding were also used to make **silver shapes** and **leaf shapes** in **soft paste porcelain**.

Relief moulding was in use in both potteries and porcelain factories by the late 1740s, shaping and decorating an item simultaneously with raised patterns and intricate shapes.

With the advent of **steam power** in the eighteenth century, new ways were devised for making large quantities of ware on a mass-produced scale. **Press-moulding** was reintroduced for all manner of objects. Stoneware and earthenware, unfired and malleable, were rolled to a uniform thickness and **stamped and pressed** out by machines. **Spouted hollow ware** continued to be made with the spouts added separately until the beginning of the nineteenth century when the shape of the whole piece was moulded in two halves and pressed together before firing.

Glaze

Natural sulphide of lead was used in making glass and was known to be transformed, when molten, into a transparent substance. To make a lead glaze, powdered **red lead** or **galena** was dusted or rubbed into the surface of earthenware before firing. In the heat of the kiln the lead melted and spread in a film over the surface, fusing to the clay in a brownish or yellowish glassy coating. Discoloration was caused by the presence of iron, manganese or other impurities in either the powdered lead or the clay body. In the sixteenth century, the addition of copper oxide to the powdered lead glaze resulted in a streaky green translucent glaze known as **Tudor green**. By the middle of the seventeenth century **liquid lead glaze** had been developed. Lead was burned to remove impurities, and the resulting **lead oxide** was ground to a fine powder with powdered sand and then mixed with water. Once this liquid glaze was developed, all earthenware bodies were fired once to a **'biscuit' stage** and then dipped in the glaze solution.

Tin glazing was more demanding. The once-fired biscuit body had to be able to absorb water from the glaze solution evenly, and so the clay was refined to a smoother consistency and some of the impurities removed. The **brilliant white surface glaze** was achieved by adding **oxide of tin** to the glaze solution. Earthenware was either dipped or brushed with the mixture, which dried and left a white powdery coating, evenly distributed over the earthenware body. When the body was fired a second time, the glaze fused to it and resulted in an **opaque white glassy finish**.

Without tin, which was only found in Cornwall and could not be transported because of the abysmal state of the roads, Staffordshire potters were attempting to produce a **white earthenware body** and a **pure, clear glaze** which would not discolour on firing. **Stoneware** was fired at higher temperatures than earthenware, and it was found that at this increased heat, **salt** thrown into the kiln at maximum temperature vaporized, and volatile particles of **silicate of soda** and

alumina were deposited in a film on the surface, cooling to a brilliant, **transparent glassy surface. White salt glazed stoneware** was therefore achieved at a single firing, using **white burning clays**. This method of glazing could only be used on **stoneware** because **non-vitreous** bodies could not withstand the high temperatures required to vaporize the salt.

The period between about 1730 and 1740 was a time of experiment. Two things were needed: an earthenware body that could be fired at a higher temperature, and a **transparent colourless glaze** that could be used as an alternative to **salt glazing.**

In about 1740 a **pure, colourless lead glaze** was developed by adding **powdered calcined flint** to lead oxide, mixed with water to a liquid solution. The earthenware was fired once to **biscuit,** dipped in the glaze solution and fired again at a lower temperature. From the early 1740s this glaze was used over cream-coloured earthenware bodies and on red stoneware.

In the search for earthenware bodies that would withstand higher firing temperatures, **mixed and mingled clays** were developed and glazed with colourless glaze. The clays were either naturally coloured or stained with pigments and were known as **agate ware.** At the same time, **cream-coloured earthenware** was streaked with metallic oxides, mottled, stained or splashed with manganese – green, yellow or slatey blue – then dipped in colourless lead glaze. The colour pigment fused with the glaze to produce **tortoiseshell ware**.

Colourless lead glaze was also used from the early 1750s over **white burning clays** to produce **cream-coloured earthenware.** A deep, **near-black glaze** was produced, too, from about 1751 onwards. Brownish-red earthenware bodies were coated at the biscuit stage with **cobalt pigment** and fired at **high temperatures** which turned the surface almost black. Smoke from the furnaces was also allowed to circulate inside the kilns, depositing **carbon** on the surface and adding a rich lustrous bloom. This was called **jet ware.**

In 1759 Josiah Wedgwood produced a reliable and consistent **clear green glaze**, which he used to make a range of **leaf-shaped** dishes and plates and, in combination with a clear glaze on a cream-coloured earthenware, green and cream together – known as **cauliflower ware**. In 1761, using **pipeclay** brought from Devon, he developed an **opaque cream-coloured glaze** which was entirely compatible with cream-coloured earthenware, and began the production of **creamware**. The glaze was still too soft to be entirely satisfactory for everyday hard wear, but in 1764 it was improved and perfected by John Greatbach, by the addition of **vitreous frit**. Much still depended on the exact composition and absorbent qualities of the once-fired earthenware body as well as the precise temperatures reached in firing, both at the **biscuit** stage and in the **glost oven** during glazing.

Before the development of the **pure white earthenware body** known as **pearlware**, the glaze was sometimes made more brilliant by the addition of a minute amount of **cobalt**, mixed with the glaze solution like a **blue whitener** and known as **under-glaze blue.** This term is more usually applied to white glazed porcelain figures and ornaments, known as **blanc de chine. Pearlware** marked the start of developments in **earthenware bodies** containing a proportion of **china clay**, when the composition of the glaze was changed radically and became more similar to the glazes used on porcelain paste.

Soft paste and soapstone porcelain were at first glazed with a **colourless lead glaze**, but by the 1760s a newer, harder glaze had been developed, similar to Greatbach's glaze. **Vitreous frit** – a mixture of white sand, gypsum, soda, alum, salt and nitre – was fused to a molten glassy mass, cooled and ground to a very fine powder and then mixed with water to a milky consistency. Because of difficulties with the composition of the paste and the incompatibility of paste and glaze unless exactly the correct formulae and firing temperatures were used, glazing presented many problems. These were overcome to a certain extent by Chelsea, where the paste was greyish and drab in colour, by adding a small quantity of **tin oxide** to make the glaze opaque and produce white and more lustrous results.

Hard paste porcelain was glazed in an entirely different manner. The paste itself had to be fired at extremely high temperatures to achieve the required **translucency**, and none of the lead-based glazes would fuse or adhere to the paste. **The glaze** developed by Cookworthy at Plymouth consisted of **pulverized china stone, lime and potash**. The paste was fired to biscuit at a fairly low temperature, then dipped in glaze and fired at very high temperatures to fuse it to the paste. The nature of the paste caused it to soften at some unspecified period during this second firing and many pieces collapsed in the kilns. A **felspathic glaze** was then developed, using **felspar, china clay and a limestone flux**, which sank into the paste and was more viscous, but as long as the second firing was at such high temperatures, results were very uncertain. When New Hall acquired the patent and licence in 1781 they reversed the firing sequence, firing the paste at a very high temperature to a **translucent biscuit**, then applying the glaze and firing a second time at a lower temperature, thus succeeding where earlier methods had failed.

Variations of **felspathic glazes** were developed by the potteries for the production of **ironstones and stone chinas. Bone china**, however, was found to be marked by blemishes and dark spots when glazed with a **lead-based glaze**, and in 1820 John Rose of Coalport developed a **lead-free, lustrous white glaze** using a mixture of **felspar, borax, sand, nitre, soda and china clay**, melted, fused and ground to a fine powder with the addition of a small amount of **calcined borax**. This glaze was expensive, and at first was confined to luxury ranges of fine bone china.

Decoration

Early decoration took the form of slip – natural-coloured clays, mixed to a creamy consistency with water and trailed or brushed over unfired earthenware bodies **before glazing**. The slip could be **joggled or combed** into simple patterns while still wet, or cut away to reveal the colour of the earthenware body it covered. Alternatively, patterns were **incised** into the unfired earthenware and a different-coloured slip of thicker consistency rubbed into the incisions – a technique known as **sgraffito**. Carved, decorative **stamps** like butter moulds were also sometimes used.

Red stoneware was decorated with little **sprigs or leaf motifs**, cut from the wet clay and **applied** by using water or thin slip as an adhesive. When fired, the applied decoration fused to the body and stood out in **relief. White pipeclay** was used in a similar manner, and was also trailed in simple patterns over the unfired body. As stoneware needed **no glazing**, white pipeclay was not discoloured by impurities in a lead glaze. Later, decorative sprigs and motifs were **stamped** out with tools like pastry cutters, and then **applied**. This technique was used in a more sophisticated form, with fine-bodied **white jasper** crisply modelled and **applied** to a coloured body by Wedgwood in the 1780s for his range of **jasper ware**.

Colour pigments were not used on English pottery until the sixteenth century, when **delftware** was being made in some quantity. Simple patterns were painted on to the powdery coating of **tin glaze** before the second firing. At first the only colour used was **blue**, made from **cobalt pigment**, prepared by roasting it at great heat to remove impurities. This form of **cobalt oxide** was known as **zaffre** and still contained elements of copper, iron and other impurities, which caused the colour to vary. The pigment was treated with hydrochloric acid at the end of the seventeenth century to remove many of these impurities and **cobalt pigment** became the mainstay for decoration at every stage of development in bodies, pastes and glazes, used **both under and over the glaze**, always turning a clear, bright blue when fired. **Yellow** from iron or antimony, **iron red, manganese purple** and, more difficult, **green** from copper oxide were all in use by the end of the seventeenth century – **metallic oxides applied under the glaze** on earthenware and compatible with the lead oxide in the glaze. These colours, as well as cobalt oxide, are known as **high temperature colours** because they can withstand high temperatures during firing in the kiln.

In **white salt glazed stoneware** firing and glazing were carried out in one operation and new methods were needed to add colour pigment **over the glaze**. Some white salt glazed stoneware was decorated before firing with **sgraffito** techniques, where **cobalt pigment** was rubbed into **incised decoration** and was known as **scratch blue.**

Cobalt pigment was imported in two forms: as **zaffre**, refined colour pigment in powder form, and as **smalt**, a more costly preparation consisting of between 2 and 10 per cent **zaffre added to molten glass**, cooled and pulverized into a flour-fine consistency. In this form it could be applied **over the glaze** in a technique known as **enamelling**. Mixed with a small quantity of oil of lavender which vaporized in the kiln, it was painted on to the glaze and fired, to fuse it to the glaze. Other **enamels**, prepared from metallic oxides, were applied in the same manner but the technique was difficult to master. When applied **over the glaze**, colours changed radically unless fired at precisely the right heat. The delicate pale pink of **'famille rose'**, for example, turned a dullish brown at too low a heat. If the temperature was too high, it changed to dark purple or puce and then to black, disappearing completely at very great heat. Other colours changed at varying degrees of heat, and it was eventually found that each coloured enamel had to be fired separately in order to achieve the desired result.

These trials on **white salt glazed stoneware** more or less coincided with the first production of **soft paste porcelain** in England. At first, **cobalt pigment** was used **under the glaze**, and decoration progressed to **enamelled colours** at the end of the 1740s for **'famille rose'** and **'famille verte'** which, owing to the nature of copper oxide, was more difficult to achieve. By this time the art of enamelling had been fully mastered on **metals**, and both Battersea and Birmingham began to make exquisitely enamelled ware. Porcelain factories soon employed professional enamellers to decorate their wares. Both porcelain factories and potteries used **cold enamels** for a brief period up to 1751. These were painted on to the glaze in a less vitreous mixture and hardened on at very low temperatures – a technique known as **japanning**. But these **cold enamels** soon wore off the smooth glazed surface, and were abandoned by the porcelain factories by the end of 1751. Staffordshire potters continued to use **cold enamels** for a considerable time on **ornamental figures** where durability was of less importance than in **useful wares.**

Other methods of colour decoration were also being employed by the Staffordshire potteries from the 1750s onwards, among them the use of **coloured glazes**, notably by Ralph Wood and his family, extending the colour palette beyond Wedgwood's **green glaze** to include most of the metallic oxide colours. Unlike early experiments by Thomas Whieldon in **tortoiseshell ware**, the Wood family stained the glaze with colour pigments and applied them over a **cream-coloured earthenware body**, perfecting the technique so that there was no running or smearing of one colour into another. **Coloured glaze decoration** on pottery is quite distinct from wares decorated **under the glaze** because the coloured glaze is itself **translucent.**

In the late 1750s, porcelain factories began experimenting with **printing** on the glazed surface. At first it was difficult to produce a rich **jet black**, owing to variations in colour at different temperatures, but the technique had been tried out in the enamel manufactories of both Battersea and Birmingham and had proved successful. By about 1754 Worcester and Bow had begun printing **over the glaze** on soft paste and soapstone porcelain. Early results with

manganese oxide produced **light purple or puce**, but once precise firing temperatures had been calculated a pure **jet black print** was produced. A similar technique was being used at a slightly later date on **creamware**, printed over the **opaque cream-coloured glaze**.

From about 1760 experiments were started by porcelain factories using **cobalt blue** printed **under the glaze**, applied at the **biscuit** stage and then covered with clear transparent glaze. There were difficulties at first, since the porcelain paste was not very absorbent, and the cobalt pigment tended to become absorbed by the glaze and produce blurred results. In the late 1760s other metallic oxides were also applied to porcelain pastes **under the glaze**, notably **iron red** for **Japan patterns** and **zaffre** for the **gros bleu** of Sèvres. These **high temperature colours** were applied in bands and panels of solid colour, often in conjunction with delicate enamels painted **over the glaze** in the white spaces **reserved** for hand-painted decoration. **High temperature colours** were also used by the potteries, in a distinctly different way from porcelain factories. This type of decoration is typical of **Prattware**: a **cream-coloured earthenware**, often **moulded in relief**, was fired to biscuit and the **relief decoration** was then painted with a limited palette before being covered with **transparent lead glaze** and fired again. This type of decoration was not suitable for **creamware**, which was coated with a rich, creamy **opaque glaze** – simple border patterns were **hand-painted** in **enamel colours over the glaze** and then fired to fuse the decoration to the surface of the glaze.

Transfer-printing in colours under the glaze proved far more successful on the absorbent earthenware bodies than on hard-textured porcelain pastes. This technique was not used much before the late 1770s on pottery, and it is possible that the methods had been learned from the Turner family who diverted their efforts from pottery to porcelain when they founded the Caughley factory in Shropshire in 1770 and produced a wide range of blue transfer-printed soft paste porcelain. Once a **near-white earthenware body** had been perfected by Spode, derived from Wedgwood's **pearlware**, the use of **transfer-printing under the glaze** was taken up by potteries making earthenware bodies containing **felspar** and **china clay**, and blue and white transfer-printed earthenware, pioneered by Spode in 1784, was made in great quantities. Later, one-colour transfer-printed ware was also made in green, puce, red and black. **Multi-colour transfer-printing over the glaze** by means of a technique known as **bat printing** was first developed in the late 1760s but was used very infrequently until the process was improved in the 1820s. The print was transferred in oil on to the glaze and was then dusted with powdered colour pigments and fired in a hardening-on kiln so that the oil vaporized and the pigments fused to the glaze. **Multi-colour transfer-printing under the glaze** dates from 1828, when several transfer prints of different colours were applied at the biscuit stage, but as each colour had to be fired separately it was costly. In 1848 a multi-colour under-glaze printing process was developed using three primary colours – red, blue and yellow – on a single transfer requiring only one firing. By this date many **artificial colour pigments** were available, made from chemical compositions and not metallic oxides. **Lithography** was first used on ceramics in 1839 using artificial ultramarine pigment which resulted in a lighter blue than cobalt. The palette soon widened to include pink, green, purple, grey and black, transferred to the glazed surface with potter's varnish, dusted with coloured powder and fired once to fix the colour to the glaze.

The two early methods of **gilding** – embellishing pottery and porcelain with gold – were **japanned gilding** and **oil gilding.** **Japanned gilding** was used on English soft paste porcelain from about 1740 onwards. **Fine gold leaf** was applied to the glaze with a mixture of spirits, gum arabic and other substances, and fired in a small furnace. It was then covered with a piece of specially prepared thin paper to protect it from damage and **burnished** with a blood-stone, agate or other hardstone. **Oil gilding** was not as durable as japanned gilding nor as brilliant. Rims, edges and patterns to be gilded were painted with a mixture of linseed oil, gum arabic and mastic, and left to dry for three days. Thin gold leaf was cut to match the pattern and pressed on to the adhesive mixture. It was then fired at a very low temperature for two to three hours. Oil gilding could not be **burnished** without damaging the surface and, though bright, it was not lasting. **Oil gilding** could also be applied **under the glaze** but the results were dull. Although abandoned by the porcelain factories by the 1750s, **oil gilding** continued to be used by Staffordshire potteries as late as the 1790s.

Honey gilding was introduced from France and was first used by Chelsea in about 1755. Gold leaf was ground to a powder and mixed with oil of lavender and honey. It was applied with a brush and, depending on the number of coats, the thickness could be varied. After fixing to the glaze with low temperature firing, it was **burnished** and could even be **chased** with a tool, like metal, if the coating was thick enough. It was duller than japanned gilding but far stronger and more durable, withstanding punishment from knives and forks without damage. **Honey gilding** was used on **soft paste, soapstone and hard paste porcelain** but it was not suitable for **bone china.**

Amber gilding, a more efficient method of **japanned gilding**, was used for a short period from the early 1760s, but was largely superseded by **mercury gilding**. This was introduced in the 1780s on Continental porcelain, but is not found on English porcelain much before 1790. Powdered gold was added to a flux of mercury which vaporized in the heat of the kiln leaving a film of dull gold, which was then vigorously **burnished**. In appearance it was more brassy than earlier forms of gilding and had less depth and lustre. But it was long-lasting and, since it was applied with a brush and flowed easily, could be used with stencils for intricate patterns, enabling whole services of tableware to be decorated identically.

Solid gilding and transfer gilding were both introduced in about 1810 and used to great effect by Spode and other makers of transfer-printed wares as well as on ironstone china.

Under-glaze gilding was used on some early nineteenth-century earthenwares instead of traditional oil gilding but its use was not widespread. **Liquid gold**, a method introduced from the Continent in about 1850, was mainly used on felspathic earthenwares. Although it required no burnishing and produced brilliant results, it could not stand up to everyday wear and tear, and an alternative method known as **brown gold** was more widely used by makers of stone china from the late 1860s. This was a gilding paste, burnished to a wonderful brilliance after firing, and was far more lasting then other contemporary methods. **Acid gilding** was introduced in about 1863 and was a complicated process which involved the use of strong acid solutions to produce a raised pattern in the glaze itself. Gilding was then applied and the raised surface only was burnished, leaving the gold dull and matt where the design had been etched into the surface. The sole rights to this process were acquired by the Minton factory.

Bodies and pastes

It will be quickly noted from the long list that follows that the two terms 'pottery' and 'porcelain' can be misleading, and that there is another group which belongs to neither – the stonewares. Furthermore, although bone china is generally grouped among the porcelains, the many developments of porcellanous wares which fall between porcelain and bone china cannot easily be placed in any category, since many of them are called 'china' but are stonewares, and others are called 'felspar', which is porcelain, or 'felspathic', which is earthenware.

In the classification of pottery and porcelain, not even the chronology can help, since developments were extremely uneven and depended on many factors not obviously connected with making crocks and pots. In attempting to reassemble the two fields, this guide to bodies and pastes does not toe the lines laid down by custom and habit; rather, in order to put each development into the category by which it is generally known by collectors, the bodies (the raw material of pottery) or pastes (the raw material for porcelain) have been categorized into not two but three main groups: earthenware, stoneware and porcelain. Some of the descriptions are, of necessity, a little technical, since the differences between one type and another often depend on very small changes in ingredients. In general, earthenware and stoneware belong under the general heading of 'pottery', while bone china belongs under 'porcelain'.

Agate ware Earthenware. Clays of different colours, either natural or coloured with pigments, mixed and mingled to produce a marbled effect. Up to the 1740s, natural buff and red clays were used together. Some clays turned white when fired, however, and Thomas Whieldon stained these 'white burning' clays with metallic oxides in greens, greyish blues and browns. By the 1750s many other Staffordshire potteries were also making marbled clays, and production continued intermittently until c.1820. In the late nineteenth century agate ware was revived with a different formula, including a variation resembling horn, which continued to be made until the 1920s.

Bamboo ware Stoneware. A dry-bodied stoneware made from c.1787 by Josiah Wedgwood and so named because his designs resembled sticks of bamboo – a very popular theme for furniture and decoration at that period. Bamboo ware contains a certain amount of Cornish china stone.

Basaltes Stoneware. Fine-grained earthenware stained black with manganese dioxide, fully vitreous; developed by Josiah Wedgwood as a refinement of earlier Egyptian black. Basaltes was fired twice, the second time at red heat, having been coated with potter's varnish to give it a permanent gloss which was further improved by polishing.

Basalts Stoneware. Similar body to basaltes, of less quality – the word is used to indicate later production and reproductions.

Biscuit Once-fired body or paste before decoration or glazing.

Bisque, biscuit porcelain Porcelain. Soft paste, soapstone and hard paste porcelain fired at a temperature high enough to cause chemical change but not high enough to vitrifiy the paste, which was left in an undecorated state – known sometimes as bisque – and unglazed. Finest examples from English factories were those of Derby, whose modelling was superb.

Black porcelain Stoneware. Loose term used by late-seventeenth- and eighteenth-century potteries to describe naturally coloured or stained clays which fired to black.

Bone china Porcelain. Ultimately developed by Josiah Spode in about 1794 from a combination of china clay, china stone and calcined bones to a paste midway between hard paste and soft paste. From about 1818 bone china was being produced by all the major factories and potteries, as well as innumerable lesser Staffordshire companies.

Bone porcelain Porcelain. Soft paste porcelain with the addition of calcined bone ash, first used by the Bow porcelain factory *c.*1750, largely for dinner and dessert ware since it was not suitable for tea ware, being unable to withstand the heat of boiling water. Also for figures and ornaments until *c.*1775, when the factory closed down.

Caneware Stoneware. Dry-bodied stoneware developed at the end of the 1770s from an earlier light-coloured fine stoneware by Josiah Wedgwood. A similar body to bamboo ware but lighter in colour. Usually decorated with a minimal palette of bright blue and green enamel with the addition *c.*1800 of red.

Castleford ware Stoneware. Porcellanous dry-bodied stoneware developed by David Dunderdale of Castleford, Yorkshire from *c.*1794. It is a generic term for white unglazed vitrified stoneware which appears to be opaque, but when held to the light can be seen to be semi-translucent.

China Porcelain. First used in England to describe delicate true porcelain imported from China. Later the word also embraced soft paste porcelain, soapstone porcelain, hard paste porcelain and, from the mid-eighteenth century onwards, all manner of wares which resembled imported Chinese wares, particularly blue and white, whether porcelain or pottery.

Cream-coloured earthenware Earthenware. Natural light burning Staffordshire clay, almost yellow in colour, lightened and refined by purifying and hand-washing to produce a lighter, cream-coloured body. Developed by Josiah Wedgwood and further improved by him by the addition of china clay and china stone in 1776, once the use of these substances was permitted for the manufacture of non-translucent wares.

Creamware Earthenware. A combination of cream-coloured earthenware and a butter-coloured opaque glaze, first produced by Josiah Wedgwood in the early 1760s. The glaze was very soft initially, but in 1764 it was improved to create a durable surface with a slightly iridescent quality. Once its success was confirmed by the overwhelming demand, it was copied by many other Staffordshire potteries. Its production continued uninterrupted until 1846.

Crouch ware Stoneware. A drab, greyish-coloured heavy stoneware made in Germany and elsewhere on the Continent and imported into England in the late sixteenth and seventeenth centuries. Possibly the name derives from the French word for pitcher, 'cruche', since many wine bottles and liquor-containers were made in this earthenware, either semi-vitrified or glazed with a salt glaze.

Delftware Earthenware. Natural clays fired once and dipped in lead glaze made white and opaque with the addition of tin. The technique was common all over Europe from earliest times – in France it is known as 'faience' and in Italy as 'maiolica'. In England it was known as 'galleyware' and used chiefly for apothecaries' ware until the fashion for copying blue and white Oriental porcelain encouraged potters to become more ambitious and attempt to copy Chinese wares. It was not called 'delftware' in England until Georgian times, when large quantities of tin enamelled ware were being made in Holland near the town of Delft. By this time tin glazed earthenware had been largely superseded by creamware.

Dry bodies Stoneware. Non-porous vitreous stoneware which needs no glaze, such as basaltes, jasper ware, red stoneware, caneware etc.

Earthenware Pottery made from natural clays which remain porous after firing and must be glazed to make them non-porous.

Egyptian black Stoneware. Vitreous stoneware stained black with iron oxide and fired once at a temperature just sufficient to vitrify the body and make it non-porous.

Encaustic ware Earthenware. Pottery decorated by means of a technique used by the ancient Greeks, Romans and Etruscans, whereby the coloured pigments are 'burnt in' to the body. The colours are usually limited to brick red and white.

'Etruscan' ware Stoneware. Wedgwood's range of black basaltes decorated by encaustic technique.

Faience Earthenware. French version of tin glazed earthenware. Doulton Faience made from about 1872, also known as Lambeth Faience.

Felspar porcelain Porcelain. A further refinement of bone china evolved by Spode at the end of the eighteenth century, whereby pure felspar was added to a body including a certain proportion of china clay and china stone. The result was an extremely hard, remarkably translucent and heat-resistant variation of bone china, which was also very costly.

Felspathic ware Earthenware. A refined clay body to which felspar has been added, resulting in a tough, almost translucent white body with a faint yellow tinge. Confusingly also known as 'semi-porcelain', 'opaque porcelain' (a contradiction in terms) and 'demi-porcelain', as well as 'ironstone', 'fling ware' and 'granite ware'.

Fine stonewares Stoneware. A group of fine-grained stonewares, glazed and unglazed, which vitrify when fired at high temperatures. The category includes the dry bodies: red stoneware, basaltes,

Egyptian black, bamboo ware, caneware, Castleford ware, jasper ware.

Flint ware Earthenware. Calcined finely powdered flint was added to clay bodies, which, when fired at high temperatures, produced a lighter-weight, more durable earthenware. Though probably used by such potters as John Astbury in the first half of the eighteenth century, the ingredient was largely ignored until the beginning of the nineteenth century, when it was used for felspathic wares and ironstone-type products.

Frit porcelain Porcelain. Almost all eighteenth-century English porcelains contained vitreous frit – a molten mixture of white sand, gypsum, soda, alum, salt and nitre which cooled to the consistency of glass and was then pounded to a very fine powder and added to the other ingredients.

Galleyware Earthenware. Early term for English and Dutch tin glazed earthenware, probably deriving from 'gallipot', an ancient word for a small earthen pot brought by galley from the Mediterranean.

Hard paste porcelain Porcelain. The nearest English approximation to true porcelain from China. Made from a paste containing kaolin and petuntse (Cornish china clay and china stone) with a glaze composed of pulverized china stone, lime and potash which fused entirely to the paste when fired at very high temperatures, resulting in a surface that was slightly duller than that of soft paste porcelain.

Ironstone caneware Stoneware. Fine-grained vitrified stoneware developed from 'piecrust' ware in the 1850s, completely ovenproof and heat-resistant.

Ironstone china Earthenware. Fine-bodied white earthenware with slight translucency, developed by C. J. Mason in 1813 and patented under the name of 'Mason's Patent Ironstone China'. A variation of felspathic ware, made by adding a finely ground glassy substance taken from molten slag to refined clay.

Ivory porcelain Porcelain. Glazed parian ware closely resembling ivory in appearance and texture, introduced in England in about 1856 for extremely expensive and delicate ornamental groups and figures. First made by Kerr & Binns of Worcester, and later the basis for Belleek, although their glaze was more iridescent and smooth.

Jackfield Earthenware. A generic term taken from one of the few known potteries making wares covered with a thick, lustrous black glaze obtained by firing cobalt at high temperatures over a brownish-red earthenware body. It was made in Staffordshire c.1751–72 and revived at the end of the nineteenth century for a range of cheaper wares on a harder, redder earthenware body, probably in imitation of the fashionable black basalts of the period.

Jasper ware Stoneware. A remarkably fine-grained white vitrified stoneware with translucent properties, developed by Josiah Wedgwood in about 1774. The unfired porous stoneware could absorb coloured metallic oxides and 'solid jasper' was made in dark blue, pale blue, lilac, sage green, olive green, black and yellow, though the last is rare. Applied relief decoration in white jasper – occasionally with touches of coloured jasper – produced the range of ornamental and decorative wares that are synonymous with the name Wedgwood today. An alternative method of colouring jasper was to dip the fine stoneware in a solution of liquid coloured jasper like slip, known as 'jasper dip'.

Jet ware Earthenware. A loose term encompassing wares glazed with a rich black glaze, also known as Jackfield.

Lambeth Faience Earthenware. Nineteenth-century revival of English, Italian and French tin glazed earthenware made by the firm of Doulton at their Lambeth potteries.

Lustre ware Earthenware and bone china. Ware decorated by an ancient technique of depositing a metallic coating – silver, gold, copper or purple lustre – on to the earthenware surface, sometimes with splashed or mottled effects. The technique was also used on creamware as well as earthenware and bone china, from the early nineteenth century onwards.

Maiolica Earthenware. Italian version of tin glazed earthenware, usually on a red or greyish natural clay which was very soft and easily chipped and broken. A 'maiolica palette' is a colour range confined to high temperature colours: blue, manganese purple, iron red, copper green and orange and yellow from antimony.

Majolica Stoneware. A range of wares introduced by Minton in 1851 owing little to the original Italian wares except the derivation of the name. Made in a fine stoneware body similar to caneware, it was dipped in tin glaze and painted in brilliant reds, pinks, blues, purples, mauves, greens, oranges, yellows, chestnuts and browns before firing, as well as being frequently pressed and moulded in high relief decoration.

Mocha ware Earthenware. A range of cheap domestic wares, tea and coffee wares, beer tankards, mugs and jugs, originally made in cream-coloured earthenware at the end of the eighteenth century. Decorated with broad bands of coloured slip – usually cream, light green or brown – into which, while it was still wet, a curious mixture of tobacco juice, turpentine, manganese and urine was dropped, flaring into moss-agate-type fronds. A cheaper version in buff or red earthenware was made from c.1820 onwards, including items used in public houses, marked from 1824 with the Excise mark for correct measure. Also known as Mokka or Moko.

Mother-of-pearl ware Porcelain. Parian porcelain similar to ivory porcelain but with a thick iridescent glaze resembling mother-of-pearl, made at Belleek, in Fermanagh, Ireland, and English potteries.

Nottingham stoneware Stoneware. Drab-coloured salt glazed stoneware made from the late 1680s, particularly by James Morley of Nottingham. Stoneware similar to Crouch ware was dipped into a liquid clay slip containing oxide of iron, which turned a rich sienna brown with a distinct metallic lustre when fired. Many pieces were decorated with incised work, and double-walled mugs and jugs, known as 'carved' stoneware, were made. From the beginning of the eighteenth century similar wares were made by many other potteries in the neighbourhood of Nottingham, including Swinton.

Parian – statuary and domestic Porcelain. Originally made by Copeland in 1842, and named for the ivory-coloured marbles from the Greek island of Paros, parian was a translucent porcelain paste containing felspar. It was taken up and used with great commercial success by Minton, among others, for quantities of busts, discreet nudes and figures from classical mythology – Venus in particular being a firm favourite. Domestic parian, developed in the late 1840s, was a cheaper harder paste, ideal for elaborately decorative jugs, vases and ornamental wares, although it picked up dirt easily on unglazed bases and was very difficult to clean.

Pearlware Earthenware. Made from c.1779 by Josiah Wedgwood as an alternative, whiter-bodied earthenware, following the success of creamware. Pearlware contained a considerable proportion of calcined flint and china clay, and proved ideal for transfer-printing. It was taken up and developed by Josiah Spode who, by 1790, had added small traces of cobalt to the formula to act as a 'blue whitener', and produced a fine white earthenware ideal for all domestic use.

Piecrust ware Stoneware. Originally made by Wedgwood as a substitute for pastry cases for crock pies and standing pies during the flour shortage and consequent high prices resulting from the Napoleonic Wars of 1793–1815. Fine-grained vitrified stoneware in 'pastry' colours, ranging from pale buff to crusty brown. Many of the finest pieces were decorated with sprigged ornament, game or trophies in high relief. These covers proved so popular that later they were made as proper dishes with lids bearing suitable pastry decoration.

Porcelain A translucent white substance made from paste containing kaolin and petuntse, vitreous and extremely tough, which rings with a metallic, echoing sound similar to glass when struck. Artificial boundaries between pottery and porcelain that have grown up over the years tend to define all translucent paste bodies as porcelain and opaque bodies as pottery.

Porcellanous Possessing the translucent qualities of porcelain.

Pottery Earthenware, stoneware and all other bodies which do not possess the properties of porcelain.

Prattware Earthenware. Made in Staffordshire c.1790–1830, named after Felix Pratt who was one of the best-known makers. Prattware is generally made in light-coloured or buff clay, decorated under the glaze with a limited range of high temperature colours – metallic oxides which could stand the heat of firing. The glaze sometimes has a bluish tinge, and apart from a series of figures, animals and Toby jugs, the most recognizable pieces are jugs, modelled in relief with borders of stylized leaves and foliage, with panels, medallions or broad bands of relief of favourite subjects such as Britannia, Nelson, the Sailor's

Return and similar traditional scenes.

'Queen's China' Porcelain. A brand name of Queen's Pottery, Longton, for their bone china.

'Queen's Ware' (Queensware) Earthenware. The name given by Wedgwood to his celebrated 'Creamware' range in honour of Queen Charlotte after she gave him a special commission in 1767. Many other potteries shamelessly took the name with alterations to the punctuation.

Red china Stoneware. Contemporary name given by Samuel Bell to his version of red stoneware which had powdered calcined flint added to the formula.

Red porcelain Stoneware. The name rather grandly used by early eighteenth-century Staffordshire potters for red stoneware.

Red stoneware Stoneware. Naturally coloured red vitreous stoneware made in England at the end of the seventeenth century and in the eighteenth century, principally in Staffordshire, in imitation of the small red stoneware teapots imported from China.

'Regent China' Porcelain. Brand name of Chamberlain's Worcester for their superior form of bone china.

Rosso antico Stoneware. Wedgwood's later verion of red stoneware of a better colour, often engine-turned after the manner of some early wares by John Astbury and his contemporaries. In the nineteenth century polished red stoneware was used as a base for copper lustre since the colour of the body enhanced the sheen and brilliance of the metallic finish.

Salt glazed stoneware Stoneware. There are two distinct varieties which often cause confusion. **Brown salt glazed stoneware** is a vitreous, drab or brown-coloured stoneware with a formula which includes sand or calcined flint. A variation is **Nottingham stoneware**. Glazing was achieved by throwing salt into the kilns at high temperature. The clays generally turned to a range of browns, from light beige to dark brown, in firing. First made in England around 1680, brown salt glazed stoneware continued production intermittently, and was revived in the nineteenth century for industrial and commercial use. It can best be recognized in the ink bottles, ginger beer bottles and spirit casks made at that time. **White salt glazed stoneware** was probably first experimented with by John Astbury, who is believed to have been the first potter to add calcined flint to clay to produce a harder body, in the 1720s. When fired at high temperatures, this body turned almost white and was non-porous with a matt appearance, which was enhanced with glazing by throwing salt into the kiln at high temperatures. By *c.*1740 it was being made extensively in Staffordshire, at first pressed in moulds, then slip-moulded in incredibly fine relief and detail. Its appearance was further enhanced by enamel painting from the late 1750s onwards.

Slipware Earthenware. Natural clays in reddish-browns and buff colours, brushed or dripped in slip – clay watered down to a treacly or creamy consistency. Thick brown slip was used over a buff-coloured surface in intricate lattice patterns, or white slip was trailed in simple designs and more elaborate patterns. Sometimes the coating of slip was scraped and cut away to make patterns showing the underlying colour of the earthenware, or incised with designs into which coloured slip or pigment was pressed. Over all the slip decoration, a lead-based glaze gave a streaky yellow colour, particularly noticeable on white slip, which turned the colour of butter.

Soapstone porcelain Porcelain. A soft paste containing about 40 per cent soapstone or pulverized steatite to make a denser, harder substance than soft paste porcelain which was resistant to the heat of boiling water. Its advantage was that it vitrified at slightly lower temperatures than other soft paste or hard paste porcelains, and was soft, malleable and relatively easy to work.

Soft paste porcelain Porcelain. A soft paste made according to a variety of complicated formulae, containing frit – a mixture of white sand, gypsum, soda, alum, salt and nitre, molten and then ground to fine powder and mixed with a fine-bodied clay. Unlike hard paste porcelain, the glaze does not fuse totally into the body and consequently it has more depth and gloss. The final quality of the objects largely depended on the quality and thickness of glaze. Soft paste is noticeably warmer to the touch than the coldness of hard paste.

Staffordshire basaltes Stoneware. A loose term covering all unattributable wares made in Egyptian black – clays stained with iron oxide and fired at high enough temperatures to vitrify the body. Also describes certain local wares made from the black-stained clays found close to coalmines.

Stone china Earthenware. Not to be confused with ironstone china, which is quite different. Stone china was first patented by Turner of Lane End in 1880, and was made using a felspathic stone or mineral which produced a finely textured, dense, opaque body, very heavy and durable, and slightly blue-grey. When Turner went bankrupt in 1806, Spode took over the formula and found it was ideally suitable for domestic wares: the enamels sank into the glaze and could not flake or wear. It was particularly suitable for Japan patterns with large areas of undecorated space, since the surface was smooth and unblemished, unlike early bone china and other felspathic wares.

Stoneware Earthenware. Natural clays with additional vitreous substances such as sand or calcined flint. The wares are rendered non-porous when fired and do not need glazing.

Terra cotta Earthenware. Unglazed natural clays, fired but still porous, made in what many Staffordshire potters called 'brick clay'. Used for architectural embellishments as well as for pottery pieces such as jardinières, cachepots, etc. English terra cotta was revived in the nineteenth century when its rich rose-red colour was achieved by spraying it with a chemical solution of iron chloride before firing.

Tin glazed, tin enamelled earthenware Earthenware. The natural clay was coated with lead glaze to which powdered tin had been added. When dry, the glaze compound formed a white powdery surface on which decoration was painted. It is a technique known from earliest times, originating in the Mediterranean, which spread through Europe and resulted in wares under various names including faience, maiolica and delftware.

Tortoiseshell ware Earthenware. After Enoch Booth developed a colourless lead glaze in *c*.1740, many potteries began to experiment with deliberately colouring it for decorative purposes, staining it with metallic oxides to produce greens, greys, slatey blues and browns which were translucent when fired. Thomas Whieldon also experimented in staining the body with pigments which were absorbed by the colourless glaze from *c*.1750. The palette was limited to metallic oxide colours – with the occasional addition of yellow. Production of less attractive 'smear' glazes continued intermittently until *c*.1820, sometimes attempting to reproduce Whieldon's agate ware with mottled surface glazes.

'True' porcelain Porcelain. Hard paste porcelain from China as opposed to European versions. The main secret of 'true' porcelain was the length of time which Chinese potters left the paste to mature – the factor that gave it such toughness and translucence. Seven years is often quoted as the inordinate time the paste was matured, during which certain chemical changes took place which were impossible to achieve by other means.

Vitreous stoneware Earthenware. Clays and bodies containing substances such as sand, calcined flints, felspars and minerals, which, when fired at high temperatures, become crystalline and render the body non-porous.

Vitrified stoneware Earthenware. The term by which vitreous stoneware is known after firing when the body has vitrified.

Welsh ware Earthenware. Large coarse earthenware dishes with simple combed, feathered or joggled slip decoration, descended from early slipware and remaining in production in rural potteries and small factories right through until at least 1820 and probably later. There was a pottery making Welsh ware in Isleworth from *c*.1795 which moved to Hounslow in 1810, and another in Lambeth from about 1811.

Whieldon ware Earthenware. Both solid agate and tortoiseshell ware are sometimes referred to as Whieldon ware, after the chief experimenter in both these techniques, Thomas Whieldon.

Prices and practices

Several events of major importance have taken place in the last few years which have caused the market for pottery and porcelain to alter more radically than anyone could have foreseen. A few years ago there was relatively little interest in English pottery except for rare and early pieces which were bought by specialist collectors. English porcelain lagged far behind the great Continental factories such as Vincennes, Sèvres, Meissen and Dresden, and was generally considered to be undervalued. A fine openwork Derby basket with applied florets dating from the mid-eighteenth century might cost between £500 and £700, while its Continental counterpart was at least a third more. Dr Wall Worcester tea bowls and saucers with blue and white chinoiserie decoration sold for around £200, while their Meissen equivalents were double the price.

English pottery at that time had just begun to come out of the doldrums, and English delft was beginning to climb, with dated eighteenth-century Bristol punchbowls already fetching £500 or more. Then the Lipski collection of English delft was sold, with each piece fetching extraordinarily high prices, and the effect was almost instantly reflected in the price of all good early English delft. Rare Lambeth pieces from the late seventeeth century rose to sell for between £1,300 and £1,800 in 1984, and by the following year fine Liverpool punchbowls were selling for £3,000 and upwards.

The sharp rise was not equalled by other categories – during that same period, English creamware was selling for as little as £100 for plain undecorated pieces, Whieldon-type and solid agate teapots could be found for less than £400 and salt glazed teapots decorated with enamels c.1755 for around £700. Prices rose steadily in 1984, and by 1985 solid agate and Whieldon-type ware had quadrupled in price to £1,600 or more. Salt glazed teapots were still about the same price, and the only indication of change was the fact that good examples with some damage had risen in price from less than £100 to between £250 and £350. Creamware had begun to increase in price, and any good pieces appearing on the market were snapped up very quickly. Good Liverpool or Leeds examples had risen to around £500 by the end of 1984.

English porcelain fared less well over the same period. Fine and highly collectable pieces have continued to rise in price, although still lagging behind Continental porcelain, and interest in the lesser English factories began to push up prices for pieces which had so far been largely ignored. Christian's Liverpool cups and saucers or tea bowls and saucers rose to sell for £250 or more, for example. But overall, by far the greatest leap in value was seen in the highly coloured nineteenth-century English majolica by Minton and other leading makers. Jardinières, plant pots and items made for Victorian conservatories suddenly raced ahead to reach staggering prices of £1,500 or more, which made Mason's Patent Ironstone China look like a bargain at around £3,000 for a dinner service.

In 1984, too, another sale had a direct bearing on prices. The first of

Michael Hatcher's salvaged treasure troves from the bottom of the South China Sea was sold in Amsterdam. Consisting of over 23,000 pieces of Chinese Ming and Transitional blue and white porcelain dating from 1620–82, the sale surprised everyone by holding a steady price throughout the marathon disposal, and indirectly stimulating other blue and white wares over the next 18 months. In 1986 Captain Hatcher salvaged a far less interesting cargo which, however, due to massive publicity, was bought by one of London's largest department stores in considerable quantities, but it is doubtful that it will have any effect on the sale of porcelain in the future beyond becoming a trendy possession for those with disposable incomes.

By the beginning of 1986 it was predicted that the price of English delftware had gone as high as the market could stand, and the nagging possibility that some of the pieces being sold might be Dutch made many collectors keep their hands firmly in their pockets. Delftware from Holland has never fetched the high prices of English pieces. Early dated and authenticated slipware had also been climbing steadily – always a collectors' market, prices have been high for several years for rare pieces in perfect condition. In June 1986 record sums of £40,000 were paid for two fine examples by Ralph Toft and William Talor, but the sale of another remarkable collection in July gave a further boost to early English pottery: £46,000 was paid for a signed piece by Thomas Toft, and an all-time record of £55,000 for a rare slipware jug c.1704. And, clearly, English delft had still not reached its peak, for the Rous Lench sale saw some staggering prices paid for rare and special items. Elsewhere too, equally high prices were paid in other salerooms, among them £3,000 for a rare pill slab and £6,500 for a Liverpool delft teapot.

Fine and rare examples of creamware and cream-coloured earthenware have seen a similar leap of almost 100 per cent in the same period – recently a fine creamware coffee pot and cover painted with young ladies in a garden sold for a remarkable £9,000. Solid agate and Whieldon-type wares have held steady, but rare and important pieces of white salt glaze dating from the mid-eighteenth century have reached an all-time record, with small figures and animals selling for prices in excess of £20,000 and fine examples of 'scratch blue' for up to £9,500. A measure of the remarkable popularity of English pottery and the comparative lack of enthusiasm for English porcelain can be seen by the £8,500 paid for a rare salt glaze model of a crouching leveret c.1750 and the £4,500 paid at the same sale for a Chelsea Red Anchor example of the same subject – both copied from a Meissen original.

However much the market may change over the next 12 months or more, it is clearly a buyers' market for porcelain. Except for rarities which will always fetch very high prices, some of the finest eighteenth-century porcelain is now extremely undervalued in comparison with almost every other category of antiques. Really fine decorative pieces such as Derby bocage candlesticks can be bought for between £300 and £500 and even rare pieces of Lund's Bristol are selling for around £1,000. While the once-despised Staffordshire animals and groups have reached unforeseen heights, with Ralph Wood lions selling for as much as £5,000 and Obadiah Sherratt circus and menagerie groups topping the market at between £12,000 and £20,000, pairs of early English Worcester partridge tureens can be bought for less than £2,000 in the white.

As always, once the prices of the best-known categories have gone beyond the reach of the average small collector, it is the unknown and unusual which take their place. Stonewares of all kinds have begun to attract attention recently, and not before time, since this can be one of the most rewarding categories for new discoveries and authenticated pieces from known late eighteenth- and early nineteenth-century makers. Here too, prices have begun to rise, although as yet the market is a long way from reaching the astronomical levels of early English pottery. But is is always the vey top of the market which influences the middle and lower levels: trends are most easily recognized when the market is at its peak. Once, there was no question of damaged pieces selling to any collector worth his salt. Today the indications are that serious collectors would sooner buy a good quality piece with some damage or restoration than settle for second best. Prices for damaged pieces in every category have been rising recently – a factor which few people could have foreseen until a very few years ago.

Good collections grow because people find a period, a theme or a particular maker which appeals to their individual taste – not because they are hoping to make money out of a fashionable trend. Almost every collector replaces a doubtful early purchase with a better one as the eye improves and knowledge deepens. Some people like to brave the market place and buy in the salerooms, though there are many who have regretted it later. Others spend time at the smaller antique fairs during slack times, talking to dealers who mostly carry on their businesses from private houses, thus cutting down on overheads and making it possible to sell for slightly less than specialist shops. Those who choose this path must be patient, for the choice is more limited, and lesser-known dealers do not go to every antique fair in their local district. For those who cannot wait too long, there are plenty of dealers with larger stocks who are only too happy to advise, offering the benefit of years of experience to anyone who shows a genuine interest in their particular specialist field.

Slipware

Historical background

In Tudor times, the bulk of domestic English pottery was glazed with a lead-based glaze which turned a yellowish colour when fired in the kiln. By adding copper oxide to the glaze, a typical 'Tudor green' colour was produced with characteristic uneven smears. The use of a liquid white-coloured slip – clay mixed with water to a creamy consistency – had been known to the Romans, who used it to decorate earthenware, but it was not rediscovered in England until the mid-sixteenth century.

Many techniques which were later used in both pottery and porcelain can be seen in slipware, particularly the sgraffito method of decoration, where a design is scratched through a layer of light-coloured slip to expose the earthenware underneath, or where slip of a thicker consistency is pressed into lines incised in the earthenware. One of the most effective methods of decoration was with white slip trailed in patterns over the dark surface of earthenware, or when the whole surface was coated with light-coloured slip and slip made from reddish-brown clay was trailed over it in intricate patterns. Many highly decorative results were achieved by these methods, believed to have originated at Wrotham, Kent, and used subsequently in Devon. In Staffordshire, where there were beds of red and buff-coloured clays, slipware was made from the end of the seventeenth century. Here, large dishes and chargers were made, up to 20 in (51 cm) or more in diameter, decorated with intricate borders and elaborate patterns, many of them by the famous Toft family.

Slipware pie plates, often decorated with simple combed patterns, were among the earliest pieces of domestic pottery which would withstand a low heat in an oven, and in many rural areas they were made and used right up to the middle of the nineteenth century.

Staffordshire slipware dish c.1720–30 with brown base over dark buff-coloured earthenware, white slip decoration coloured yellow by lead glaze. 16½ in (42 cm) diameter.

Signs of authenticity

1. Distinctive yellow colouring of glaze, sometimes with traces of green.
2. Surface ranging from uneven to knobbly, where the slip decoration stands out from the surface.
3. Limited variety of shapes, coarsely potted.
4. Early plates fairly deep, often without rims.
5. Rims of chargers often highly decorated as well as centres.
6. More than two colours of slip extremely rare, then usually only variations in tone of slip colour.
7. Rims on chargers broad, curved. Narrow flat rims denote first half of eighteenth century or later.
8. Objects usually of relatively large size due to clumsiness of materials – rare to find small objects of early date.
9. Glaze only on underside, showing colour of natural fired earthenware.
10. Staffordshire wares most commonly with slip-coated ground.
11. Staffordshire slipware on both red and buff-coloured earthenware – most other potteries in varied red clays.
12. Patterns and designs correct for period.

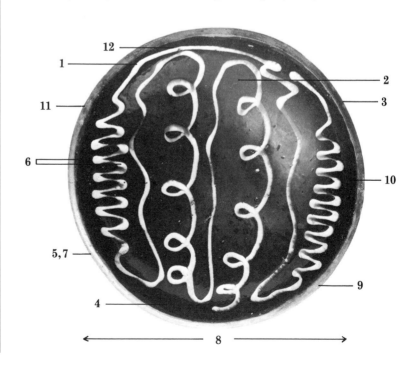

Materials and decoration

Coarse earthenware, red or buff-coloured, with trailed contrasting slip decoration standing out from the surface, glazed with yellowish-coloured lead glaze, always turning the white slip to cream colour or butter colour. Simplest decoration was no more than a series of dots, lines and outlines, applied with a quill used like a tube in the same way as icing on a cake. Combed patterns and marbled effects, sometimes known as 'joggled', were also common in local potteries.

Popular subjects were naive, usually full-length portraits of Charles II, William III, simple birds, particularly owls, heraldic animals, stylized flowers – tulips being most popular after the accession of William of Orange in 1689.

Wrotham ware, usually in red earthenware, was sometimes decorated with small designs stamped from different-coloured clay and applied; dishes, mugs and tygs have survived from this area.

Sgraffito decoration was largely made in the Devon potteries and ships were a popular subject, as well as the royal coat of arms and naive flower patterns.

Principal producers and products

Kent, especially Wrotham; Devon, especially Bideford, Barnstaple; Sussex; Essex; Derbyshire; Somerset; Wiltshire; Warwickshire; Glamorgan; Yorkshire; North Staffordshire.

Mugs, tygs, puzzle jugs, dishes, chargers, marriage cradles, harvest pitchers, pie plates, ewers, posset pots, bowls.

Period of manufacture
*c.*1600 and earlier to *c.*1800 and later.

Variations

As with oak furniture, purely functional pottery, such as harvest jugs, pie plates, mugs, ewers and jugs, continued to be made in many parts of the country for rural use long after more sophisticated wares were in everyday use in towns and cities. One of the most enduring shapes was the oblong pie plate with a simple combed decoration or a simple outline of a bird, sometimes with an impressed 'rope' pattern round the edge, which was still being made and used well into the middle of the nineteenth century. The other most common traditional object was the 'marriage cradle', which continued to be made and given to newly married couples right through to the 1830s and probably even later.

A. *Staffordshire slipware baking dish, late 18th century, with red body, brown slip ground and cream slip decoration coloured by lead glaze.*

B. *Rare North Staffordshire slipware mug of thistle shape, with a low-set small loop handle. The buff-coloured body is decorated in 'feathered' cream and brown slip, and it is glazed with typical translucent yellow-tinted lead glaze. The neck is inscribed 'RC' on one side and dated '1711'. 4 in (10 cm) high.*

Reproductions

The shapes of objects nearly always betray their late origins: well-turned foot-rims to plates, flat rims instead of curved ones, strap handles on mugs instead of small, rounded ring-shaped handles. The yellowish glaze is too uniform in colour, and the decoration either too sophisticated or overly naive. Above all, there are small objects which were never originally made, such as egg cups and cruets, as well as salt 'kits'.

Most deceptive are genuine well-used nineteenth-century pie plates, honestly made by some local pottery and used for making 'plate pies' well into this century. The generic term for these dishes is 'Welsh ware' although they were made at Isleworth and then Hounslow from 1810 and Lambeth from 1811.

Price bands

Loving cups:
17th century £6,000–£8,000;
18th century £1,500–£2,000.

Mugs (dated) £1,200–£3,000;
(undated) £400–£900.

Dishes (named, dated) £10,000 and over; (undated) £6,000–£8,000.

Welsh ware £120–£400.

A

B

Delftware

Historical background

The technique of adding tin oxide to lead glaze to produce a brilliant white surface on earthenware was an ancient one, known to the Syrians, the Moors, the Spaniards and the Italians, who called it 'maiolica'. From about 1550 onwards tin glazed earthenware was being made in England, where it was known as 'galleyware',

possibly from the same origin as 'gallipot'. It only became known as 'Delftware' in Georgian times, when more of this type of ware was being made in the Netherlands than in England.

In 1567 Jasper Andries and Jacob Jansen established a galleyware pottery in Norwich, later moving to Aldgate. Their principal range of products was apothecaries' ware and tiles. A similar range was also made at Lambeth from the end of the sixteenth century onwards, and in Southwark from about 1620–30. Early syrup jars were fairly squat and had a handle at the back and a spout in front, but later jars stood on more slender stems and had no handles. The spouts were at the back, leaving the front free for decorative labels embellished with birds, cherubs, angels, baskets of flowers, sprigs and ribbons. Commemorative plates and chargers were made from

about 1630 onwards, as well as barrel-shaped mugs and wine jars.

From about 1600, when Chinese porcelain began to come into Bristol through the East India Company, many painters copied designs of Ming blue and white wares on tin glazed earthenware. Potteries were established at Brislington and in and around Bristol. Bristol delft is often decorated in manganese as well as blue. Wincanton delft, in production for a very short time from about 1736, excelled in decorated wares in manganese. Delftware was also made in Liverpool from about 1710. In particular, towards the end of the eighteenth century, Liverpool made great punchbowls and plates decorated with ships in full sail.

Bristol delft charger with Adam and Eve naively and boldly painted in blue on white, with some green, yellow and red. 13¼ in (33.5 cm) diameter.

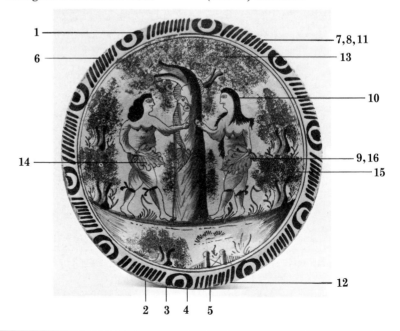

Materials and decoration

Natural earthenware body, fired once, then coated with lead glaze mixed with tin oxide and left to dry, leaving a white powdery surface. Cobalt pigment was painted on to this powdery surface, and then the piece was fired again. Yellow from antimony was the next colour to be used successfully, but only in small quantities. Manganese, the next pigment, was mainly used by Bristol, Brislington and Wincanton. In the early eighteenth century, iron reds, copper green and dark brown from manganese were also used for a growing number of decorative and commemorative wares.

Some Lambeth and London delft followed the Italian maiolica style of extremely rich all-over decoration, mostly in varying tones of blue with small quantities of other colours. In general, however, English delft was decorated with pleasing if slightly confused images drawn from the Chinese, the Dutch, or native traditional patterns, with Bristol using the widest colour palette.

Principal producers and products

London, especially Lambeth, Southwark; Bristol and Brislington; Wincanton; Liverpool.

Drug jars, syrup jars, apothecaries' pots, jars and pill slabs, barbers' bowls, bleeding bowls, large serving dishes, chargers, plates, dishes, posset pots, vases, flower bricks, caudle cups, fuddling cups, puzzle jugs, wine jars, mugs, jugs, tiles and rare tea bowls, teapots, tea ware.

Period of manufacture
*c.*1550 to *c.*1800.

A royal portrait dish, Brislington delft, painted with a portrait of Queen Mary, with initials 'Q M' and showing signs of wear round the rim. 9¼ in (23.5 cm) diameter.

Reproductions

Nineteenth-century quasi-delftware was made in the 1850s by Herbert Minton, and copied by other contemporary potteries. Similar ware was made at John Doulton's Lambeth pottery from 1872. If any confusion arises, it is likely to be with delftware made in England after the Italian maiolica style, but the colours are more strident, being made from different pigments produced chemically or artificially, and in general the shapes are more ornate than simple early English wares. French faience also has common roots with the ancient technique of tin glazing, but again bears only a superficial resemblance to early English delftware.

A delft flower brick remarkably finely painted with flowers and tendrils in manganese, sage green, yellow and iron red, possibly Liverpool, c.1760. 5 in (13 cm) long.

Variations

Dutch delft bears a more than superficial resemblance to English ware, but closer inspection reveals that the earthenware itself is generally more stone-coloured than the warm buff of Bristol or the beige of Liverpool. The confusion may be more noticeable with apothecaries' ware – the 'singing bird', for example, used on drug jar labels with two birds, probably originated in the Netherlands, but English birds are altogether plumper, and the cherubs' heads more childlike and less like Renaissance chubby-cheeked versions. Italian tin glazed wares of similar period are quite different in shape, and the body is much more reddish-coloured.

Price bands

Drug, syrup jars: Lambeth £400–£1,200; London £300–£800. Dry drug jars less.

Sack bottles
Lambeth £1,500–£3,500; London £800–£2,500.

Bleeding bowls £1,000–£2,200.

Mugs £600–£1,000 and upwards.

Early 18-century apothecaries' drug jar for dry or powdered drugs, the mouth slightly out-curved to allow a parchment cover to be tied over it. 6¾ in (17 cm) high.

Early blue and white

Signs of authenticity

1. Typical small size for period.
2. Flat, flush-fitting lid – domed lids of later period.
3. Lid slightly too small where shrinkage has occurred in firing.
4. Blue may be blurred in outline where pigment has sunk into unglazed powdery surface before firing.
5. Lid with simple decoration and finial, matching teapot in age and wear.
6. Earthenware with buff-coloured body indicates Liverpool.
7. White tin glaze with pinkish tone usually indicates Lambeth.
8. Liverpool blue softer, more greyish in tone, with matt appearance where it has formed small pools and sunk into the glaze.
9. Bristol blue much brighter, more vibrant.
10. Slight pitting of glaze on base indicates Bristol.

Early tin glazed earthenware blue and white teapot with chinoiserie decoration, in a shape clearly influenced by Staffordshire designs, with curving spout and crabstock handle. $3\frac{1}{4}$ in (8 cm) high.

Historical background

The first attempts at reproducing the costly and much-prized Oriental blue and white porcelain using the brilliant white tin glazed surface of delft-type earthenware in England began some time between 1620 and 1630. 'Hollandsche Porceleyn', the Dutch version, came a little later. All kinds of Chinese symbols were painted by English artists with varying degrees of success on the difficult, absorbent powdery surface of the unfired glaze: peonies, prunus, willow, pine tree, pagodas, fences and Chinese figures, as well as many of the classic Chinese border patterns.

There was little demand for tea ware at this period: the cost of tea was prodigious, and in 1658 it cost anything from 16 to 50 shillings a pound, today's equivalent of between £80 and £450. Towards the end of the century, and certainly at the beginning of the eighteenth century, however, tea had ceased to be regarded as a purely medicinal drink, and was drunk socially, in very small quantities. It is not surprising that early English teapots are often mistaken for miniatures, since they seldom measure more than four to five inches in height. Quite a large number of delftware teapots were made in fashionable blue and white, although they cannot have been very satisfactory, since the earthenware body could not withstand the heat of boiling water and frequently cracked.

It is interesting that these early delftware teapots with their high-set spouts follow the shape of Chinese teapots, while the later, traditional Staffordshire shape with an almost L-shaped curving spout is derived from the shape of Chinese wine pots.

66

Materials and decoration

Earthenware of red, brown or buff colour, with a white tin glazed surface decorated under the glaze with cobalt blue pigment in Oriental, Chinese and charmingly mixed patterns which may include traditional English elements – border patterns of small sprigs of flowers and early diaper patterns. Octagonal plates, made with press-moulding techniques, are of later date and more commonly made in Liverpool or late Bristol than from the London potteries, which made deeper dishes with wide rims. Flower bricks, which were also made with wells in the centre and holes for quill pens, were favourite subjects for Oriental designs, and were made by Lambeth, Liverpool and Bristol, the bases often shaped into simple curves. Most Oriental designs were used by all potteries although some, such as a man fishing from a bridge and one or two men in a skiff-shaped boat, are particular to Bristol.

Variations

The most common confusion arises with Dutch delft of similar period and design, but the painting is less fluid and robust, the designs are more mechanical and spindly in execution, and the earthenware is often of a far lighter colour than any English delft. The glaze on Dutch delft is more deeply and profusely pitted on the underside than any English ware, even Bristol, which generally shows some signs of pitting. Dutch delft continued to be made in greater quantities and far later through the eighteenth century than English delft.

Principal producers and products

Bristol and Brislington; London, especially Lambeth; Liverpool from 1710.

Tea boxes or caddies, flower bricks, plates, dishes, bowls, tiles, mugs, teapots, vases, tulip vases, jugs.

Period of manufacture
c.1685 to c.1740.

Rare delft jug in blue and white with a 'sparrow-beak lip' and blue dash decoration to the handle, from the early 18th century. $4\frac{1}{2}$ in (11.5 cm) high. On either side, a pair of early 18th-century salts decorated with Oriental flowers and little insects. $3\frac{1}{4}$ in (8 cm) diameter.

Reproductions

Some pseudo-Oriental designs were revived by Lambeth in the nineteenth century, but in general the pottery revival of the Victorian era favoured the more highly decorated polychrome wares, particularly those derived from early Italian maiolica. Some copies of early Oriental blue and white were made by Spode too, and bear some resemblance visually to early tin glazed blue and white wares, but handling them should be enough to establish that these are not made of earthenware.

Price bands

Punch bowls:
Bristol £2,000–£3,000;
London £1,200–£1,500;
Liverpool £1,000–£3,000.

Flower bricks £180–£400.

Plates from £200 (prime condition).

Mugs £1,000–£1,800.

Royalist portrait chargers:
Lambeth £1,800–£4,000;
Bristol £2,000–£3,000.

Early Oriental polychrome ware

Signs of authenticity

1. Early eighteenth-century polychrome in bright, clear colours.
2. The deep puce of later wares is found on some tin enamelled ware.
3. Oriental polychrome painted with far more sophistication than earlier blue and white.
4. From mid-eighteenth century, colours become more muted, less bright.
5. Many designs, while still Oriental in flavour, much more Europeanized in later wares.
6. Shapes of plates, dishes conform with other makers of the same period.
7. Plates, dishes glazed with white glaze on underside as well as surface.
8. More elaborate shapes of wares from mid-eighteenth century onwards.
9. Some pieces with over-glaze decoration – usually Liverpool.
10. Use of gilding, usually on rims only, on some later tin glazed wares.

Historical background

By the beginning of the eighteenth century, K'ang Hsi porcelain in the delicate colours of 'famille verte' and 'famille rose' had come into the country and begun to eclipse the fashion for blue and white. While still nowhere near the translucent porcelain from which the designs were taken, tin glazed earthenware was very skilfully decorated by painters and artists in a bright, clear palette. The colours were still essentially the metallic oxide pigments and, when compared to the delicately coloured enamels on Oriental porcelain, are far too bright and crude to be mistaken for any enamelled decoration. By this time, the artists had become extremely proficient, executing each piece with swift, sure brushstrokes – a similar technique to Chinese calligraphy, allowing no room for error. Colour pigments were still applied on to the glaze in its unfired state, although on some much later tin glazed earthenware, usually from Liverpool, occasionally some decoration was applied over the glaze. But this is rare, as is gilding, which was also used on some Liverpool pieces.

Decoration was by no means confined to Chinese and Oriental designs. In addition to commemorative dishes and chargers, there were grand polychrome posset pots with twirling crowned covers, loving cups painted with the arms of city companies and guilds, as well as flowers, leaves and more abstract designs. It must always be remembered that although tin glazed earthenware was one of the earliest forms of pottery made for domestic use, it did not cease to be made as the next development appeared on the market. Many shapes, patterns, styles and objects which were made in the potteries and porcelain factories were also made in humble tin glazed earthenware. Like oak furniture and country furniture, traditional potteries continued to make plates and dishes for the local population long after they had been superseded in towns and cities.

Rare Liverpool delftware plate decorated in Chinese export 'famille rose' style with an inner diaper border, with a garden scene that is a quaint mixture of European and Chinese, the border with sprays of flowers alternating with rather curious birds and sprigs, with gilding round the rim. 9½ in (24 cm) diameter.

Materials and decoration

Earthenware with opaque white tin glaze, decorated in bright colours in designs derived from Oriental 'famille rose' and 'famille verte'. Detail and quality of decoration is much more skilled and fine than on early blue and white. The growing use of a simple diaper border becomes more evident as techniques of painting on the soft, porous surface improved. There is much less blurring and a much crisper effect is achieved. There are even some extremely sophisticated examples painted with panels or 'cartouches' with early versions of pheasants and birds with sprigs of blossom. Towards the middle of the eighteenth century the colours become more muted, more like pastel painting or watercolour, as better control of pigment, powdery glaze and firing temperatures were developed. Gilding is usually unfired oil gilding and is generally confined to the rims.

Principal producers and products

Bristol; London, especially Lambeth; Wincanton; Liverpool.

Plates and dishes (sometimes in several sizes with same designs), jugs, mugs, cups, saucers, puzzle jugs, loving cups, chargers, punch bowls, punch ladles, small dishes, bleeding bowls, barbers' bowls, vases, flower bricks, tea caddies, tea boxes, candlesticks.

Period of manufacture
*c.*1720 to *c.*1780 and later.

Variations

Dutch delft decorators kept far more rigidly to the Oriental designs which they copied, unlike the artists who decorated English polychrome delft. Interpretations are very fluid, often mixed with distinctly English ingredients. These brightly coloured later designs were also made in French faience, but in England the use of over-glaze decoration was an exception, while on the Continent it was far more common. It is as well to remember the distinctive colouring of English earthenware and the regional clays when comparing with later Dutch or Continental versions.

Price bands

Tin glazed plates £200–£450; chargers – blue dash, tulips, oak leaves etc. £800–£3,000.

Mugs £350–£850.

Jugs from £400.

Later periods lower prices.

A. *Staffordshire salt glazed stoneware teapot, probably by John Toft, with crabstock handle and green diaper border, with a simple landscape design on the lid. 3½ in (9 cm) high.*

B. *Tin glazed dish with a narrow rim decorated with a version of diaper and dots with a bird perched in a rooted flowering shrub by the side of a lake, in yellow, orange, blue, green and manganese. 9¼ in (23.5 cm) diameter.*

Reproductions

Nineteenth-century so-called delftwares are most commonly decorated with the Japanese designs that were popular in Victorian times, which have quite a different appearance. Liverpool continued to make delftware through to the beginning of the nineteenth century, though the smaller potteries which continued this traditional product mostly reverted to early blue and white designs of earlier periods, in keeping with the nineteenth-century trends.

White salt glazed stoneware

Signs of authenticity

1. Glaze pitted like an orange skin.
2. Light in weight.
3. Decoration in applied relief usually indicates period between 1720 and 1740.
4. Brilliant clear enamel colours from *c.*1745.
5. Many intricate pierced, latticed and curiously shaped moulded wares, usually undecorated.
6. Sharper, crisper modelling, more elaborate decoration in low relief from *c.*1745.
7. Later decoration in too wide a range of colours.
8. Palette limited to mauves, pinks, yellows, greens and turquoise.
9. Palette including iron reds, green, turquoise, yellow and black only may indicate Dutch decoration, not English.
10. Base unglazed.

Historical background

By the beginning of the eighteenth century two problems concerned the English potteries: the continued searches for a fine-bodied clay which would more closely resemble the translucent Chinese porcelain and for a substance which would stand up to the heat of boiling water. Teapots and teaware as well as tableware were now being imported from Germany, where Meissen had discovered the necessary ingredients for making 'true' porcelain. In addition, a whole new colour range had been introduced with porcelain in 'famille rose' and 'famille verte'.

In Staffordshire, where kilns were fired with coal and reached a greater heat than charcoal-fired kilns, some stoneware had been made towards the end of the seventeenth century. The stoneware body was made by adding powdered calcined flint to light-coloured clay. It was found that if salt was thrown in when the kiln was at maximum temperature, it vaporized and fused to stoneware, giving it a glaze which was colourless and characteristically pitted like the skin of an orange. Salt glazed stoneware proved to be able to withstand the heat of boiling water.

The earliest known dated piece of salt glazed stoneware of this type is 1720, but the greatest period of production was between 1740 and 1760, after Enoch Booth had developed a colourless lead glaze and techniques of enamelling were discovered. Early salt glazed decoration in applied relief, or using the sgraffito technique and rubbing cobalt pigment into incised decoration, gave way to enamelled colours in about 1740–45. Colour pigments were mixed with the colourless lead glaze compound and added after the first firing, then fired again at a lower temperature to produce clear, bright colours – usually mauve, pink, yellow, green, black and a vivid turquoise, all made with metallic oxides.

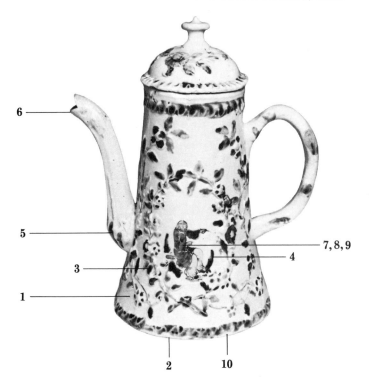

Salt glazed stoneware coffee pot with moulded relief and moulded crabstock handle and 'dragon' spout, with enamelled polychrome decoration in clear bright colours, rather unevenly painted.

Materials and decoration

Opaque stoneware, greyish white, light in weight and thinly potted, glazed by throwing common salt into the kiln at maximum temperature, resulting often in a pitted appearance like an orange skin. From *c.1720* decoration was usually limited to stamped applied relief, as well as 'sprigged' relief of floral and fruiting vine branches. Incised decoration was sometimes heightened by the addition of cobalt pigment rubbed into the incisions. This is known as scratch blue or sgraffito, and is usually found on jugs, mugs, teapots and coffee pots. Slip-casting methods produced extraordinarily fine, intricate designs and shapes, particularly in later teapots, which were often moulded in wildly eccentric shapes, including camels and houses. From *c.1745* when moulds were made from plaster of Paris instead of clay, detail is finer and crisper, often following the lines of contemporary silver.

Reproductions

Lightweight salt glazed stoneware was not reproduced as such – only the shapes and patterns, which continued to be made in a variety of bodies throughout the eighteenth century. Easily differentiated is nineteenth-century Lambeth stoneware with scratch blue decoration, heavier in weight and altogether more clumsy.

Principal producers and products

John Toft; Enoch Booth; Aaron Wood; John Astbury; Thomas Heath; Thomas Whieldon; Wedgwood Snr; William Littler; Leeds; Liverpool.

Teapots, coffee pots, chocolate pots, punch pots, dishes, plates, puzzle jugs, mugs, food warmers, night lamps, cream jugs, sauce and butter boats, spoon trays, dessert baskets, serving dishes, chestnut warmers, tureens, jelly moulds, mousse moulds, pickle dishes.

Period of manufacture
*c.*1720 to *c.*1760.

Slip-cast white salt glazed tankard covered with intricate scenes of drunken revelry entitled 'Midnight Conversation' after Hogarth, with armorials on the other side, and a band of acorns and sprigs round the bottom, c.1745. 7 in (18 cm) high.

Teapot with scratch blue decoration with rouletted herringbone border, moulded ware, c.1760–60. 8 in (9.75 cm) high.

Finely moulded white salt glazed spoon tray or dish decorated with birds and double rope border in low relief.

Price bands

Basket-moulded, lattice plates £300–£800.

Mugs, tankards £300–£600.

Slip moulded wares £1,800–£5,000.

Rare collectors' pieces £9,000 and upwards.

Sauce and butter boats (silver shape) £450–£550.

Cream jugs £400–£500.

Variations

The shapes of many items of salt glazed stoneware remained unchanged for decades, particularly those of teapots with crabstock handles and curving spouts – a shape derived from Chinese wine pots. These teapots were also made with a thicker colourless lead glaze, and in vitrified stoneware. Pierced ware, lattice-rimmed plates, basket-moulded dishes and many other items made in white salt glazed stoneware were also made in almost identical shapes in creamware, but confusion would only arise from the patterns and shapes – the body and glaze of creamware are completely different from salt glazed stoneware.

Creamware

Signs of authenticity

1. Early cream-coloured earthenware extremely light in weight.
2. Piercing and lattice work very characteristic.
3. Very distinctive shapes and patterns.
4. Early cream glaze almost iridescent when held to the light – glaze rich, thick and almost brilliant yellow.
5. No crazing of the glaze from c.1764.
6. Handles on coffee pots, teapots, chestnut tureens made by Leeds characteristically made with double twist, secured to the body with crisply modelled leaf or flower in applied relief.
7. From c.1764 creamware usually decorated with painted or enamelled border patterns only.
8. Painting in two colours only – black and brick red – typical of Leeds.
9. From c.1760 transfer-printing in black, particularly Liverpool, embellished by hand-painted sprigs of flowers, festoons etc.
10. Authentic early Wedgwood 'Creamware' and 'Queen's Ware' marked with impressed mark **WEDGWOOD**.

Historical background

With the tremendous increase in wealth in the country as a whole, the expanding middle classes of mid-eighteenth-century England moved into newly built Georgian town houses and country houses and began to adopt fashions which had been brought into court circles on the accession of George I. One of the greatest pressures on the potteries was for matching dinner services for the new custom of dining *à la Berline* at a single table, instead of the rather haphazard collection of small tables, with unmatched crockery and glasses, served from long buffet-style sideboards.

Staffordshire potters had discovered that by firing some light-coloured earthenware at a lower temperature, an almost white body could be produced, which was then glazed with a colourless lead glaze, but it was not very durable or satisfactory. In 1761, Josiah Wedgwood succeeded in producing a strong, near-white earthenware body and, almost simultaneously, developed an opaque, thick, cream-coloured glaze, and thus made the first range in his celebrated 'Creamware'. At first, the glaze was too soft and scratched easily, and was not entirely suitable for everyday use. Nor, in its early stages, was it able to withstand the heat of boiling water, so it was unsuitable for making teapots and coffee pots. However, Wedgwood continued to refine and improve the earthenware body and strengthen the cream-coloured glaze, until by 1764 it was durable, strong, did not scratch or craze, and was resistant to boiling water. After a royal commission, Wedgwood renamed the range 'Queen's Ware'.

Both Leeds and Liverpool began making creamware in about 1765, and some intricate pieces have survived, many of them pierced and latticed, most of them undecorated. Their creamware was not, in its early states, as strong and durable as Wedgwood's and on the whole pieces were of the more decorative kind, such as chestnut warmers, dessert baskets and pierced plates and dishes.

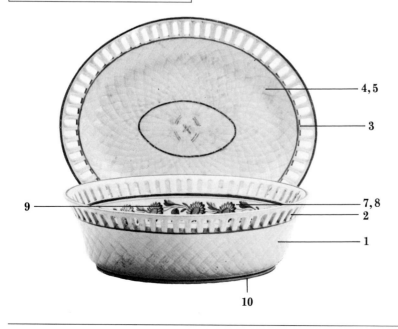

— 4, 5

— 3

— 7, 8

— 2

9 —

— 1

10

Wedgwood 'Queen's Ware' dinner service decorated with hand-painted blue daisies and a pink line border, in pierced and moulded lattice, c.1765–70.

Materials and decoration

Light-coloured earthenware or stoneware with a transparent glaze, or coated with a rich, cream-coloured, opaque glaze. Cream-coloured earthenware coated with transparent glaze was made for a short period at the Leeds, Cockpit Hill and Melbourne potteries, and was often very similar in appearance to white salt glazed stoneware, with much piercing and lattice work, some applied ornament and characteristic twisted handles.

Creamware coated with a rich, silky, butter-coloured glaze was developed by Wedgwood at about the same time, and was used for a huge range of useful wares. The first version of creamware might be called 'transitional' since, although it was an important breakthrough technically, it was not very durable or practical, and was soon discontinued by many potteries in favour of Wedgwood's creamware. The 'transitional' version was seldom decorated in colours – on Wedgwood's creamware painted decoration was limited at first to simple border patterns, painted over the glaze and fired again at a lower temperature.

Rare commemorative Wedgwood creamware jug with baluster-shaped body and blue line decoration, inscribed 'C. Barker 1790' with floral decoration on one side and an amusing rural scene on the other. Impressed **WEDGWOOD**. *8¾ in (22 cm) high.*

A cruet stand in pearlware with a design closely related to early creamware. Apart from the surface decoration of the stand itself, the blue line borders are almost the only embellishment except for small sprigs of flowers on the individual containers. c.1785. 8½ in (21.5 cm).

Reproductions

A common trap to fall into is to mistake creamware marked **WEDGWOOD & CO** for the work of Josiah Wedgwood. It is in fact from the Burslem pottery of Ralph Wedgwood, who made quantities of good creamware in the eighteenth and nineteenth centuries.

The name and mark **WEDGWOOD & CO** was also used by a Tunstall pottery in the nineteenth century. Other misleading marks include **VEDGWOOD, WEDGWOOD WARE** and **QUEEN'S WARE** or **QUEENSWARE** – Wedgwood's 'Queen's Ware' was impressed **WEDGWOOD**.

Variations

From the late 1770s Josiah Wedgwood introduced 'pearlware', which he considered to be merely an improvement on creamware. It is a harder-bodied earthenware with an almost white glaze and a slightly iridescent appearance, resistant to boiling water and particularly suitable for transfer-printing. Many other potteries made pearlware, including Josiah Spode at a slightly later date. Today it is a highly collectable field, because it was made for a very short period – probably only about ten years from the 1770s to the 1780s.

Price bands

Teapots: Leeds £400–£600; Wedgwood £500–£800; Cockpit Hill £450–£750.

Tureens: Leeds £250–£500; Liverpool £350–£500.

Bowls £250–£550 and upwards.

Higher prices for collectors' pieces.

Principal producers and products

Wedgwood; Leeds; Liverpool; Spode; Minton; Swinton; Swansea; Sunderland; Melbourne; Cockpit Hill; Turner of Lane End; Castleford; and many other unmarked Staffordshire potteries.

Sweetmeat and pickle dishes, bowls, cream jugs, sauce and butter boats, tureens, pharmaceutical jars, jugs, dessert plates, chestnut warmers, food warmers, pierced plates and dishes, strainers, ladles, slices, shell dishes, cruets, candlesticks, screw-top ointment jars, snuff boxes, centrepieces, mousse moulds, jelly moulds, shapes, ice cream moulds, night lamps. From c.1764 teapots, coffee pots, chocolate pots, tableware.

Period of manufacture
c.1761 to 1846.

Soft paste porcelain

Historical background

'True' porcelain is made from a paste containing china clay (kaolin) and china stone (petuntse), both related to granite. From about 1710, when the formula and its ingredients were discovered on the Continent, diligent searches began in England – particularly in Cornwall, rich in granite – for these two essential elements. Chemists, scientists and analysts also experimented with all manner of substances which might provide a substitute for china clay and china stone, neither of which appeared to be present in the substrata of England.

Opaque white glass was being made in Europe at that time as a form of counterfeit porcelain, which may have prompted experiments in English glass factories. Soft paste porcelain was first manufactured in about 1745, at Edward Heylin's Glassworks at Bow, Middlesex. At Bristol, it is believed that 'porcelane' was first made at 'Lowd'ns Glass House'. At first Bow soft paste was drab and only semi-transparent, but from 1749 the addition of bone ash produced a whiter, more satisfactory paste. At about the same time, the manufactory at Chelsea began making a similar paste with greater success. Some soft paste porcelain was made at Liverpool, but unmarked, and the only other porcelain manufactories that produced soft paste porcelain successfully were Longton Hall (in Staffordshire), Derby and Lowestoft.

As always, the stumbling block was the ability of the paste to withstand the heat of boiling water, and it was not until the 1760s that Bow developed a paste suitable for tea and coffee wares.

A Bow saucer dish decorated in 'famille verte' colours of an Oriental figure in a rocky landscape, with the rim divided into compartments in Japanese style. Scalloped rim and gilt line borders, with gilding on a deep blue ground in two panels, c.1758–60. 7 in (18 cm) diameter.

Signs of authenticity

1. Early paste hard, dense, not very translucent, greenish.
2. First wares generally decorated in blue only, to c.1749.
3. Bow from c.1750 cream-coloured, dense, thickly glazed and showing 'moons' or grease spots.
4. Early Chelsea 1745–9 creamy with satin-like texture, flawed with specks of more translucency like pin holes, visible when held to the light.
5. Glaze on Bow, Chelsea uneven, settling more thickly in hollows, centres of plates, dishes etc.
6. From c.1755–9 new formula paste at Bow produced wares with sparkle and clarity.
7. Chelsea paste of same period more opaque, whiter from addition of some tin oxide as in delftware.
8. From c.1759 Bow glaze more ivory-tinted, enamelled colours include distinctive puce or maroon.
9. Gilding soft, warm, never metallic.
10. Bow glaze discoloured with age, often shows brownish patches towards base, or pinkish tinge, almost iridescent.
11. Liverpool soft paste distinctively greyish compared with other potteries.
12. Lowestoft largely blue and white, enamelled wares more rare.
13. Longton Hall recognizable by thick glaze, particularly brilliant blue.
14. Enamelled colours softer in tone than on hard paste because of porous nature of soft paste.
15. Early Derby soft paste lumpy, poorer quality.
16. Chelsea/Derby wares recognizably better, finer quality.

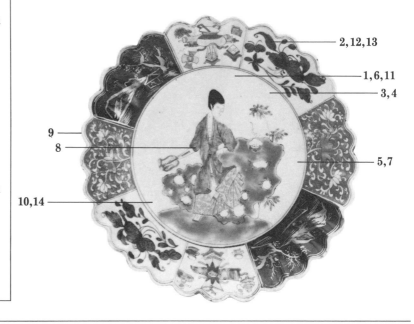

Materials and decoration

Early products from English soft paste porcelain manufactories were decorated in blue on white, not only because of the fashion for Chinese designs but also because cobalt was known to withstand the heat of the kilns, higher than the heat needed to produce stoneware, although considerably less than temperatures required to make hard paste porcelain. Enamelled colours were applied not to the 'biscuit' but to a once-glazed surface, and then fired again at a lower temperature to fix them.

In soft paste can be seen the progression of influences working on English potteries: first the Chinese, in blue and white, then in 'famille rose' and 'famille verte', followed by the German influence, first of Meissen, then of Dresden, and then the French influence of Vincennes, later known as Sèvres. Soft paste porcelain is more porous than the hard paste used in Europe, however, and the colours are softer and more delicate, and can easily be distinguished.

Principal producers and products

Bow 1745–55, ornamental ware, writing and toilet table objects, flatware. From 1755, tea ware, tea bowls, coffee ware, domestic objects. From *c*.1765 to 1775, tableware, dessert services, tea services, coffee services, dinner services.
Chelsea 1745–9, cream jugs, sauce and butter boats, embossed relief ware, silver shapes. From *c*.1749–53, tableware, figures, ornamental wares. *c*.1753–6, leaf shapes, applied flowers, raised border patterns, tableware. 1756–69, figures, ornamental wares, table services, tea and dessert services, highly decorated wares.
Longton Hall 1749–60, leaf shapes, pierced flatware in Staffordshire salt glaze tradition,

figures, vases, tea and coffee ware.
Lowestoft *c*.1757–1802, tea ware, sauce and butter boats, largely in blue and white, chinoiserie designs. From 1765, trifles, souvenirs, commemorative wares.
Derby Derby Porcelain Co. 1749–55, mainly ornamental ware and figures. Duesbury-Derby 1755–86, some tableware, improved quality figures, finest in 'bisque' without glaze. Chelsea-Derby 1769–75.
Swansea 1750–1820, main production of soft paste from 1813, with typical Billingsley roses, pierced work, tea ware.
Nantgarw 1813–20, similar range to Swansea.

Period of manufacture
c.1745 to 1802.

A fine early Chelsea dish of cruciform shape known as the 'Hans Sloane' pattern, c.1755. Lobed, oval shape, painted with leaves and flowers surrounded by butterflies and insects, with gooseberry-like fruits below and a rim edged with brown. Red anchor mark. 10¾ in (27.5 cm) diameter.

A Bow bowl and cover painted in Japanese Kakiemon style in a partridge or quail pattern with plump birds and flowers, with an iron red and gilt border, c.1758–60.

Reproductions

Many lesser nineteenth-century porcelain factories used versions of Chelsea's anchor mark on their wares. The New Chelsea Porcelain Co. Ltd, which was established in 1912, made reproductions of Chelsea, Bow, Lowestoft, Plymouth, Bristol and Swansea soft paste and hard paste, as well as copies of Meissen, Sèvres and some early Oriental wares. The most deceptive period is 1912–19, when all their products were marked with an anchor. From 1919 to 1951, when the company ceased production, reproductions were in bone china and marked **New Chelsea, Chelsea** or **Royal Chelsea.**

Variations

In the early stages, paradoxically, all the variations are better made than English work of the period. Dresden figures, Meissen tableware and services from many German manufactories were copied by English factories with varying degrees of success. The enormous production of the Worcester factories in soapstone porcelain, following all the same influences, bears the closest resemblance to the relatively small output of soft paste – and of this, Chelsea and Bow are most likely to be confused with Worcester, both in shape and in decoration.

Price bands

Small bowls: Bow £180–£300, Chelsea £250–£400; Longton Hall £250–£350; Lowestoft £150–£250.

Mugs: Bow £450–£600; Lowestoft £180–400.

Prices vary depending on period, object and pattern.

Rare patterns, shapes, enamels, periods from £1,800 upwards.

Soapstone porcelain

Signs of authenticity

1. Denser, harder and heavier than soft paste or hard paste.
2. No crazing to the glaze, or shrinkage of glaze round foot-rim or rim of plates, dishes etc.
3. Early Worcester slightly greenish in tinge when held to light.
4. Liverpool slightly grey-coloured body, milky glaze which is faintly blue, also slightly greenish translucency.
5. Caughley quite different in tone, tending towards a pinky orange or straw-coloured tinge when held to the light.
6. Caughley glaze rich, thick, clear and brilliant white with bluish tint.
7. Liverpool blues darker, more inky than Worcester, Caughley.
8. Worcester, Caughley extremely similar in shape and design, moulded and shaped in contemporary silver shapes.
9. Worcester and Caughley cabbage-leaf jugs distinguished on sight: Worcester low-bellied, rounded like a football; Caughley with more slender, tapering base, like a rugby ball.
10. Bases of Liverpool during Richard Chaffer's period inevitably glazed – Worcester and Caughley usually neatly cleaned off.
11. Liverpool enamelled colours usually limited to pale yellow, brick red, emerald green and blue, with red line border round rims of hollow ware very characteristic.
12. Liverpool 'beaked' jugs have lips raised above the rim; Worcester, Caughley continue same level around entire rim.
13. Some Worcester cabbage-leaf jugs of larger size have no lips – presumably resembling ewers for pouring water into containers, either hot or cold.
14. Teapots continue small capacity – increased size is slight and due to added height of domed lids.
15. Later, New Hall paste very similar to Caughley in colour.

Historical background

In about 1749, Benjamin Lund obtained a licence to quarry soapstone near the Lizard in Cornwall, and established the Bristol China Works to make 'porcelane' using pulverized 'soapy rock' as a substitute for china clay and china stone. This variation of soft paste porcelain proved able to withstand the heat of boiling water, unlike other pastes being made in England at this period.

By 1751 the celebrated Dr John Wall had formed a partnership which amalgamated with the Bristol China Works, and thus was founded the famous Worcester Porcelain Company. Dr Wall was evidently a shrewd businessman as well as an accomplished chemist, for one of his partners was Edward Cave, editor of *The Gentleman's Magazine*, which greatly assisted in publicizing their merchandise. The first anouncement for a sale of china was at the Worcester music meeting in 1752. By 1756 there was a warehouse in London taking orders for 'Home and Foreign Trade' and by the 1770s, when tea gardens were all the rage, Mr William Bird was running his very successful 'Bird's Gardens' in Worcester, on the other side of the river from the porcelain factory. No doubt the tea ware was gladly supplied by the management.

Liverpool teapot and cover from the 'Christians' period when Philip Christian took over from Richard Chaffers. It is enamelled in bright colours with sprays of peony and prunus in panels separated by kiku mon, *a stylized Japanese-type flower on a diaper ground, with gilt line embellishment. 5 in (12.5 cm) high.*

Materials and decoration

The paste of soapstone porcelain contains steatite from Cornwall instead of the china clay and china stone used for making hard paste porcelain. Decoration was in blue, painted under the glaze, for Oriental blue and white, followed by enamels in 'famille rose' and 'famille verte' palettes, used with increasing skill as techniques of firing at different temperatures were found to produce different tones and colours. Transfer-printing was used at Worcester from as early as *c.*1751, at first in brick red, dark purple or brown, and then in black. Gilding, either 'japanned' or honey gilding, was also used, to great effect.

From *c.*1760 the word 'ground' appears, denoting areas between cartouches or panels: the ground colour was painted on with a brush under or over the glaze and fired at very high temperatures so that it would not be affected by subsequent firings. It was difficult to avoid brush-marks showing in the ground colour, and possibly the characteristic 'scale' ground developed by Worcester helped to conceal them.

Principal producers and products

Lund's Bristol 1748–52; Worcester 1751–1820s; Liverpool (Chaffers and Christian) *c.*1756–early 1770s; Caughley 1775–1799.

Tea ware, coffee ware, tableware, services and all manner of useful wares as well as some decorative vases, leaf dishes, dessert baskets.

Period of manufacture
1748 to 1799.

A. *Caughley miniature tea set, hand painted in blue with chinoiserie scenes, in a standard design used on 'toy' porcelain pieces. The teapot is just over 1 in (2.5 cm) high.*

Right *Worcester teapot and cover enamelled with chinoiserie scenes in panels 'reserved' on an iron red scale diaper, scattered with red and black florets, the cover matching in panels and red scale diaper. 5¾ in (14.5 cm) high.*

Variations

Possibly the most deceptive pieces are those 'improved' during the nineteenth century, since the additional enamels have acquired a convincing age – but there is usually a bubbling of the glaze and almost always small black specks occur on pieces which have been fired again at a later date.

Occasionally there have been cases of 'clobbering' to increase the value of blue and white wares with the addition of coloured enamels which may deceive the uninitiated, but with a knowledge of which patterns were originally made in polychrome it is an easy pitfall to avoid.

Price bands

Tea bowls: Worcester, Dr Wall First Period £400–£600; Liverpool £250–£500; Lund's Bristol (extremely rare) £2,000–£3,000.

Caughley mugs, tankards £500–£1,000.

Worcester cabbage-leaf jugs from £500–£850.

Caughley cabbage-leaf jugs £250–£450.

Rare patterns, shapes, enamels, periods from £1,500 upwards.

Reproductions

The Worcester Porcelain Company copied its own wares in bone china over the years, although it seldom reproduced wares from the First Period of Dr Wall Worcester. Like the Chelsea reproductions, many copies of early patterns were made at the beginning of this century, mainly on the Continent, particularly of rich blue-scale patterns with exotic birds. These are made in a hard, cold porcelain which is generally lighter in weight than soft paste and has the consistency almost of solid icing sugar where the body is left unglazed.

Hard paste porcelain

Historical background

In the same year that the Bow factory began to make soft paste porcelain, using substitutes for china clay and china stone, these two elusive elements were found in Cornwall. William Cookworthy, a Plymouth chemist, discovered 'both the petuntse and kaolin' on Carloggas Moor in 1745. It was not until 1768 that he was finally able to take out a patent for making hard paste porcelain, which he made at Plymouth between 1768 and 1770, when his company got into financial difficulties. In 1774 Richard Champion acquired the patent and the licence, and Cookworthy's Plymouth manufactory then transferred to Bristol; though it seems that he continued to use his established mark – the chemical sign for tin – before he retired, leaving Champion to continue on his own.

From 1774, Richard Champion began to make 'Champion's Hard Paste Porcelain' and, hoping for a vast improvement in his profits, succeeded in extending his monopoly on china stone and china clay until 1796. Hard paste porcelain withstood the heat of boiling water, and Champion's output consisted mainly of tea ware which was much in demand. Hard paste was extremely difficult to work with – more pieces were thrown out than sold – and Champion was soon in trouble financially. Production virtually ceased in 1778, and Champion sold his monopoly to a group of Staffordshire potters, who established the New Hall factory and began to manufacture hard paste porcelain in 1781.

New Hall teapot of characteristic straight-sided shape, with a simple border pattern of blue scrolls intertwined with gilt leaf pattern, with pineapple or pine-cone finial with a vent hole. Pattern No. 170, c.1782–9. 6 in (15 cm) high.

Signs of authenticity

1. Translucent quality of paste.
2. Undetectable glaze, fused to body on first firing.
3. Ribbing, wreathing on inside of bowls, jugs, cups etc.
4. Straight, simple lines due to difficulty of manufacture.
5. Handles often with herringbone moulding and arrow-shaped or leaf-shaped terminals where they join the body.
6. Thick streaks of glaze to be found under base of early teapots, tea ware.
7. Reeded, faceted and fluted bodies of pots, teapots, with pineapple or pine-cone-like finials.
8. Knobs of early teapots with central vent hole for steam – later lids had perforated hole in lid itself.
9. Rectangular-shaped teapots mark the period just before introduction of bone china – last period of hard paste.
10. Tea bowls with slightly out-turning rim, slight rounding to foot-rim where glaze was cleaned off from bottom edge.
11. Minute bubbling in glaze on flat and open-shaped bowls, cups, round rim where glaze is thicker, streaked with 'curtains' where glaze has run down, suggesting that objects were turned upside down after glazing, before firing.
12. Teacups only introduced in last phase of hard paste c.1795.
13. Coffee cans from about same period, both with finger rings to handles.
14. Under-glaze blue transfer decoration exclusive to New Hall – none made at Plymouth or Bristol, but blue of poor quality and brilliance compared with soft paste, soapstone and refined earthenware bodies.

Materials and decoration

Hard paste porcelain is extremely thin, has a metallic ring when tapped, and its structure is almost crystalline. Unlike soft paste porcelains, the glaze, containing pulverized china stone, was applied before the first firing. At very high temperatures, glaze and paste fused together, forming an integral, glassy surface which is duller and colder than that of soft paste porcelain, where the coating of glaze is clearly visible.

A characteristic of Cookworthy, Plymouth and Champion's hard paste porcelain is the 'wreathing' similar to hand-potted earthenware which spirals up the sides. This device helped to prevent the wares collapsing in on themselves in the kiln. Very little hard paste porcelain from these factories survives, and it is generally of poor quality, though valuable for its rarity.

Early New Hall tea ware, dating from about 1781, is generally decorated in simple border patterns, often blue under the glaze, with gold embellishment. Early shapes are often ribbed, perhaps also to reduce the risk of collapse in the kilns. Some early wares have enamelled chinoiserie decoration on rounded, slightly squat shapes with quite thickly potted handles, often with an overlapping thumbpiece. Transfer-printing was also used on New Hall hard paste porcelain, and examples decorated with willow pattern are not uncommon. New Hall switched from hard paste to bone china in about 1812, and care is essential to differentiate between the two. Pattern numbers are a useful guide – the highest number recorded on hard paste porcelain is believed to be 1048.

Principal producers and products

Plymouth 1768 – c.1771; Champion's hard paste 1774–82; New Hall 1781–1812.

Figures, groups and cabinet ware, tea ware, tableware, coffee ware.

A

A. A rare dessert basket in Cookworthy's Plymouth and Bristol hard paste porcelain, c.1770–2, with pierced latticed sides and applied with small blue florets and leaves, twig handles and trailing leaves. $8\frac{1}{2}$ in (21.5 cm) from handle to handle.

B

C

B. *Bristol christening mug, Champion's hard paste, c.1775. The barrel-shaped body has panels of pink roses between gilt line borders, and the handle shape is typical of coffee cups from the same producers, as is the scalloped border, on this mug in blue and gilt. 3 in (7.5 cm) high.*

Period of manufacture
1768 to 1812.

C. *A fluted coffee cup in the style of hard paste, from Lund's Bristol China Works, c.1751–2. It is more likely that the paste is a soapstone porcelain that true hard paste, since Lund obtained a licence in 1748 to quarry soapstone near the Lizard in Cornwall.*

Variations

Robert Chamberlain left Worcester in about 1786 and began making wares remarkably similar to New Hall, using an adulterated form of hard paste, greyish, hard and often marred with black spots. The production dates from c.1791 and was presumably illegal until the licence expired in 1796.

Hard paste porcelain in direct copies of New Hall ware was also made at Thomas Turner's Caughley factory, either just before or just after it was acquired by Coalport. Many of these items have typical spiralled, reeded, fluted and faceted shapes. The imitations are more or less contemporary, presumably dating from 1796 onwards.

Three other factories made deliberate copies and imitations of New Hall, and left them unmarked. Specialists and experts in the field have called them simply Factory X, Y and Z.

Price bands

Small mugs, bowls:
Champion's Bristol £600–£800;
New Hall £150–£300;
rare early Plymouth £600–£1,200 and upwards.

New Hall teapots £100–£360.

Reproductions

Thomas Minton, who worked with Spode before starting his own factory in about 1798, made some hard paste porcelain, but his wares were marked, the paste was whiter, and only half a dozen or so of his wide range bear close resemblance to New Hall.

It could be said that New Hall bone china, made from c.1812, was the first reproduction ware, since many shapes and patterns were continued using the new paste. The factory continued until 1835, though running down, and with a gradually declining production.

18th-century blue and white

Historical backbround

All early blue and white wares made in England had been painted with a cobalt pigment discovered in Saxony in 1545. It was imported either in an unrefined state, when it was known as 'zaffre', or in its more costly, prepared condition, called 'smalt'. When the Seven Years' War broke out between Saxony and Prussia in 1756 supplies were cut off, and England had to turn to her own deposits of cobalt. English cobalt, when properly prepared, was considered by many to be superior to zaffre and smalt, but frequently it was inexpertly prepared and the results often produced a very dark colour tinged with indigo, violet or purple which was not evident until firing, when it streaked through the colour in varying degrees of strength, making it extremely hard to make matched sets and services.

Dr Wall of Worcester succeeded in preparing cobalt pigment of such excellence that practically every pottery in England bought their 'blue' from him and, since his source of supply was Bristol, it became known as 'Bristol blue' and was also used by the glass-houses. As blue was the only colour that could be successfully applied under the glaze, and because the techniques of enamelling were still in their infancy, the lack of cobalt pigment would have been a severe blow to all the newly established porcelain factories engaged in making soft paste, hard paste and soapstone porcelain. Some designs first used on tin glazed earthenware are still recognizable in very similar form in early blue and white porcelains, though at first they may seem almost inexpert compared to the high degree of skill achieved by the artists working on tin glazed earthenware.

Signs of authenticity

1. Soft paste, hard paste, soapstone porcelain with varing degrees of translucency.
2. Slight shrinkage of glaze on some soft paste.
3. Liverpool blues darker, more inky and smudgy than Worcester or Caughley.
4. Worcester slightly greenish tinge of glaze when held to light.
5. Longton Hall soft paste wares particularly brilliant, sharp blue known as 'Littler's blue'.
6. Lowestoft likely to be in plainer, simpler shapes.
7. Worcester, Caughley, Derby often decorated in Chinese patterns on moulded silver shapes.
8. Liverpool blue and white soapstone in ornate moulded shapes, stiffer, more upright lines.
9. Blue may be blurred in early wares, particularly Lowestoft, where pigment has sunk into the body, fused to the glaze.
10. Pseudo-Chinese marks used by more than one porcelain manufactory easily differentiated from genuine Oriental marks.
11. Both Worcester and Caughley used crescent mark – colour of body and glaze determine the origin.
12. Caughley more straw-coloured paste with bluish tinge to glaze.
13. New Hall hard paste blue and white later than other producers, and in less brilliant blue, transfer-printed decoration and not hand-painted wares.
14. New Hall paste similar to Caughley in colour.

*Rare Bow mug, c.1751, painted under the glaze in vivid blue, with a pierced rock with peony flowers and pines and a border of diaper pattern interspersed with floral panels, with a typical indented strap handle. Marked **g** in blue. 4¾in (12cm) high.*

Materials and decoration

By definition, blue decoration under the glaze, on a white or whitish ground with varying translucency depending on the paste. There was no gilding on early eighteenth-century blue and white wares, and shapes were frequently moulded with relief decoration in silver patterns. Rarely but occasionally, Oriental motifs are moulded into the body, but more commonly swags, festoons, reeding, fluting and shapes of cartouches are found. The largest number of teapots and coffee pots are found in soapstone porcelain, though some were made in soft paste and in hard paste, the latter by New Hall, the former by Lowestoft in general.

Teapots were largely made by Worcester at this period, since this factory combined the use of a hot-water-resistant paste with experienced artists from the Bristol factory with which it amalgamated.

Motifs are exclusively Oriental and include early versions of willow pattern, prunus, peony, sprigs of blossom, figures in fenced gardens and tall, thin ladies known as 'Long Elizas' or 'Long Lizzies'. Variations of a small diaper pattern border are common, both on inner and outer rims and bases.

Period of manufacture
c.1749 to c.1810.

Principal producers and products

Bristol 1748–52; Worcester 1751 – c.1760; Caughley 1775–99; Liverpool (Chaffers and Christian) c.1756 – early 1770s; Lowestoft c.1757–1802; Longton Hall 1749–60; New Hall 1782–1810; Bow 1745–75; Derby 1749–55.

Teapots, tea services, tea bowls, saucers, teacups, coffee pots, coffee cups, cream jugs, sauce and butter boats, pickle dishes, sweetmeat dishes, tea caddies, sugar boxes, mugs, jugs, dessert baskets, centrepieces.

B. *Worcester butter boat in moulded silver shape with a chinoiserie scene of rocks, a pagoda and shrubs, the interior rim with a diaper and half-floret border, c.1756–8.*

A. *Fluted tea bowl and saucer with prunus root pattern. Worcester, c.1756–8.*

C. *Early Worcester double-lipped sauceboat with silver shape, scroll handles and button thumb-rests, decorated with red and under-glaze blue, c.1760.*

Reproductions

Transfer-printed bone china was made extensively from c.1812 onwards in traditional Chinese designs and patterns, but generally the actual wares are completely different in shape and purpose. Plates, dishes, cups and saucers had all evolved from early shapes and are easily distinguished. The deceptive Continental reproductions of Dr Wall's Worcester made in the early part of this century are still around, having gained some spurious age, but the consistency of the body is that of the hard, cold Continental porcelain and not the softer pastes of eighteenth-century England.

Variations

Many Staffordshire potteries made good 'blue and white' on a creamware base, but the difference in colour and texture is obvious. Early Spode patterns in earthenware often included very limited numbers of 'replacement' china, copied precisely from pieces sent to the factory, and made in a white-bodied stoneware, or in pearlware from c.1780. Pearlware was an improvement on creamware developed by Josiah Wedgwood in the 1770s, and by 1790 the whiteness had been markedly improved by the addition of a small quantity of cobalt to the glaze, in much the same way as washing powder has a 'blue whitener'. For a short period, pearlware was used extensively for blue and white wares – it has a slightly pearly sheen in imitation of soapstone porcelain, but no transparency.

Price bands

Mugs: Bow £750–£950; Caughley £200–£300; Derby £250–£350; Liverpool £350–£500; Longton Hall £750–£950; Lowestoft £150–£250; Worcester £550–£650; New Hall £120–£300.

Rare patterns, shapes, periods £800 upwards.

Early polychrome enamel

Historical background

The new pastes or 'porcelains' which were being made by the middle of the eighteenth century produced a whole new crop of problems, not only with the paste itself and the glaze, but also with pigments that produced polychrome wares – pieces decorated in more than one colour. The new pastes were fired at a far higher temperature than earthenware bodies, hard paste in particular requiring extremely high heat. Coloured pigments made from metallic oxides which had remained clear and fixed at lower temperatures either changed colour radically or disappeared completely at these higher temperatures, and a whole new technique had to be evolved for the delicate colours of 'famille rose' and 'famille verte' palettes, which were much in demand.

Some early porcelain factories in England began using cold pigments, painted over the glaze and then hardened-on at a low temperature, but these colours were impermanent and soon flaked away because the pigments were not fused to the glaze. By the 1750s the enamelling process was being used, inexpertly at first, and then with more confidence as techniques were mastered, and distinctions were made between 'japanned' wares and 'true enamel'. The delicate rose pink of 'famille rose' was found to be produced when coloured pigments, mixed with a flux of glaze, were painted over the glaze and fired at a very specific temperature – any lower and the colour turned reddish-brown, any higher and it turned purplish. Similar experiments with copper oxide produced the delicate green of 'famille verte', and it was found that colours needed different temperatures to 'fix' them. It is no wonder that the majority of porcelain factories in the second half of the eighteenth century were sited near the coal fields instead of on the banks of rivers which in earlier decades were harnessed for power.

Very rare Longton Hall loving cup c.1755, campana-shaped with double scrolled handles, painted with a scene of Chinese magicians in lime green, bright yellow, greyish blue and raspberry red, with some detail and outline picked out in black. 4½ in (11.5 cm) diameter.

Signs of authenticity

1. Paste, not earthenware, bodies in soft paste, hard paste, soapstone porcelain.
2. Translucent, not solid colours, of delicate tones.
3. Uneven application of colours which were applied to the glasslike surface of once-glazed wares.
4. Correct shapes, styles for the period.
5. Enhanced with gilding, usually japanned, which may have worn away leaving only traces of original richness.
6. Very limited colour palette in early wares.
7. Areas of colour imperceptibly raised from surface of glaze where pigment mixed with glaze adds a layer of thickness.
8. Colours limited to the spectrum of purples, pinks, browns and black from manganese, green and pale yellow.
9. Japanned over-glaze painting seldom survives in good condition – generally badly flaked.
10. Printed outline not in general use before c.1765.
11. 'Pen work' or 'pencilled' black and white Oriental subjects shown previous stage of development – from c.1760.
12. Typical blue and white decorative borders change to single iron red line border and gilded patterns – polychrome inner border patterns not found.

Materials and decoration

These typically delicate polychrome enamels were used by porcelain manufactories making soft paste, hard paste and soapstone porcelain, still in Oriental tradition. The wares are quite different from early 'Japan' patterns, which are far more bold and bright. In contrast to blue and white wares, the shapes of tea bowls, saucers, jugs are much more simple, rarely in moulded decorative relief, and rely entirely on the effect of the pale, glowing colours of the enamels, highlighted by gilding. Richard Chaffers of Liverpool produced a range of distinctive patterns, including birds and robed figures as well as the rock and peony theme. Colours are brighter and more emphatic; brick red, emerald green, dark blue and pale yellow, and frequently borders are lined with iron red. The old diaper pattern of blue and white was carried over to polychrome wares by Liverpool, in black or red.

Principal producers and products

Worcester; Liverpool; Longton Hall; Chelsea; Derby (Cockpit Hill); Plymouth.

Tea bowls, teacups and saucers, cream jugs, mugs, teapots, coffee pots, tea cannisters, jars, vases; flatware rarely in early period.

Period of manufacture
c. 1755 to 1770s.

Variations

The range of Worcester wares with black outlines printed under the glaze is markedly different from the 'free-hand' outlines and painting of early polychrome enamels.

A. *Early Derby coffee pot with fluted body and acanthus leaf decoration to the base and top of the spout on which some gilding remains. The Chinese figures are painted in strong enamel colours, with a repetition of the low table with bowl and flowers on the lid. From the Cockpit Hill works, c.1756–68. 9¼ in (23 cm) high.*

Spode's early range of bone china included many Japan patterns, richly enamelled and usually embellished with burnished gold. Large quantities of stone china, too, were made from about 1800 onwards, many of the pieces decorated with enamels over the glaze over a pattern printed usually in sepia, but both these variations are more in the tradition of early polychrome earthenwares than the delicate, translucent wares in porcelain.

B   C   D

Reproductions

Here there are two possibilities which make what appears to be an extremely valuable piece of porcelain almost valueless: the practice of 'improving' or adding coloured enamels to a piece of the right period, glaze and body, or the less likely encounter with Continental copies in hard porcelain.

If 'improvements' are added to a piece with blue under the glaze, either printed or painted, the slightly blurred outlines of blue contrast with the more transparent coloured glazes which have been re-fired over them. It is unlikely that any 'pencilled' wares from Worcester have been treated this way, since there is too much detail in the drawing for additional colour to be convincing, and they have a high value of their own.

Price bands

Mugs, tea bowls: Bow £500–£700; Chelsea (Red Anchor) £500–£900; Liverpool £400–£600; Longton Hall £500–£700; Worcester (Dr Wall First Period) £600–£800; Plymouth £900–£1,400.

B. *Worcester jug with sparrow-beak spout, crisply printed in black outline and coloured with enamels of two Oriental figures, with an under-glaze diaper border on the inner rim, c.1770. 3½ in (9 cm) high.*

C. *Worcester tea bowl and saucer printed in black with the 'Red Cow' pattern, coloured with enamels and with an iron red line round the rim.*

D. *Worcester trio, almost matching, of tea bowl, saucer and coffee can of similar design to the Derby coffee pot (above) with printed outline coloured in enamels, of Oriental figures and furniture, with a red line and hoop border on the tea bowl and saucer, gilt border on the coffee can, c.1770.*

Japan patterns I

Historical background

The growing web of canals at last began to link Staffordshire with the rest of England and for the first time the huge output from the potteries came into direct competition with the porcelain factories. In the 1770s a commentator from Nottingham wrote: 'People here are not without their Tea, Coffee and Chocolate, especially the first, the use of which is spread to that Degree, that not only Gentry and Wealthy Travellers drink it constantly, but almost every Seamer, Sizer and Winder will have her tea in the morning....' The rich still insisted on porcelain, but the less expensive tea services from the potteries were very beguiling. Tea-time became an English institution – the potteries revived Chinese blue and white patterns for the prosperous middle classes, and the porcelain factories turned to Japan for inspiration.

The first range of 'Kakiemon' Japan patterns, taken from silk or paper paintings of flower sprays, birds, rocks and blossom, were enamelled in delicate pale colours and proved expensive to produce. Japanese export porcelain was all the rage – brightly coloured 'Imari' patterns based on Japanese brocaded silks, made specially for the European market. Using 'high temperature colours' English manufacturers began to copy the Japanese Imari patterns, applying a limited palette straight on to the 'biscuit', firing, then glazing and finally enriching with gilding – all of which required far less skill and could be done at far greater speed than the delicate enamelled colours.

Dozens of versions of Imari, Kakiemon and other Japan patterns were produced by all the major procelain factories. The only drawback was that Japan patterns were just as easy for the potteries to produce, once they had mastered the techniques of high temperature colours, and from about 1790 Staffordshire too began to produce inexpensive Japan patterns for a less exclusive market.

Signs of authenticity

1. Soft paste, soapstone porcelain with translucent qualities of both paste and glaze.
2. Colours applied under the glaze.
3. Limited palette of iron red, yellow and burnt orange from antimony, manganese purple, occasionally pea green from copper.
4. Gilding either 'japanned' and burnished, or harder-wearing, longer-lasting honey gilding, slightly duller in appearance.
5. Small sizes of teapots, cream jugs.
6. From c.1768 onwards Worcester mazarine blue, deeper and more similar to deep 'gros bleu' of Vincennes, later Sèvres.
7. Chelsea blue even darker, more lustrous.
8. No teapots from Bow, Chelsea before c.1760.
9. Characteristic tilted flower finial of Worcester hollow ware with Oriental patterns.
10. Vent hole in centre of floret.
11. Liverpool unmarked wares with quite distinctly different colour palette, particularly green, which was more emerald.
12. Bow used characteristic puce line border, scrolling.
13. Caughley made very few, if any, Japan pieces. (Factory bought out by Coalport c.1799 and wares made by Caughley decorated and finished under Coalport management.)
14. Shapes, styles correct for period.
15. Bow factory acquired by William Duesbury of Derby in 1776 – no Bow porcelain after that date.

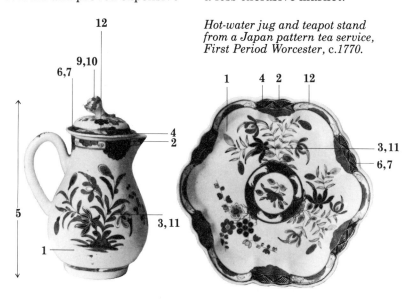

Hot-water jug and teapot stand from a Japan pattern tea service, First Period Worcester, c.1770.

Materials and decoration

In soft paste and soapstone porcelain, for a relatively short period between c.1700 and c.1796 when china stone and china clay became freely available and bone china began to challenge the exclusive porcelain market. Worcester had by far the largest range of variations of both Imari and Kakiemon patterns, from early, simple, almost floral designs to the bold quartering in iron red, or 'rouge de feu' as it became known rather grandly, and the brocade patterns which merged gradually with new decorative techniques brought by Chelsea workers from c.1768 onwards. Thus the bold panels were also translated into the famous dark blue grounds that owed their origins to Sèvres, interspersed with Imari branches, rocks and flowers. The stylized flowered centres of *kiku mon* on fan pattern Worcester were also transposed and used in combination with an iron red diaper ground. Above all, the key to recognizing these last vigorous products of eighteenth-century porcelain factories is their translucent quality, lightness in weight, and the immensely skilful decoration and intricate gilding.

A. *Worcester fluted dish decorated with two Imari-type panels and two panels of chrysanthemum, separated by iron red gilt diaper and* kiku mon, *c.1770. 7½ in (19 cm) diameter.*

B. *Tea canister of similar pattern.*

C. *Worcester Japan pattern c.1770 tea bowl and cup, fluted and painted with three orange gilt diaper bands, separating panels of demi* kiru mon *above scrolling foliage.*

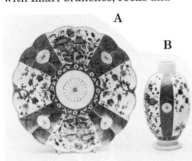

A

B

C

D

Principal producers and products

Bow c.1770–6; Worcester c.1770–1800; Chelsea c.1765–70; Caughley-Coalport c.1799–1820; Liverpool (Christian) c.1770–1800; Chelsea-Derby c.1770–5; Derby 1775–1810.

Tea ware, teapots, tea bowls, teapoys, tea caddies, coffee pots, coffee cans, milk and cream jugs, dessert dishes and bowls, toilet ware, vases, garnitures.

D. *Fan pattern tea and coffee service, decorated with under-glaze blue, iron red and green, with gilt diaper pattern and with* kiku mon *in the centre, First Period Worcester.*

Reproductions

If the repetitions of Japan patterns on bone china and stoneware constitute reproductions, then these are legion. For contemporary versions of Japan patterns in coarser wares, undoubtedly reproducing fine porcelain for the mass market, the following section provides details.

Variations

Spode's fine-bodied high-quality stone china is probably the closest to Worcester wares visually, except for an excess of gilding. On close inspection this proves to have been transfer-printed under the glaze and coloured with flat washes of pinks, blues and reds. It would appear that Josiah Spode II went into production with bone china from 1803, Minton from 1805, Chamberlain of Worcester in 1811 and Derby from 1816.

Period of manufacture
c.1770 to c.1820.

Price bands

Mugs, tea bowls: Bow £400–£600; Chelsea £800–£1,000; Derby £350–£600; Caughley-Coalport £180–£350; Worcester c. 1770 £320–£480.

Japan patterns II

Historical background

Bitter legal proceedings in 1775 over Champion's monopoly on china stone and china clay resulted in a ruling that the two substances could be used in the manufacture of non-translucent pottery but were forbidden to all makers of translucent porcelain. In the late 1770s Wedgwood obtained supplies of china clay, legally and independently, and included it in his formula for pearlware.

Between 1780 and 1810 a bewildering variety of bodies were produced, including felspar porcelain, ironstone and stone china, some of which included china clay, while some used substitutes. This burst of experimental activity culminated in the resoundingly successful production of bone china in 1796, when Champion's monopoly, owned by New Hall since 1781, finally ran out.

Japan patterns were highly suitable for the coarser, heavier ironstones and stonewares. The off-white colour of the body could be completely covered with bright all-over patterns which also hid any flaws in the surface or glaze. During this period the similarity of patterns and designs shows quite clearly the results of direct competition between the two groups of manufacturers in the potteries and the porcelain factories.

By about 1820, all the porcelain factories had gone over to bone china, and some of the potteries too. Others continued to make cheaper ranges of ironstones and stonewares as the Industrial Revolution brought new methods of manufacture into the potteries and mass-production finally became a reality.

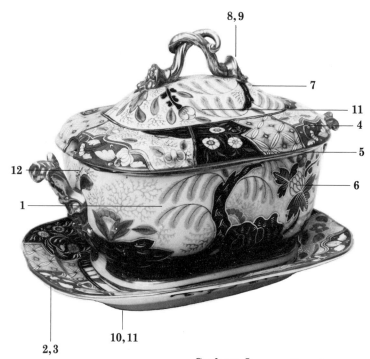

Coalport Japan pattern tureen, c.1805–10, from a dinner service in early bone china in a peony and rock pattern of the same design as that supplied to Brighton Pavilion.

Materials and decoration

In translucent felspar porcelain, opaque stone china and ironstone, all earthenware derivatives and much heavier than porcelain or bone china. In 'high temperature colours' of cobalt blue, iron red, antimony yellow and copper green, with additional chemical pigments from c.1820. These include a more brilliant green, bright orange, bright pink, scarlet red and an artificial ultramarine blue. Inexpensive mercury gilding, more brassy in appearance than earlier forms of gilding, also contributes to the rather crude richness of many Japan pattern wares from Staffordshire. Where the old copper-based green on porcelain derivatives would not take gilding, the bright apple green of ironstones and stonewares could – a point to note in later wares. With the advent of mass-production techniques, outlines of the pattern were often printed in light reddish brown to act as a guide for the less skilled artists employed by some potteries.

Principal producers and products

Spode from c.1803; Minton from c.1805; Chamberlain's Worcester from c.1811; Derby from c.1816; Coalport from c.1805; Davenport from c.1815; John & William Ridgeway & Co. from c.1814; Masons of Lane Delf c.1813–29; Turner of Lane End 1800–6; and other unmarked Staffordshire potteries.

Tableware, table services, tea services, ornamental vases, potpourri jars, spill jars, garnitures.

Period of manufacture
c. 1803 to 1825.

A. *Early 19th-century Spode dessert service tureen in modified Japan pattern in dark blue, scarlet and gilt on an orange ground. Pattern No. 1694. Impressed mark.*

B. *Chamberlain's Worcester dessert service in Japan pattern of considerable similarity to the Coalport version, c.1805.*

Reproductions

In a sense, the felspar porcelain and stone china services made in the first quarter of the nineteenth century are themselves reproductions of the original Worcester fan, brocade and other patterns drawn from Japanese original wares. Much of the mass-produced wares made by unnamed Staffordshire potteries from c.1825 to 1875 is generally degenerate in colour, form and taste, and in this sense pieces from this period could be said to be reproduction in its derogatory sense.

Variations

Japan patterns continued in production after 1825, but the quality fell disastrously as chemical pigments and cheap gilding became available, and standards were not raised again until the end of the century. Debased forms of the Imari patterns were more popular than versions of Kakiemon, with its sparser decoration which in some cases presented problems, particularly when the body was flawed or the glaze uneven.

Price bands

Part services: Coalport £450–£700; Davenport £800–£1,200; Derby £850–£1,500; Chamberlain's Worcester £800–£1,100; Minton £600–£800; Ridgway £900–£1,600; Spode £1,600–£1,800.

Full Worcester tea service £4,200–£5,500.

Dessert services usually less than tea, dinner services.

Mason's Patent Ironstone China

Historical background

The most successful nineteenth-century Staffordshire pottery was undoubtedly that of the two brothers George Miles and Charles James Mason. Sons of an established importer and manufacturer of porcelains, they took over their father's business in 1813, when Charles took out a patent for 'a process for the improvement of the manufacture of English Porcelain'. This he called 'ironstone china' – which, as experts at the time were quick to remark, was a contradiction in terms, since ironstone is earthenware and china is porcelain. In fact it was made by using a molten, greenish, glassy slag from the furnaces which was pulverized and added to the whitish clay body, resulting in an even-textured, faintly transparent earthenware with a metallic ring to it. Ironstone china was instantly successful and in a very short time the Mason brothers expanded their premises to cope with the demand.

George Mason left the firm in 1829 and Charles continued with a new partner, who left the business in 1845. By 1848 the company was in the hands of the liquidators, and in 1854 the moulds and copper plates were purchased by Francis Morley, who had married into the famous potteries family of Ridgway and taken over the company from his father-in-law. With Taylor Ashworth as his partner, Francis Morley continued to trade under his own name until 1862 when the name of the business changed to Geo. Ashworth & Brothers, whose descendants still own the firm. Only recently has the name been changed to Mason's Ironstone China Ltd.

The name is so strongly associated with richly gilded brightly coloured versions of Japan patterns that many people are unaware of the wide range of Mason's wares made during the nineteenth century, many of which were extremely fine and followed many porcelain patterns of the eighteenth century. In addition, huge quantities of blue and white transfer-printed wares were made.

Signs of authenticity

1. Hard, heavy, smooth-textured body, very dense.
2. Metallic ring when tapped with fingernail.
3. Bright high temperature colours, lavish gilding.
4. Patterns including one or more characteristic motifs: large peony-like flowers and full-blown roses, prunus twigs and blossom, daisies, birds of paradise, butterflies, flying insects, diaper and scale patterns, birds on the wing.
5. More delicate colours of Kakiemon patterns applied in flat washes filling transfer-printed outlines.
6. Transfer-gilding under the glaze from c.1813.
7. Correct mark, printed, impressed for period.
8. Typical shapes, forms of wares.
9. More jumbled motifs, patterns indicate later dates.
10. From c.1840 change in formula – mark includes words **improved patent ironstone china.**

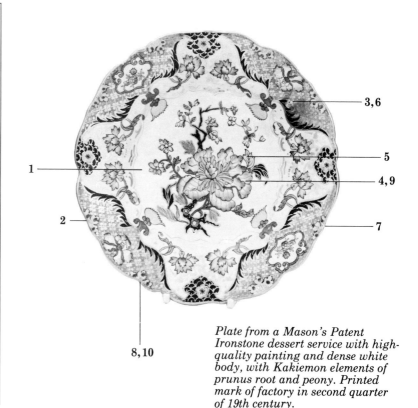

Plate from a Mason's Patent Ironstone dessert service with high-quality painting and dense white body, with Kakiemon elements of prunus root and peony. Printed mark of factory in second quarter of 19th century.

Materials and decoration

In the early years of production, Japan patterns were in rich, bright, high temperature colours of reds, blues, greens, with lavish gilding, but from the time that the new artificial pigments became available around the 1830s, colours became more strident – in particular the orange and the green, which was able to take gilding, unlike the copper-based green of previous decades. By c.1825 colours were ground mechanically instead of expensively by hand, and a more slapdash approach can be seen in the flat-washed infilling of transfer-printed outlines. Later gilding is mechanically repetitive in contrast to early good-quality handwork, and more brassy, tinsely in appearance. While the shapes of early Mason's wares were ornate, with exaggerated form owing to the thickness of the ironstone, they were still in relatively good taste and proportion. Later wares degenerated into meaningless curves and dips, together with jumbled images which no longer related directly to the fine early versions of Imari and other patterns.

Principal producers and products

Mason's Patent Ironstone China 1813–40; Mason's Improved Ironstone China 1840–62; Geo. Ashworth & Brothers from 1862.

Tableware, dessert services, dinner services, tea services, jars, garnitures, jugs, bowls. From 1845–48 conservatory seats, vases up to 5 ft (152 cm) high, graduated octagonal jugs, fireplace surrounds.

Period of manufacture
1813 to 1848.

A

A. Geo. Ashworth & Brothers ironstone tureen from a dinner service painted with Japan pattern composed of mixed elements from both Imari and Kakiemon. Pattern No. B 3694.

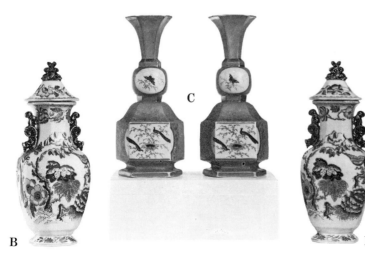

B. Fine pair of early Mason's Ironstone octagonal vases and covers decorated in mixed 'rococo revival' cartouches with Europeanized leaves, peonies and birds. The handles are known as Korean lions. c.1813–25. 15¼ in (39 cm) high.

C. Fine pair of Mason's Ironstone flared hexagonal vases with powder-blue ground and gilt-edged panels of butterflies and a pair of peacocks and their nest, c.1813–25. 14 in (35.5 cm) high.

Variations

Mason's manufactory made wares of almost every conceivable pattern in its heyday, and large quantities of blue and white as well as printed landscapes, houses, flowers were produced. It is worth turning over almost any piece of 'household china' from the first half of the nineteenth century to see if it is marked with Mason's mark – though it will not necessarily turn out to be a piece which has much value on the market.

Reproductions

Since the firm is still producing a wide range of wares, and has done so continuously since its inception in 1813, the marks define the early and the late, which are reproductions of themselves.

Price bands

Octagonal jugs – sets of four £800–£1,100. Singles from £110.

Dinner services £3,000–£5,000. Dessert services £2,000–£3,000.

Ashworth Bros dinner services £1,800–£2,500.

Staffordshire imitations – part services from £450.

Red and brown stoneware

Historical background

The English subsoil may have been deficient in the ingredients necessary for making true porcelain, but it was rich in red clays with a wide variety of compositions. Some of the first teapots to come into England, packed with the tea in teachests, were Chinese Yi-Hsing ware made of hard red stoneware, produced by mixing sand with red clay and firing it at a high temperature so that the sand vitrified, producing a very hard body which could then be turned on a lathe.

There is some argument over where red stoneware was first produced in England: John Dwight of Fulham took out a patent for making stoneware including the words 'red porcelane' in 1684, but two brothers by the name of Elers are more likely candidates. They came to England in 1688 and discovered fine beds of red clay in Staffordshire, and soon began to make copies of Yi-Hsing teapots and other wares. John Dwight's Fulham pottery concentrated more, it seems, on producing a coarser form of stoneware, similar to the 'Cologne ware' being made in Germany at that time. Most surviving red stoneware is usually referred to as Elers ware, although in later years John Dwight issued writs against the Elers brothers for infringement of his patent.

From c.1700 Nottingham made similar stoneware to John Dwight, with a curious metallic-looking semi-matt surface, achieved by dipping drab-coloured stoneware into liquid slip containing oxide of iron. When fired, the surface turned a rich brown with a faint metallic lustre.

Many surviving pieces of Elers red stoneware are imprinted with a mock Chinese stamp, impressed on the base.

Red stoneware coffee pot and cover in contemporary silver shape with moulded rococo scrolled spout and applied decoration of flowers and sprigs, with a traditional Staffordshire crabstock handle. c.1760. $6\frac{3}{4}$ in (17 cm) high.

Materials and decoration

Hard, stone-like, unglazed wares in varying tones of red brick, decorated in relief, usually stamped and then applied. John Astbury decorated his redware with white pipeclay, copied later by other potters using natural light-coloured clays glazed with lead-based glazes which turned the applied decoration a smeary yellow. Red stoneware was also decorated and finished by turning it on a lathe before firing, known as 'engine turning'. From c.1729 Samuel Bell made red stoneware which was harder and capable of being polished, and very dense in texture. Any chipping will show

as a smooth blemish, more like a dent than a chip.

Brown stoneware is drab-coloured or yellowish brown, with a semi-matt finish, and was used for less sophisticated domestic ware. The exception is Nottingham which produced a range of 'carved' jugs and mugs with double skins to reduce the weight. The outer skin was pierced in simple patterns, joined with incised decoration on the surface – mugs and jugs often have neat rings of turning round the collar and neck.

A

B

Above left *Elers red stoneware teapot of similar shape to Chinese Yi-Hsing ware with silver mounts to the spout and chain attaching the lid to the silver sleeve on the handle, c.1690. 5 in (13 cm) high. Also Elers red stoneware mug c.1690. 3½ in (9 cm) high.*

A. *Nottingham stoneware 'carved' jug with double-walled body, the outer wall pierced with stylized leaves and flowers and incised decoration, with a grooved neck and ribbed loop handle. c.1700–10. 4 in (10 cm) high.*

Reproductions

Brown stoneware was revived at the Fulham Potteries by John Doulton from 1820 onwards – nineteenth-century copies of 'bellarmines' and late versions of harvest jugs are often mistaken for early wares. Many purely functional objects were made in the nineteenth century in brown or drab-coloured stoneware – ginger-beer bottles and ink bottles being among the most common.

Variations

From c.1760 Wedgwood made a version of red stoneware called 'rosso antico', which generally had fine crisp moulded relief decoration, in contrast to Astbury and earlier wares with applied sprigged decoration. Wedgwood teapots, though often made in traditional Staffordshire shapes with crabstock handles and flush-fitting lids, are easily distinguished from small early examples by their larger capacity. Considerable quantities of red stoneware covered in dark brown glaze and with rather poorly defined cream-coloured applied decoration were also made from the mid-eighteenth century through to the end of the nineteenth.

B. *Brown salt glazed stoneware jug from the Mortlake factory, dipped in brown slip containing oxide of iron to cover the top half of the body, c.1800. 10¼ in (26 cm) high.*

Price bands

Astbury-type red stoneware coffee pots £600–£1,000. Elers-type teapots £700–£1,200.

Later period pieces £450–£800.

Nottingham carved mugs, jugs £600–£1,000.

Bellarmines £300–£500.

Harvest jugs from £130.

Mortlake tankards, mugs £175–£320.

Principal producers and products

Red stoneware John Dwight of Fulham; Elers Brothers of Staffordshire; unnamed Staffordshire potteries; Samuel Bell of Newcastle-under-Lyme c.1729 – 1750s; Josiah Wedgwood c.1760 – 1780s; Enoch Wood; Josiah Spode; Samuel Hollins; John Astbury.
Brown stoneware John Dwight of Fulham; John Morley of Nottingham; Brampton and Chesterfield potteries (in the

nineteenth century).

Red stoneware Teapots, coffee pots, chocolate pots, punch pots, spoon trays, cream jugs, sugar bowls, tea caddies, teacups and saucers.
Brown stoneware Mugs, jugs, harvest jugs, ewers, loving cups, posset pots, plant pots.

Period of manufacture
c.1690 to c.1780s.

Agate and tortoiseshell ware

Historical background

Visually these rather curious products seem to be unconnected with the main development of 'china' in the English potteries. Apart from the fact that they were considered to be extremely decorative and desirable at the time, they were in fact an important advance technically, and proved to be a turning point in the progress towards producing real 'china'. In the early decades of the eighteenth century Thomas Whieldon and many other potters were endlessly experimenting with different clays and glazes, striving to produce a refined white-bodied earthenware and new ways of glazing.

There were two reasons for developing new glazes. Firstly, even at that period the dangers of lead poisoning were well known and the use and preparation of lead glaze had proved fatal to workers in the potteries. Secondly, in order to produce a white-bodied earthenware, it was necessary to fire at a much higher temperature, which lead glaze could not withstand. Salt, sand and flint in one form or another had so far been the only materials, either incorporated into the body or fused to the surface, which would produce a glassy finish and render pottery non-porous.

In the early 1740s Enoch Booth produced a clear fluid glaze by grinding lead powder together with flint and clay. Thomas Whieldon had been working along similar lines, mixing clays together and combining metallic oxides with glazing substances and firing them at varying temperatures, searching for the right combination of glaze and body. In 1754 he took Josiah Wedgwood into the firm as a partner, and Wedgwood succeeded first in producing a rich green-coloured glaze. The partners continued to experiment, with both 'solid agate' made from mingling clay bodies and 'tortoiseshell' wares using coloured glazes, constantly refining the body and experimenting with cream-coloured glazes.

Signs of authenticity

1. In solid agate, colours of marbled clays usually in tones of blue, grey, cream and brown.
2. In solid agate, base the same colour marbling as rest of body.
3. Tortoiseshell glazes mainly in browns and greens for early examples.
4. Bases unglazed or clear glazed only.
5. Plates in tortoiseshell of silver shape, with gadrooned moulded rims.
6. Moulded plates with rococo cartouches round rim rarer, with more variegated glazes.
7. Teapot size slightly increased – 6 in (15 cm) high as well as smaller sizes.
8. Modelling, moulding clear and crisp – poor modelling or blurred moulding probably indicates later date.
9. Finials, details of teapots, cream jugs often innovative, original, not found on contemporary wares.
10. Early palette of coloured glazes limited – generally in green and brownish grey, or brown, green and slate blue, occasionally with some yellow.
11. Rare solid agate with salt glaze – very high prices compared with lead glazed examples.
12. Silver shapes of later period, twisted handle, leaf modelling characteristic of Leeds potteries and of later date.

Staffordshire solid agate teapot with three small feet and rather stocky shape in marbled colours of brown, pale yellow, cream and blue. $4\frac{1}{2}$ in (11.5 cm) high.

Materials and decoration

These fall into two separate categories: solid agate, which has a marbled body composed of mingled clays, with a colourless lead glaze, and tortoiseshell wares, where different-coloured glazes produce a mottled effect. Of the two, solid agate is more rare and its uses were confined to knife handles, teapots and coffee pots, tea caddies, and milk and cream jugs. These were often in fine copies of silver shapes, and some early pieces were made with Chinese 'Dog of Fo' finials, raised on lion's-paw feet.

Tortoiseshell wares are more common and vary in quality and attractiveness depending on the mixtures of coloured glazes.

Plates and many other pieces were moulded with fine modelling, and then glazed with tortoiseshell glaze. Some of the most successful designs were mottled glaze over the traditional Staffordshire teapot shape, often with moulded sinuous designs of trailing creepers, leaves and flowers. The mottled glaze suits the crabstock shape particularly well. Rare cow creamers are found in solid agate, finely modelled after the original silver design. More often they are in tortoiseshell with a brindled or dappled effect. Many small experimental animals were made with different coloured glazes, applied in black or brown spots, with green bases.

Reproductions

At the end of the eighteenth century the Wedgwood company used a marbled glaze to make a limited range of simulated agate ware, and one or two unnamed nineteenth-century potteries also made wares with similar surface decoration.

A deceptive range of excellent copies of tortoiseshell wares were made in the 1920s which have even taken in experts. Arbour groups, milkmaids with cows and other early models were among the most successful copies and any of these rare groups should be treated with great suspicion. More recent copies of tortoiseshell wares have been made, detectable by the soapy, slimy appearance of the glaze and the stiffness of modelling.

Variations

Leeds potteries produced a fine range of solid agate ware and tortoiseshell, but in shapes and designs quite distinctive to Leeds and of a later date than Wedgwood/Whieldon. Various other Staffordshire potteries made small items, usually ornamental animals and small figures in similar 'smear' glaze, as late as the 1820s, but usually the colouring is not the limited early palette of green, dark brown, mottled grey and yellow used originally by Whieldon and Wedgwood. Later 'smear' glazes often include a distinct orange and a far more acid green.

A

A. *Whieldon cow creamer, beautifully modelled, in brindled coloured glazes, with a square lid in the centre of the back, c.1760. 6½ in (16.5 cm) nose to tail.*

Price bands

Solid agate teapots £400–£700; jugs £350–£500; seated cats £300–£1,500 depending on condition, glaze, rarity.

Tortoiseshell Whieldon-type teapots £700–£1,200; jugs £280.

Whieldon-type cow creamer £550–£850.

B. *Wedgwood/Whieldon teapot in 'egg and spinach' yellow and green, with engine-turned body, ribbed spout with acanthus leaf decoration, and crabstock handle, c.1765. 6½ in (16.5 cm) high.*

B

C

C. *Solid agate model of a seated cat in marbled clays with the eyes dotted in with dark brown slip, glazed with transparent lead glaze, c.1750. 4¼ in (11 cm) high.*

Principal producers and products

Thomas Whieldon; Josiah Wedgwood; Leeds potteries; Thomas Astbury; Samuel Bell.

Teapots, cream jugs, milk jugs, animals and small ornamental objects, knife handles, plates, tea bowls and saucers, tea caddies, wall pockets, coffee cans and saucers, coffee pots, cow creamers, tureens.

Period of manufacture
*c.*1740s–1820s.

Jackfield ware

Historical background

At one time this rich black pottery was thought to be an imitation of Wedgwood's grand black basaltes but in fact it predates this range and was one of the many experimental wares made from as early as 1751 at Jackfield, Shropshire. It is related both to Wedgwood's green glazed wares and to the refined red stonewares being made at the time. Clues to this latter connection can be seen in the applied sprigged decoration, a feature of the original Elers red stoneware and Samuel Bell's products.

The earthenware body of Jackfield ware is of a brownish-red colour and is almost at the same stage of development as Whieldon's lighter-coloured bodies achieved by firing red clays at high temperatures. The glaze was produced by firing cobalt at a high temperature until the deepest blue turned black. The lustrous sheen was partly due to the carbon-filled smoke from the furnaces being directed into the kilns and further blackening the earthenware.

A later version of this glaze is known as 'Rockingham glaze' and was developed in about 1790 by the Rockingham pottery established in 1745 by Edward Butler, at Swinton, where there were fine beds of yellow clay. The factory enjoyed little distinction until it was acquired by Thomas Bingley and William Brameld, who began to make a range of tea and coffee ware in brown, mottled colours known as Swinton pottery. The so-called Rockingham glaze was produced by staining lead glaze with oxide of manganese and firing it until it acquired a deep, purplish-black bloom.

Fine, rare example of richly decorated Jackfield baluster jug painted in oil colours and oil gilding, inscribed 'Iames Hall – Brazier – Oversley Green', c.1770. From the Glaisher Collection, Fitzwilliam Museum. 7 in (17.5 cm) high.

Signs of authenticity

1. Rich black lustrous glaze.
2. Body light reddish buff or brown – rare but sometimes found, body with marbling like coarse agate ware.
3. More yellowish-buff body denotes later period Staffordshire.
4. Hard red earthenware body denotes late period Staffordshire black ware revived at the end of the nineteenth century.
5. Some shrinkage of glaze round base with Jackfield wares.
6. Unglazed or clear glazed base only.
7. Originally decorated with oil gliding, oil colours generally much worn.
8. Some Jackfield originally decorated with cold enamels, painted on after firing, generally visible only in traces, where colours, gilding have not worn off.
9. Later Rockingham glaze browner, with almost purple bloom.
10. Typical Jackfield baluster-shaped jugs often inscribed – Rockingham blackware sometimes with religious texts from the time of John Wesley towards the end of the eighteenth century onwards.
11. Many Jackfield-type teapots, jugs raised on three small feet.
12. Later Jackfield-type blackware often with moulded decoration in low relief with traces of gilding.
13. Finials to teapots sometimes moulded in distinctive shapes of birds, seldom flowers.
14. Small size of teapots – 5 in (13 cm) or less usually denotes eighteenth century.

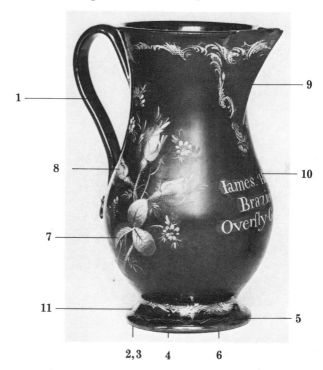

Materials and decoration

Earthenware body sometimes containing similar ingredients to some stoneware, covered in a rich black glaze made by staining the glaze with manganese oxide or firing cobalt at a high temperature, which turns it almost black. To this group must be added some unmarked wares made at various periods from the time of John Astbury's 'black porcelane' onwards, which was made from clay found in and around the coal mines, containing a high proportion of coal dust. When fired, this body is extremely heavy and dense, not unlike Samuel Bell's polished red stoneware, for it will take a shine from polishing, and except for the unsophisticated objects made in this material, might be mistaken for Wedgwood's basaltes.

Some Jackfield ware was decorated in cold enamels painted over the glaze after firing which have not survived well. Most typical early Jackfield tea and coffee wares are raised on three small feet, similar in style to Wedgwood/Whieldon agate and tortoiseshell wares, and teapots have simple rounded handles and low-set spouts. Most jugs have large pointed lips and are pear-shaped, on rounded plain bases. Rockingham glaze is more brownish purple and generally made in shapes not found until the end of the eighteenth century: flattened globular shapes, often with bands of moulded decoration in low relief instead of the freer, sinuous decoration of leaves and flowers of early wares.

Principal producers and products

Jackfield; Swinton; unnamed nineteenth-century Staffordshire potteries.

Tea and coffee ware, teapots, coffee pots, cream jugs, milk jugs,

sucriers, jugs, mugs, loving cups, tea caddies.

A

A. *Jackfield-type teapot of octagonal shape with panels decorated in low relief with flowers. The handle is an elaborate version of the traditional Staffordshire crabstock shape, and the lid has a scrolled flower finial. $5\frac{1}{2}$ in (14 cm) high.*

B. *Baluster-shaped milk jug on three small feet with glossy black glaze and relief decoration of flowers and tendrils picked out in cold enamels, rather pot-bellied, with looped strap handle, c.1760. $5\frac{1}{4}$ in (13 cm) high.*

B

Reproductions

Many potteries in the nineteenth century produced a range of 'Egyptian black' made by staining earthenware black with iron oxide before firing, and covering it with clear glaze. With the Victorian passion for useless objects and trinkets, all manner of curious items from toilet and writing articles to plant pots and flower pots were made in this black-stained earthenware, most of it roughly modelled or press-moulded in factory conditions.

Variations

Black glazed wares were revived in Staffordshire at the end of the nineteenth century, possibly as a result of the fashion for black basaltes and 'Egyptian black' as an inexpensive version of an expensive range. Larger capacities for teapots mark these later revivals. Some of the most amusing pieces are the 'barge' teapots in large sizes and capacities, in lustrous, brownish-black glaze decorated with applied sprigs and mottoes such as 'Home Sweet Home' in panels of yellowish white. The lids were topped with miniature teapots, and these imaginative pieces, known as 'Measham ware', were a great favourite of people living on the canals and working the narrow boats.

Period of manufacture
*c.*1751 to *c.*1825.

Price bands

Baluster jugs with decoration and gilding intact £500–£1,000; worn £350–£700; undecorated £280–£400, depending on condition.

Mugs, tankards £300–£700; with inscription, gilding £450–£750.

Black glaze Staffordshire from £140.

Black basaltes & Castleford ware

Historical background

Although quite dissimilar to look at, both these types belong to a category known by specialists as 'dry-bodied wares', and they fall somewhere between earthenwares and stonewares. Black basaltes is a particularly handsome type of 'Egyptian black' which was principally made in its most refined state by Josiah Wedgwood. The body is a mixture of refined ball clay from Dorset, the same sort of glassy slag used by Mason for making ironstone, and manganese. It was fired once at high temperatures, then coated with a particular kind of varnish and fired again to red heat. It was a versatile material, for it could be thrown on a wheel or, when moulded, would take very clear impressions. In addition, traditional-type sprigged decoration could be applied to the surface, and it could also be engine-turned. Wedgwood's range of black basaltes was in production by the 1770s, and many other potteries were soon producing similar wares, though the quality of some black basaltes was far less fine, and the bodies were often of a gritty consistency.

The body known generally today as Castleford ware was originally made by the Turner family using felspathic stone as well as experimenting with the addition of china clay and china stone to stoneware bodies. The 'dry body' is white and porcellanous, has a degree of translucency and is vitrified, not glazed. Most of the very finely moulded and decorative teapots, jugs and mugs made in this white porcellanous body are today credited to David Dunderdale, who opened a factory at Castleford, not far from Leeds, in about 1790. Clearly, as with so many developments, other potteries were experimenting along similar lines and similar wares have been found from a number of other factories.

*Black basaltes coffee pot, with engine-turned chequered decoration on the lower half of the body and steeply domed lid with low relief acanthus leaf decoration and a swan finial. Impressed **LEEDS POTTERY**, c.1775–85.*

Signs of authenticity

Black basaltes
1. Extremely dense, hard body.
2. Unglazed, but with surface shine produced by polishing.
3. Crisp definition on wares with moulded relief.
4. Vitrified body, same density and colour on base and solidly through thickness.
5. Any slight chipping will show stone-like quality of body.
6. Silky, fine-grained surface.

Castleford ware
1. Hard, dense, white body with distinct translucence when held to the light.
2. Unglazed, non-shiny surface typical of vitrified stonewares.
3. Remarkable definition of moulded relief decoration.
4. Distinctive shape of Castleford teapots, jugs quite unlike any other wares.
5. Most commonly found without painted decoration except for blue lines edging panels of moulded relief.
6. Rarely found medallions or panels containing painted landscapes in several colours.
7. Body identical on base to rest of the piece.

Materials and decoration

Dry-bodied wares include the early vitreous stonewares such as red stoneware and 'black stoneware'. They are unglazed and made of vitreous bodies which are transformed by firing into a nonporous substance that is extremely hard and dense. Most of them can be moulded as well as thrown, and the moulding is always remarkably fine and crisp – although some of the unmarked wares of both the Castleford type and other versions of black basaltes were made in moulds which were used too often, so that the definition became blurred. Some pieces which have been identified as black basaltes may have been made from the clay found round coal mines as described with Jackfield, and this black gritty clay is still used today in some local potteries in Staffordshire.

Principal producers and products

Black basaltes Josiah Wedgwood; Humphrey Palmer of Hanley *c.*1760–78; Neale & Palmer *c.*1769–76; James Neale & Co. 1776–86; John Turner of Lane End 1762–87; Herculaneum, Liverpool *c.*1800; E. Mayer *c.*1780–1800.
Castleford ware David Dunderdale *c.*1790–1821; John Turner *c.*1780–1806; Clulow & Co. *c.*1802; Heath & Son, Burslem *c.*1797; Benjamin Plant, Longton *c.*1780–1820; Sowter & Co., Mexborough *c.*1795–1804.

Black basaltes Tea ware, toilet articles, ornamental vases and urns, busts, figures, cabinet ware, plant pots, writing articles.
Castleford ware Domestic articles, teapots and tea ware, mugs, jugs, sugar boxes, cream and milk jugs.

Period of manufacture
*c.*1780 to *c.*1820.

A. *Distinctively shaped teapot by Heath & Co. in dry-bodied white vitrified stoneware, with crisp acanthus leaf moulded decoration and central medallion of classical figure in low relief, and with blue enamel lines highlighting outline and moulding, c.1800–5. 5⅝ in (14 cm) high. City Museum & Art Gallery, Stoke-on-Trent.*

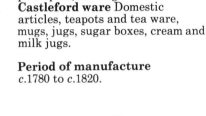

A

B

Reproductions

Victorian revivals of the classical 'Etruscan' ware abound, but the quality is poor and the articles were mass-produced. These are generally known as 'basalts' and also include black-dipped wares in a variety of dry bodies, which, when chipped, show a dingy half-stained, lighter centre to the ware and not the dense, solid-coloured true basaltes body. Perhaps the nearest reproduction of Castleford wares are those in domestic parian made in Victorian times, usually very ornate jugs, vases and mainly ornamental items, but they have none of the smooth glossy finish of Castleford.

Variations

For black basaltes, the obvious variation is the 'Egyptian black', which is made by staining an earthenware body with manganese which turns almost black with firing. Another version is stained with iron oxide, which produces a rather crumbly-textured body. 'Egyptian black' was made by many Staffordshire potteries after Wedgwood's black basaltes became fashionable, in imitation of his elegant highly polished wares.

B. *Wedgwood and Bentley black basaltes hedgehog bulb pot c.1800, engine-turned mug c.1775 and boat-shaped cruet with a ram's-head terminal and a swan handle, decorated with classical scenes in moulded relief.*

Price bands

18th-century black basaltes rare fine examples, marked from £420; unmarked, later dates from £80.

Castleford type teapots: unmarked £220–£350; marked £230–£500.

19th-century black basalts from £40.

Wedgwood

Historical background

Josiah Wedgwood was born in 1730 and began his career in the potteries at the age of 14 when he was apprenticed to his brother. In 1752 he set up on his own with two partners and made an undistinguished range of domestic stonewares. After two years the partnership dissolved and Wedgwood joined Thomas Whieldon. From 1754 his name recurs again and again in association with every major breakthrough in the development of earthenware

and stoneware, first with agate and tortoiseshell wares, quickly followed in 1758 with a remarkable green glaze and, in 1760, a cream-coloured glaze over a cream-coloured body which became the celebrated 'Creamware'. As this was clearly a tremendous commercial proposition, Wedgwood set up on his own at Burslem in partnership with Thomas Bentley and, in association with a former aquaintance, William Greatbach, made a range of tableware in the form of fruit and vegetables to compete with the range of leaf patterns being made in the porcelain factories. Known today as cauliflower ware, it used the green and cream-coloured glazes together, with

remarkable effect.

In its initial stages, creamware was not resistant to hot water, and first products were services of tableware and domestic and kitchen products. After 1765, when Wedgwood was commissioned by Queen Charlotte, he called this range 'Queen's Ware' in her honour, although he continued to use his standard mark.

Two Liverpool men, John Sadler and Guy Green, were producing transfer-printed tiles and basic flatware from

continued overleaf

Solid blue jasper ware vase by Wedgwood, impressed marks, late 18th century, with coiled snake handles and a rim of bay-leaves, decorated with scenes from classical mythology.

Signs of authenticity

1. Solid jasper with smooth, silky surface.
2. Body evenly stained and coloured throughout, and polished.
3. White decoration in low relief always applied to the surface.
4. Relief very slightly undercut, standing out very crisply.
5. Typical 'Wedgwood blue', faintly smoky with slight tendency to lilac tinge – strong but not vivid.
6. Brighter tones of cobalt blue indicate Turner's wares, always with extremely fine, crisp modelling.
7. Jasper dip only a coating of colour, but relief crisp, sharp and applied.
8. Wedgwood jasper ware made in distinctive pale cobalt blue, sage green, olive green, lilac, a rare yellow and silky black, not to be confused with his black basaltes.
9. Brighter, less sublte lilac may indicate William Adams wares.
10. Late, poor reproductions moulded in relief, with colour stained round areas of white relief, less crisp, more blurred.
11. Correct marks for Wedgwood & Bentley, impressed on base.

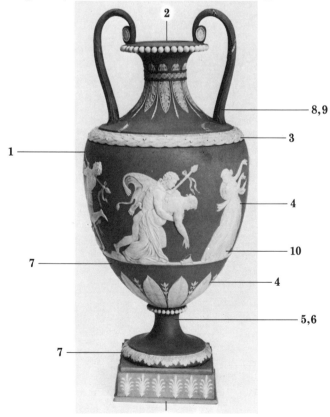

Variations

With so many successful developments in so many fields, it is not surprising that Wedgwood had his imitators in practically everything. It is only fair to say that in the early years, many other potteries were experimenting along similar lines and may have arrived at their own versions without deliberately copying Wedgwood, and in later years many famous potteries were set up by men who had once been apprenticed to or worked with Wedgwood before breaking away to start up on their own.

The principal names connected with variations of Wedgwood's extremely successful lines in each field were the following:

Agate and tortoiseshell John Astbury; Samuel Bell; Leeds pottery; Keeling & Morris from 1773; Britannia Pottery Co., Glasgow 1920s.

Green glaze ware Poole, Stanway & Wood from c.1860; Banks & Thorley from c.1873; Daniel & Sons, Longton 1863–75.

Creamware Leeds pottery from c.1765; Liverpool from c.1773; Herculaneum from c.1790; Swansea from c.1765; Minton c.1793–6; Spode c.1770–7; Sunderland from c.1780.

Black basaltes Humphrey Palmer of Hanley 1760–78; Neale & Palmer of Hanley 1769–76; James Neale & Co. 1776–86; John Turner of Lane End 1762–87; and Elijah Mayer.

Jasper ware William Adams, Greengates from 1789 (lilac).

Pearlware Spode c.1777–95; Leeds pottery from c.1777.

Principal periods of manufacture

Agate and tortoiseshell ware with Thomas Whieldon from c.1754. Green glaze ware from c.1759. Cauliflower ware with Whieldon from c.1759. With William Greatbach at Burslem, in partnership with William Bentley from c.1760. 'Rosso antico' red stoneware from c.1760. Creamware from c.1761. Transfer-printed creamware with Sadler & Green from c.1764. Black basaltes from c.1765. Marbled and 'Etruscan' were at Etruria from c.1769. Caneware from c.1770. Jasper ware from c.1774. Improved pearlware from c.1776. Bamboo ware from c.1790. Bone china from c.1812 to 1822 and from 1878 onwards. Polished red stoneware from c.1820.

A

A. Wedgwood black basaltes candlestick with moulded reliefs of classical scenes, with anthemion scrolls and formal borders with bronze and gilt details. Impressed mark, c.1900.

B. Piecrust ware with relief decoration of musical instruments in classical manner, with pipeclay border decoration.

B

Reproductions

It is interesting that Continental copies provide one of the greatest traps for unsuspecting buyers: 'Creamware' was copied by potteries in France, Germany, Holland, Denmark, Italy and Sweden, many of whom acknowledged their debt to Wedgwood with the word 'anglaise' or 'inglese' to describe the body and/or the glaze. Even Russian potters made replacement 'Creamware' in the nineteenth century for original wares supplied to Catherine of Russia in 1770. Contemporary facsimiles of jasper ware cameo plaques were made by John Voyez, mainly in black basaltes, marked indistinctly **WADGWOJD** – which at first glance can be mistaken for Wedgwood. Other similar names and markes used on similar wares include Tunstall's **WEDGWOOD & CO** and other Staffordshire nineteenth-century potteries, who marked their wares **WEDGEWOOD, VEDGWOOD, WEDGWOOD WARE** and **QUEENSWARE.**

Price bands

Agate, tortoiseshell from £400.

Green glaze ware from £180.

Cauliflower ware from £350.

Early creamware decorated by named artists £1,000–£1,600; transfer-printed from £320.

Early black basaltes from £400; later periods from £130.

Etruscan and marbled vases £1,500–£2,300 pairs.

Jasper ware: small plaques from £180; green, yellow, lilac more expensive; jasper dip from £65.

Caneware from £240. Bamboo ware from £320.

Pearlware from £180.

Polished red stoneware from £90.

Wedgwood

about 1756 onwards, and when Wedgwood realized that this method of decoration would greatly reduce the cost of creamware, he entered into a business agreement with them in about 1761, sending cartloads of creamware to their factory to be printed, instead of employing artists to hand-paint each individual piece. His original factory at Burslem outgrown, in 1769 Wedgwood opened new premises with the ambition of making vases and grand ornamental wares in the classical manner which was then so fashionable. He named it 'Etruria' and, still in partnership with Thomas Bentley, developed his great range of 'Etruscan' wares in an incredible range of marbled bodies which imitated all manner of decorative stones and marbles, as well as reviving an ancient technique of encaustic decoration for black basaltes with iron-red scenes from classical antiquity.

But of all his immense range of creamwares, pearlwares, fine stonewares and earthenwares, the one he is remembered by most is his 'Wedgwood blue'. This was known as jasper ware, and was quite similar to Castleford ware in many respects, since it was dense, vitrified and porcellanous, although its formula was a complicated and sophisticated compound. Jasper ware could be coloured right through the body with various metallic oxides or, less expensive, dipped in a solution of coloured jasper slip. Solid jasper was made in blue, sage green, lilac, lavender, olive green and black. Occasionally a rare yellow solid jasper was made, but it is not common. Embossed ornament in high relief was applied on these varied grounds, in pure white jasper. Wedgwood began making solid jasper in about 1774, and the full range of colours was in production by about 1777. Jasper dip was introduced in 1785.

Josiah Wedgwood's lifelong partner from his early days at Burslem, Thomas Bentley, died in 1780. After ten years, during which time he worked alone, Josiah took his three sons John, Josiah II and Thomas into partnership, together with his nephew William Byerley. The firm, originally called Wedgwood and Bentley, changed to Josiah Wedgwood from 1780 to 1790, and then to Wedgwood, Sons and Byerley until 1793. Two of Josiah's sons resigned at that time, and the firm became Wedgwood, Son and Byerley, a name which continued after Josiah's death in 1795 until William Byerley died in 1810.

Josiah Wedgwood II made bone china for a brief ten years between c.1812 and 1822 without great enthusiasm, but production was revived at Etruria in about 1878 as a commercial proposition and bone china is still made today by the Wedgwood company.

C. *Wedgwood cabinet cup, cover and stand in black and white chequered jasper, sprigged with yellow ochre florets with white garlands. Early 19th century.* **Impressed WEDGWOOD.**

C

D
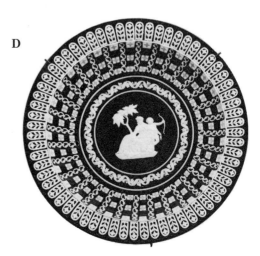

E

F

G

D. Black jasper dip cabinet plate from the mid-19th century, with yellow florets and central scenes from classical mythology.

E. One of a pair of black basaltes vases with Bacchic mask handles and acorn finials, with a border of swags round the tapered engine-turned body, c.1770. Wedgwood & Bentley. 10 in (25.5 cm).

F. Extremely rare Wedgwood and Bentley black basalte fox-mask stirrup cup (left) and a metal mould for a slightly different pattern.

G. One of the six 'First Day' black basaltes vases made to commemorate the opening of Wedgwood and Bentley's factory at Etruria. Inscribed with the date 'June 13th 1769' and commemorative legend.

Majolica

Signs of authenticity

1. Correct mark for Minton pottery.
2. Correct serial number – year code instituted from 1842.
3. Fine, crisp modelling.
4. Rich, thick glaze with deeper patches of colour where it has collected in small indentations.
5. Correct colour palette: red, pink, blue, green, purple, mauve, orange, yellow and brown.
6. Glaze and pigments integral.
7. Under-glaze pigments denote work from Staffordshire potteries.
8. White or pale cream-coloured body denote under-glaze-coloured earthenware.
9. Biscuit-yellow cane colour of body.
10. Minton majolica palette includes range of pinks, reds, mauves, absent in under-glaze-coloured earthenware.
11. Hard white body of almost crystalline texture denotes later wares in domestic parian.
12. Variety of objects more sophisticated than Staffordshire under-glaze-coloured earthenware.

Historical background

Majolica is often dismissed as a poor nineteenth-century version of original seventeenth-century Italian maiolica. In fact it is a considerably superior product in technical terms, though the results may not please everyone aesthetically. This rather stridently coloured range of ceramics was first produced by the Minton factory from 1851 onwards and its body closely resembles caneware, one of the succession of fine stonewares first developed by Josiah Wedgwood in 1770. Its decoration, however, is derived from early tin glazed techniques used for embellishing delftware.

Herbert Minton developed his majolica by using a version of Wedgwood's fine cane-coloured stoneware which was dipped in a tin-based glaze before firing. The colours, as with delftware, were applied on the powdery unglazed surface and the interaction of the stoneware with both glaze and pigments greatly enhanced the bright colours with which it was decorated, producing spectacular results. Many pieces were made of truly enormous proportions: jardinieres, conservatory seats, great bowls on towering stands, many of them as much as 4 ft (1.22 m) tall, as well as purely decorative birds and animals, flowers and fruit. On a smaller scale, Minton majolica cheese stands, bread trays, tazzas, table centrepieces and fruit baskets are perhaps more pleasing. And it is the designs of tureens and dishes which come closest to Wedgwood – in spirit at least.

Minton majolica tureen with moulded basket-weave decoration interlaced with leaves, with dead game on a bed of ferns and leaves. Impressed mark. 13¼ in (33.5 cm) wide.

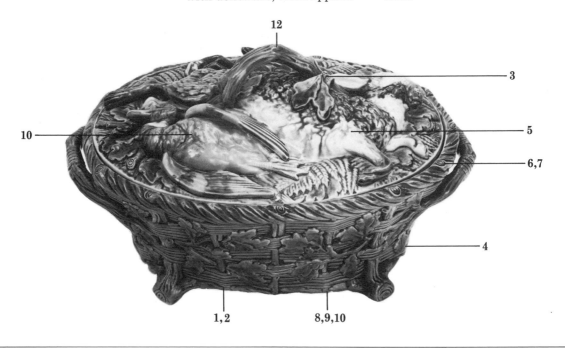

Materials and decoration

Fine cane-coloured stoneware with thick tin glaze into which the coloured pigments sank and fused. Majolica is moulded in elaborate shapes often more decorative than functional, and uses a similar palette to seventeenth-century Italian maiolica of blue, green, orange, yellow, brown and black, with the addition of a rather strident range of pink to mauve, and with more variations in blues and greens, including a vivid sky blue and a turquoise. The pieces were finely modelled under the thick glaze, which tends to blur over the crisp detail. The cane-coloured stoneware was so strong that it could be used for extremely large objects bearing considerable weights. Jardinières of great capacity, filled with earth and towering plants, stood on stands of the same ceramic, and many conservatory seats easily bore the weight of ample Victorian ladies.

Principal producers and products

Herbert Minton 1851–62.

Domestic wares, tureens, teapots, vases, ornamental jugs and vases, table centrepieces, dessert baskets, tazza, jardinières, conservatory seats, giant bowls on stands, ornamental birds etc., umbrella stands, cheese stands, bread trays, decorative plates.

Period of manufacture
1851 to 1862.

Variations

The manufacture of Minton's majolica spanned just over ten years from 1851 to 1862. After this date, a form of domestic parian was used instead of cane-coloured stoneware – a completely different composition originally made by Copeland & Garrett for ornaments and statues. Parian is a glossy, translucent soft paste, ideally suited to the Victorian passion for ornamental busts, nudes and classical figures. A coarser version of parian, tougher and harder, proved to be resistant to hot water and was easier, quicker and cheaper to use for elaborately moulded wares of all kinds, particularly ornate jugs and vases. This domestic parian has a completely different texture from cane-coloured stoneware, easily detected by the fact that it is extremely difficult to clean when left without glaze, as the bases testify.

Reproductions

Once the success of Minton's domestic majolica was established, many other manufacturers made similar ranges, but of lower quality. Italian maiolica in earthenware with traditional maiolica palette was made in the nineteenth century using a soft reddish or greyish clay body.

Price bands

Game, fish dishes £500–£1,000.

Jardinières £800–£1,800 and upwards.

Pedestals, plant stands £500–£1,100; pairs desirable and more than double the price.

Vases, jugs, dishes £400–£600 depending on design, colour, pattern.

Cheese stands, bread trays etc. from £50.

A. *Minton majolica teapot in the shape of a cockerel in bright colours. Impressed mark for 1872. 8 in (20 cm) high.*

B. *Minton majolica chestnut dish and spoon in green, brown and ochre, the interior of the bowl a rich turquoise, and decorated with chestnut leaves, with a horse-chestnut finial.*

A   B

Silver shapes

Historical background

Up to the seventeenth century, few people in England ate from anything else but a trencher – a slab of wood hollowed out to take the sloppy stews and 'spoon meats' which made up most of the dishes of the day. Rich and powerful households ate from plates of silver or pewter – sometimes even gold or silver-gilt. Crude earthenware mugs and jugs were used by the lowly; horn beakers, silver goblets and pewter tankards by the more privileged.

Plates were not easily made on a potter's wheel, and by the time pottery was needed in any quantity, they were made in a mould of wood or stone, onto which a flat pancake-shaped disc of clay known as a 'bat' was pressed. This remarkably primitive method of making flatware remained unchanged in England until around 1730, when new techniques of moulding and casting were introduced from the Continent. Of all the varied types of earthenware and paste manufactured in this way, none surpassed the incredibly fine and intricate patterns achieved in salt glazed stoneware. The first designs of moulded wares, destined to be used in banqueting rooms and state rooms of wealthy houses, followed the lines of the silver they were to accompany. Scrolling handles, rococo cartouches, gadrooning, scrolling and scalloping were impressed into the surface before firing. Both soft paste and hard paste porcelain were often made in contemporary silver shapes and then decorated in fashionable chinoiserie blue and white, apparently with no thought of the incongruous mixture of the two cultures on a single piece. The one exception to the use of silver shapes was tea ware, which copied Chinese teapots, bowls and saucers and developed a style of its own until it, too, followed the line of silver in the mid-eighteenth century.

Worcester pickle dish in 'famille rose' enamels in the typical silver shape of a shell. 4½ in (11.5 cm) diameter.

Worcester sauceboat, moulded in relief with rococo panels, of classic silver shape with scrolled handle and shaped rim. First Period c.1753. 6½ in (16.5 cm) long.

Materials and decoration

The shape of contemporary silver was followed in red and white stoneware, salt glazed stoneware, soft paste, soapstone and hard paste porcelain. Bodies and pastes were pressed or poured into moulds, left to dry, removed, and fired. Master moulds were carved from Derbyshire alabaster, or made in costly brass. A second mould was taken in porous clay and fired at a fairly low temperature. Thick slip was poured into the mould which instantly began to absorb the moisture and leave a layer of the 'body' solidified against the wall of the mould. When a thick enough layer of body had built up inside the mould, the surplus slip was poured off and the mould and its contents left to dry. The body shrank as it dried, so that it was easy to remove once it has reached the leathery consistency required for the first firing. In the 1740s, plaster of Paris replaced porous clay moulds and resulted in even crisper detail.

Principal producers and products

Red stoneware Elers brothers; John Astbury.
Salt glazed stoneware John Astbury; Leeds pottery; Liverpool.
Solid agate Whieldon/Wedgwood.
Creamware Wedgwood; Leeds.
Soft paste porcelain Bow; Chelsea; Derby; Longton Hall; Lowestoft; Liverpool.
Hard paste porcelain Bristol/Plymouth.
Soapstone porcelain Bristol; Worcester; Liverpoool; Caughley.

Teapots, coffee pots, sauce boats, butter boats, sweetmeat dishes, cream jugs, milk jugs, decorative tableware.

Period of manufacture
*c.*1720 to *c.*1780.

Reproductions

Few silver shapes were made by the more lowly potteries, with the exception of cow creamers, originally made in silver in the early eighteenth century, and then in agate and in tortoiseshell ware. Towards the end of the eighteenth century, cow creamers were made in Staffordshire potteries, where they joined the range of decorative, charmingly naive wares being made for the growing industrial towns and cities.

Variations

Silver shapes continued to influence the design of pottery and porcelain almost throughout the eighteenth century, particularly for rims of plates and services. At the beginning of the nineteenth century there was a noticeable revival in this design in table services of Regency proportions.

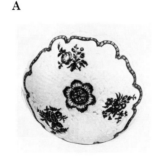

A

C

A. *Pair of Worcester junket dishes with silver-related moulded patterns, decorated in blue and white with sprays of flowers.*

B. *Rockingham dessert plate with hand-painted border, with gilt acanthus moulding to the rim in silver style and shape. Puce griffin mark inscribed* **Rockingham Works, Brameld. Manufacturers to the King**, *c.1831–5. 9¼ in (23.5 cm) diameter.*

C. *Duesbury Derby dessert plate of typical silver shape with gadrooned edge to rim and simulated beaded decoration around the central decoration, in gilt. 19½ in (26.5 cm) diameter.*

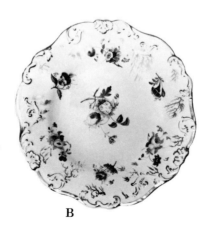

B

Price bands

Red stoneware from £500. White salt glazed stoneware from £300. Solid agate from £400. Creamware from £300.

Porcelain: Bow from £480; Chelsea from £500; Liverpool from £350; Longton Hall from £200; Worcester from £380; New Hall from £100.

Leaf shapes

Historical background

Meissen had discovered the secret of making 'true' hard paste porcelain in about 1710, and was making wonderful tureens, dessert baskets and dishes in the shapes of leaves, fruit and vegetables. This was the first European influence to have a marked effect on English manufacturers –

creamware was one example of attempts at imitation. English porcelain factories, still labouring to produce hard paste porcelain, began to imitate the delicate leaf shapes – Chelsea made a highly decorative range of leaf dishes from about 1753 onwards. The Worcester porcelain factory first produced their well-known cabbage-leaf jugs in about 1757 – a shape which proved so popular that it continued to be made with progressive decoration from blue and white onwards.

Small leaf dishes for pickles, sweetmeats and all manner of garnishes were opportunities for experiment, and those from Chelsea showed a cheerful sense of reality with their tiny caterpillars almost hidden down the central spine of the leaf. In England at that time, customs were changing under the influence of the House of

Hanover, and households began to adopt the custom of dining *à la Berline* – one course at a time, served by an army of footmen, with pretty little dishes set out on the table. Many well-bred middle-class and provincial households, however, continued to set out all the food on the table at the beginning of a banquet, and desserts were piled in a dazzling show on the sideboard, with centrepieces mounting in a series of tazza, or built up on a 'rocaille' base of rocks and shells with little dishes hanging or balancing on the silver or porcelain edifice.

Chelsea leaf dish from the Red Anchor period c.1752–5 with brownish-red veining, painted in bright enamel colours with butterflies, moths and insects and a characteristic caterpillar along the main vein. 9 in (22.5 cm) diameter.

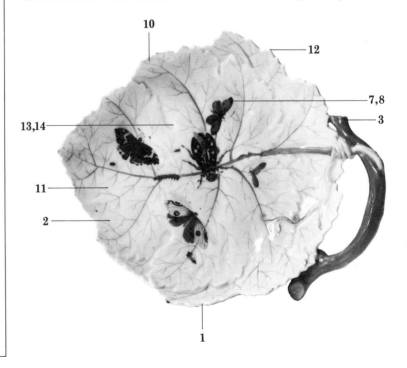

Materials and decoration

Soft paste, hard paste and soapstone porcelain with white ground and enamelled decoration painted in limited palette. Many patterns and shapes have names, such as 'Hans Sloane' for Chelsea lobed oval shapes, and 'Blind Earl' made by Worcester *c.*1765–70, said to have been commissioned by the Earl of Coventry, although he did not finally lose his sight until 1780. The famous porcelain artist of the time, James Giles, worked for both Chelsea and Worcester, which makes the two factories easy to confuse unless close attention is paid to marks and characteristic details of body and glaze.

Principal producers and products

Green glaze leaf dishes Wedgwood.
Cauliflower ware Wedgwood.
Creamware Melbourne; Leeds; Wedgwood.
Soft paste porcelain Bow; Chelsea; Derby; Longton Hall; Lowestoft; Liverpool.
Hard paste porcelain Plymouth (Champion's hard paste).

Soapstone porcelain Bristol; Worcester; Liverpool; Caughley.

Leaf dishes, tureens in leaf shapes, partridge tureens, shells, melon shapes, leaf butter boats and sauce boats, cabbage-leaf jugs.

Period of manufacture *c.*1756 to 1780.

A. *Worcester leaf dish of the 'sunburst' pattern with puce scrolling rim decoration, painted in brilliant enamels with sprays of flowers, butterflies and insects.*

B. *One of a pair of Worcester basket-moulded oval dishes with pierced rims and twig and vine handles moulded in relief, decorated with good colours in enamel with fruit and flying insects, c.1760–5.*

C. *Rare Bow sauceboat crisply moulded with overlapping vineleaves with a bound stalk handle, painted in enamels with a Japanese quail pattern, c.1752–8. 6¼ in (15.5 cm).*

Reproductions

The original fine porcelain leaf dishes have not been reproduced in any form which would be confused with a genuine piece. Green glazed ware, on the other hand, has become almost a standard range for many of today's makers of bone china and it is doubtful if there has ever been a period since its first introduction in the 1760s when it has not been made in some form or another.

Variations

The variation that has become synonymous with leaf dishes is Wedgwood's range of green glazed earthenwares in leaf shapes, made from *c.*1760 to *c.*1790. It was revived in the Victorian period, with a thicker glaze on a more refined earthenware body, and was also made in fashionable 'majolica' green by Poole, Stanway & Wood in the 1860s. In the 1870s a much finer version was produced by Banks & Thorley. Daniel & Son of Longton also made a wide range of green glazed wares from 1863 to 1875.

Price bands

Sauce and butter boats from £380.

Leaf dishes: Chelsea Red Anchor period £750–£950, pairs £1,600 upwards; Derby £400–£600.

Bow pickle dishes £600–£800.

Longton Hall peony dishes £2,800–£3,200 pairs.

European influence – Meissen

Historical background

In Germany the passion for Oriental blue and white porcelain was less overpowering compared with English porcelain factories, and Meissen and other leading manufacturers made relatively little Chinese and Japan pattern porcelain. Designs were closer to silver patterns of the period, but less ornate and more pure, with delicate, restrained enamelled decoration. What first caught the imagination of English porcelain manufacturers were the exquisitely modelled tureens in the shape of lettuces, fruit, animals, and those with partridges nesting on the lids. Chelsea was among the first to copy these decorative wares, with considerable success. Leaf dishes and relief decoration followed, and then Chelsea began to imitate the delicate colouring and restrained shapes of Meissen tableware, often combined with rims and borders in moulded basket relief, or with bands of relief decoration. The detail was not very crisp, however, since Chelsea was using a thick, creamy glaze, perhaps to cover up the slightly greyish colour of the paste and the visible imperfections caused by greasy spots. From 1749 to 1756 a considerable quantity of extremely fine tableware was made at Chelsea, with hand-painted sprays of flowers and sprigs in delicate, soft colours.

Worcester contented itself with Chinese and Japanese patterns, except for a brief period from 1765 to 1780 when it included a range of Meissen-influenced patterns and designs, hoping to attract a richer class of customer. The scattered flowers and sprays were less free, more stilted than those of Chelsea but Worcester's range of colouring was fine and delicately painted.

Early Meissen figures, such as the famous Monkey Orchestra, first made in 1747, had elaborate, gilded rococo bases – a form which clearly appealed to Chelsea, for soon their tableware began to curl, scroll and glitter with burnished gold.

One of a pair of Chelsea dishes in Meissen style, with band of relief decoration almost obscured by the glaze, iron red rim and sprays of flowers, scattered with sprigs. 9 in (22.5 cm) diameter.

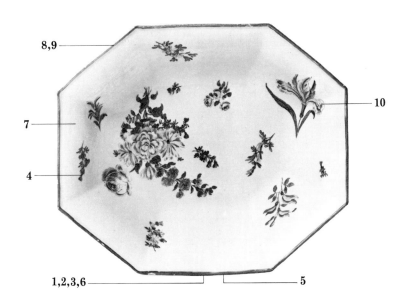

Materials and decoration

In soft paste, soapstone porcelain and hard paste, with a richer, more cream-coloured glaze than blue and white and Oriental patterns. The first Chelsea products were limited, and excluded tea services – it was not until about 1760 that an improved version of soft paste was able to withstand the heat of boiling water. Since it was genuine Meissen and, shortly after, Vincennes and Dresden that were so much in demand, the English factories were not above putting the marks of these noble factories on their copies – just as many of them had marked their Oriental wares with pseudo-Chinese marks. Gilding on Chelsea was a rich, deep, burnished gold of honey gilding, easily differentiated from later mercury gilding, which was not brought over to England from Europe until the 1780s.

A. *Part of a First Period Worcester tea service painted in enamels in Meissen style, with characteristic Worcester flower finial on the elegant teapoy, and flowers in cartouches, sprinkled with feathery sprays. c.1775–80.*

B. *Chelsea mug painted in brilliant enamels with sprigs and a spray of flowers. Red anchor mark, c.1752–6. $5\frac{1}{2}$ in (14 cm) high.*

C. *Hand-painted Meissen teacups and stands, marked with blue crossed swords, and a mug with similar decoration impressed* **IK** *with pink lustre mark for Hochst.*

D. *Vincennes ewer decorated with sprays of flowers and flying insects, with gilded rim and detail. Marked with interlaced Ls and date letter for 1754. $11\frac{1}{2}$ in (29 cm) high.*

Principal producers and products

Chelsea; Worcester; Longton Hall; Derby; Nantgarw; New Hall.

Full ranges of tableware, tea ware, dinner services and dessert services.

Period of manufacture
1749 to 1813 and later.

Variations

In a sense, Nantgarw, Swansea and almost all the later makers of flower-patterned bone china based their early designs on the Meissen flower sprays and sprigs, although as time passed and an English style began to emerge, the patterns became more highly coloured and covered more and more of the surface – the aesthetic sprinkling of well-spaced, beautifully painted flowers was presumably too restrained both for the manufacturers and their customers.

Reproductions

The most common and confusing are pieces marked with the Chelsea anchor mark, many of them made by a large factory in Italy which used a large red anchor. Derby and Worcester wares decorated outside their works, mainly in London, also often added a Chelsea-like anchor. Bow, too, used an anchor, but with a dagger. Familiarity with Chelsea in terms of glaze, colour and body are essential before placing one's trust and one's money on the evidence of 'Chelsea marks'.

Price bands

Plates: Chelsea £200–£320; Derby (unmarked) £35–£80; Longton Hall (rare) £500–£750; Worcester £50–£120; Nantgarw £350–£500; New Hall £80–£150.

Prices escalate depending on rarity to £1,000 upwards.

Fabulous birds

Historical background

As early as 1750 there were independent artists who had set up as enamellers and painters, to whom porcelain factories sent their undecorated wares. William Duesbury, who later set up the Derby Porcelain company (which in due course acquired the Chelsea Porcelain Factory), began his association with porcelain as an independent enameller, but it is probably to James Giles that we owe a series of porcelain painted with his improbable 'dishevelled bird'. He was known to be decorating 'china' some time before 1760 in London, where he had a studio of artists working for him. There are some recorded exotic bird patterns that were produced by Chelsea, Derby, Plymouth and Worcester dating from c.1755, but the 'dishevelled bird' is quite different. It reappears in varying but unmistakable form, on everything from the early leaf shapes right through to the end of the century, including a transfer print of almost identical design on Wedgwood's creamware decorated by Sadler and Green.

Another bird painter, James Rogers, worked for the Worcester Porcelain Company in the late 1750s – and Oriental-inspired birds, particularly the ho-ho bird which Chippendale used again and again in gilt mirror frames, feature in some of Worcester's named patterns, such as the 'Sir Joshua Reynolds'. Quails, too, appear in many derivations of Oriental decoration. But the enchanting 'dishevelled bird' owes little or nothing to the rich and heavy painting of naturalistic birds on Meissen porcelain.

One of a pair of Worcester leaf dishes in the shape of cos lettuce leaves moulded in relief, with veins of the leaves in pink, and with a gilt rim. The 'dishevelled bird' is accompanied by a chick on a bed of hedgerow leaves and creepers, with butterflies, moths and insects surrounding it. c.1770. 10½ in (26.5 cm) diameter.

Signs of authenticity

1. In soft paste, hard paste and soapstone porcelain with typical translucent body.
2. Both Worcester and Chelsea frequently combined fabulous birds with moths and winged insects.
3. Painted in enamels in remarkable detail, wide colour palette.
4. Iron red rim distinctive of Chelsea.
5. James Giles birds have a startled air and ruffled feathers.
6. Chelsea birds sleeker, often with long trailing tails and crest feathers, faintly resembling cock pheasant.
7. Longton Hall birds fill more of the centre, leave less undecorated, and are seldom seen with associated moths and insects.
8. Birds on Plymouth hard paste relate more directly to derivations from Japanese designs, often with heavy peony and prunus root – frequently associated with simple gilt border.
9. Derby, Chelsea often with osier- and basket-moulded relief on dessert ware, some wares with applied florets.
10. James Giles worked for Chelsea, Derby and Worcester – his work found on pieces from all three factories.
11. Later work from studio of James Giles may be overpainted on transfer-printed engraved plates in 'off black' tones printed specifically for the purpose of painting.
12. Use confined to dessert services – no tea services with dishevelled bird.

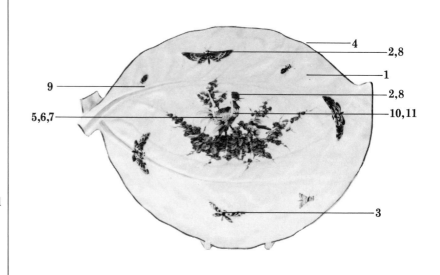

Materials and decoration

On soft paste, soapstone porcelain and some rare hard paste examples. The 'dishevelled bird', once seen, will not be confused with the Oriental ho-ho bird, with its exaggerated crest feathers and broad sweeping tail-feathers; nor with the naturalistic birds or the plump little quails, also derived from Oriental designs. These fabulous and unlikely 'dishevelled birds' occur in a wide variety of shapes and designs; sometimes in pairs, more often singly with small perching birds or with

A. *Chelsea plate painted with fabulous birds in a landscape, surrounded by flying moths and winged insects, with osier-moulded rim with gilt edge, c.1755–60.*

Variations

The naturalistic birds that appear on early porcelain from about 1755 following Meissen's series of birds are a separate development. They are richer in colouring and use of enamels, and belong to the botanical, ornithological series from all the major porcelain factories. The true dishevelled bird was continued by Worcester, and later by Longton Hall, in association with rich panels of ground colours, as well as by Chelsea in its rococo phase.

chicks. Worcester and Chelsea (both of which used James Giles) frequently have additional winged insects, moths and butterflies – certainly in early examples. Derby birds are often associated with the flowery Meissen-type decoration. Inevitably such a popular design was copied by contemporary potteries seeking to emulate the expensive wares of soft paste and other porcelains – but generally in transfer-printed versions.

B. *One of a pair of Chelsea dishes with rococo scrolled edge, gilded and painted with a fabulous bird among shrubs in a landscape, c.1760–5. 9½ in (24 cm) diameter.*

C. *Chelsea plate with panels of deep blue in gilded cartouches and gilt moths and insects in the centres, linked by festoons of flowers and foliage, with a fabulous bird in the centre in a landscape with a town on the horizon, surrounded by moths and winged insects, c.1760–5.*

Principal producers and products

Chelsea; Derby; Worcester; Plymouth; Longton Hall.

Mainly decorative and dessert ware – glaze was soft and crazed with use. Display pieces and

cabinet ware – baskets and leaf dishes.

Period of manufacture
*c.*1757 to 1770 and later.

Reproductions

Those later porcelains from Worcester, using transfer-printed outlines and then enamelled in colours, are again worth mentioning since the quality was variable, with a fine bubbling of the glaze similar to the telltale signs of later 'clobbering' but in fact contemporary. The transfer-printed wares of Wedgwood and other Staffordshire potteries in creamware were a deliberate attempt to reproduce more cheaply the expensive porcelain of the time.

Price bands

Dishes: Chelsea £500–£700; Derby £550–£750; Bow (quail pattern) £350–£500; Worcester First Period £450–£650; Longton Hall £550–£800; Plymouth (rare) £480–£700.

Condition of prime importance. James Giles, named artists more.

D. *Two Derby dessert baskets with moulded basketwork handles and applied leaves and flowers on the inside, and applied florets on the moulded trelliswork body, painted in enamels with exotic birds in a landscape with trailing sprigs and sprays of flowers.*

European influence – Sèvres

Signs of authenticity

1. In soft paste and soapstone porcelain.

2. Sequence of introduction: 'gros bleu', mazarine blue 1759; pea green 1759; claret, turquoise 1760; yellow 1761.

3. Worcester ground colours from 1769 after Chelsea craftsmen joined the company.

4. Exceptions from Worcester are yellow from 1758, and a powder blue ground which pre-dates 1769.

5. From 1769 Worcester produced a full range of ground colours: mazarine blue, sky blue, pea green, French green, sea green (turquoise), purple, scarlet (claret).

6. Worcester ground colours less vibrant than Chelsea.

7. Both Chelsea and Worcester versions of pea green and yellow could not take gilding – gilt borders stop short by a hairline from grounds, panels in these two colours.

8. Coalport early nineteenth-century copies of early Chelsea with chrome green ground, easily gilded.

9. Quality of gilding rich and burnished – honey gilding until *c.*1780 when mercury gilding introduced.

Historical background

Between 1770 and 1780 there was a marked change in the style of decoration and shape of porcelain. The simple designs and sprigged flower decoration of Meissen were now being made in Wedgwood's creamware far more cheaply and in direct competition with the porcelain factories. Catering as they did for a far more exclusive class of customer, the porcelain factories began to try and copy the elegant, rich colours and formal patterns associated with the Sèvres porcelain factory.

Their ambition was to produce the deep 'gros bleu' panels of Sèvres, formally spaced and joined by swags and garlands of more stylized flowers and foliage. 'Gros bleu' was achieved by applying cobalt pigment to the 'biscuit' paste in predetermined panels

of colour, reserving spaces for flower arrangements in panels, cartouches or symmetrical spaces. The cobalt pigment used by English potters was imported from Saxony, either as smalt, prepared with ground glass as an enamel, or as zaffre, pure refined cobalt pigment. There had been a dearth of good Saxony cobalt between 1756 and 1763, when supplies ceased due to the Seven Years' War. During that time, English deposits of cobalt were mined and used, but this was not entirely satisfactory because it tended to have a strong purple ingredient which sometimes appeared during firing. Although some potteries used English cobalt to great effect, the porcelain factories managed to acquire small quantities of Saxony smalt, which they preferred for enamelling. It was Dr Wall of Worcester who refined and prepared both smalt and zaffre for 'gros bleu' to such a high quality that it became known as 'Bristol blue', named for the chemist in Bristol who was the sole source of imported cobalt. It was only possible to produce significant quantities of the much-admired 'gros bleu' when supplies of good cobalt were again available. Dr Wall was, of course, in the forefront of the move towards producing high-quality porcelain in the French manner.

Worcester milk jug and cover with mottled scale blue ground, domed cover, characteristic small flowering bud finial and cartouches painted with Japanese-influenced flowers. c.1770.

Materials and decoration

Soft paste porcelain, soapstone porcelain and bone china, decorated at first with bands of dark blue, almost always with some gilding, with the rest of the piece decorated over the glaze in coloured enamels. Sèvres designs were first successfully produced by Chelsea during the Gold Anchor period, but soon afterwards the Chelsea factory closed down and its craftsmen were employed at the Worcester Porcelain factory. From that time, 1769, Worcester began to produce a full range of ground colours.

None of the wares produced at this time were painted or decorated in any of the later chemical pigments and colours which are much harsher and have less depth. Only the green continued to cause problems, and it was not until Rockingham produced its rare and distinctive apple green that this colour became really effective.

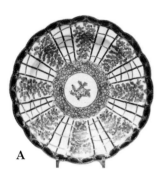

A. *Worcester 'Hop Trellis' pattern plate with deep blue border with gilded swags, pure trellis and vivid turquoise leaves and central border.*

C. *Worcester cup and saucer with mottled 'gros bleu' ground with fan-shaped and gilt foliage-edged panels with polychrome birds and insects.*

D. *Teacup and saucer with single studies of exotic birds within gilt-edged panels reserved on a wet blue ground, c.1765–70.*

Period of manufacture
c.1758 to 1783 and later.

Principal producers and products

Chelsea 1758–69; Worcester 1768–83; Chelsea/Derby 1769–84; Chamberlain's Worcester from c.1798; Coalport from c.1814; Davenport from c.1850;

Rockingham 1830–42.

Full ranges of tableware, dinner services, dessert services, tea and coffee ware.

B. *Worcester bowl with deep blue scale ground, gold rococo scrolls and shield-shaped panels with gilded surrounds, painted with sprigs and flowers. Square mark for First Period. 9 in (22.5 cm) diameter.*

E. *Worcester cup and saucer painted with gilt-edged panels on a dark blue ground, with brightly coloured birds and insects.*

Reproductions

Many famous makers in the nineteenth century made bone china in copies of eighteenth-century Sèvres designs, but although many books on this convoluted subject classify 'bone china' among the 'porcelains', strictly speaking bone china is in a class by itself, neither pottery nor quite porcelain.

Variations

Makers of felspar porcelain produced versions of these wares with 'reserves' or panels decorated with fruit, flowers, birds and many other themes, but none of them have the real depth and vividness of soft paste and soapstone porcelain, and all of them are heavier in weight, with far more naturalistic renderings of themes than eighteenth-century decoration. Nineteenth-century forms and shapes are quite distinctive too – more elaborate, usually with more gilding.

Price bands

Plates (blue ground): Chelsea £800–£1,200; Chelsea/Derby £280–£320; Worcester (early dates) £500–£750; Chamberlain's Worcester £50–£120; Rockingham £180–£250; Coalport £80–£140; Davenport £90–£250.

Green, yellow grounds rarer, more costly.

Black transfer-printing

Signs of authenticity

1. Early wares often with unsatisfactory black – Worcester, Bow tend towards purple spectrum with lilac, puce, brown.

2. Earthenwares with early printed decoration more brick red, with greenish brown or dull green.

3. Both pottery and porcelain printed over the glaze in black or near black.

4. From c.1764 both pottery and porcelain additionally decorated with colour washes and enamels.

5. Worcester, Chelsea porcelain from c.1770 transfer-printed on coloured ground – particularly associated with clear yellow.

6. Longton Hall and Liverpool porcelains decorated with Sadler's transfer prints from c.1760.

7. Frederick the Great, King of Prussia and William Pitt commemorative prints from c.1756–63 with accession of George III.

8. Transfer-printed commemorative wares from Liverpool followed by other Staffordshire potteries from c.1762 onwards.

9. Transfer-printed armorial services from Worcester, c.1756 onwards.

10. Bow transfer-printed wares in puce as well as black.

Historical background

The two worlds of the porcelain makers and the potteries were still very much separated from each other, but the demand for both pottery and porcelain was growing, and both fields were looking for ways of cutting the cost of their wares. The use of costly hand-painted enamels, which needed several firings in the kiln at the expense of quantities of fuel, was troubling the makers of porcelain, while hand-painting individual pieces of Wedgwood's steadily improving earthenware was expensive and time-consuming.

It seems clear that the technique of printing engraved designs on any surface other than paper originated with the makers of enamel, either in Battersea or in Birmingham, and that first trials were not entirely successful. The first recorded evidence is a patent taken out in 1751 by an Irishman, John Brooks, and the Battersea works were opened in 1753 for printed enamels. In 1754 an illustrator, Robert Hancock, was engraving plates for Battersea and also for Bow, the results in each case being printed in red or purple – a pure black was difficult to achieve and depended on precise heat in the kilns. Meanwhile, two Liverpool men, Sadler and Green, were also working on the same process. As soon as Josiah Wedgwood had perfected his creamware in about 1764, he sent quantities of it to be decorated by Sadler and Green and in a short time took them on as permanent employees in his enlarged works at Burslem. Both Worcester and Wedgwood used coloured washes of enamels over transfer-printed designs, and this sophisticated decoration brought them for the first time into direct competition.

Worcester transfer-printed mugs with engravings by Robert Hancock of (left) *Frederick the Great,* (centre) *William Pitt and* (right) *the King of Prussia,* c.1760. $3\frac{1}{2}$ in (9 cm) to 4 in (10 cm) high.

Materials and decoration

On soft paste, soapstone porcelain and on creamware. Transfer prints were applied over the glaze and then fired at a lower temperature to fix the design to the glaze. An engraving on copper plate was made, printers' ink was mixed to a flux with enamels, and the plate was inked and transferred to a paper specially developed for the process. The paper bearing the transfer was then pressed on to the glazed surface after it had been moistened in soapy water so that it would slide off, leaving the print transferred to the glaze. The properties of early pigment frequently produced a change in colour during firing, and it was some time before a true 'jet black' was achieved.

Transfer prints were used with variable results in conjunction with coloured enamels, and the process was later taken up by manufacturers of stoneware and used as a guide to applying colours with new techniques.

Reproductions

Some early pieces originally printed in black and white have been 'clobbered' or embellished by the later addition of coloured enamels, which considerably enhances their value. This is more commonly found on wares with imperfect black printing, which can resemble genuine wares with outlines printed as a guide to hand-colouring.

Variations

In the nineteenth century new techniques of printing on ceramics were developed which were cheaper and easier to apply. These included the various techniques of printing more than one colour under the glaze, either with a series of transfers or from a single transfer in three colours. Genuine black and white transfer-printed wares can be detected by the slight unevenness of the surface where the additional layer of enamel has only partly been absorbed by the glaze.

Period of manufacture
c.1754 to c.1824 and later.

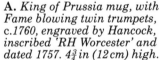

A. *King of Prussia mug, with Fame blowing twin trumpets, c.1760, engraved by Hancock, inscribed 'RH Worcester' and dated 1757. 4¾ in (12 cm) high.*

B. *Rare Worcester tea canister, c.1765, printed with 'The Tea Party' on one side and 'Lady Watering a Garden' on the other. 5½ in (14 cm) high.*

C. *King of Prussia mug with war trophies and Fame with two trumpets on a curved cylindrical shape, c.1760. 4¾ in (12 cm) high.*

D. *Sunderland creamware jug commemorating the building of the cast-iron bridge, begun in 1795 and completed in 1796, with a verse on the other side. 7½ in (19 cm) high.*

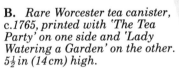

E. *Rare Derby jug and mug printed with engravings by Richard Holdship and signed with the anchor rebus, of the regiment of the First Foot Grenadier Guards, c.1760–5.*

Price bands

Mugs (plain cylindrical):
Bow (rare) £750–£1,250; Derby £280–£600; Longton Hall £550–£950; Worcester £300–£1,200; creamware from £80.

Higher prices for rarer shapes, named engravers.

Principal producers and products

Worcester from c.1756; Wedgwood from c.1761; Liverpool from c.1760; Bow from c.1754; Longton Hall c.1756–60; Chelsea from c.1760; Derby c.1760–9.

Commemorative and landscape, pastoral scenes – on mugs, jugs, plates, services, tea ware, armorial services.

Early blue & white printed ware

Historical background

Transfer-printing in blue and white was a logical step from black enamel printing. Cobalt oxide, as has been seen repeatedly with every advance, was the one colour that could be applied under the glaze and maintain its colour through successive firings. It seems that the credit for the first successful printing in blue under the glaze must be accorded to Robert Hancock at the Worcester factory, though the precise date is not clear. Early examples seem to have been made around 1760 and run almost parallel with wares which have been painted in blue. Of the two, it is the painted decoration that has the clearest, crispest lines in the early stages, and the printed decoration that is more blurred and uncertain. Once the technique was perfected, however, the clarity of line and detail became remarkably fine, and printed patterns include Oriental subjects as well as sprays of flowers, fruit and vines. Among the best-known Worcester printed patterns is the pine cone or mulberry pattern.

Robert Hancock left the Worcester factory when Thomas Turner started the Caughley Factory in the 1770s, and from that date blue printed wares from Caughley closely followed those of earlier Worcester, both in shape and design and in the printed patterns used. Caughley produced a range of pine cone pattern wares, as well as a particularly fine print known as the 'Pleasure Boat' or 'Fisherman' pattern. Lowestoft, too, produced a version of the pine cone pattern, but the prints were often improved by additional brushwork.

Some Staffordshire potteries produced a small quantity of experimental blue printed wares – Thomas Turner, for example – but it was left to Josiah Spode to take the technique to a remarkably high level of development for the mass market, thus beginning the long line of commercially produced Oriental blue and white earthenware from about 1781 onwards, including the celebrated willow pattern.

Signs of authenticity

1. On soft paste, soapstone, hard paste porcelain and stoneware, limited number of manufacturers.
2. Distinctive straw colour of paste identifies later Caughley from earlier, more blue/green Worcester.
3. Limited number of printed patterns used, repeated on different pieces.
4. Unlike black-printed wares, printed under the glaze at the 'biscuit' stage.
5. Soft, rich tones of cobalt blue distinguish this period from later, harsher shades of artificial and chemical blues, with the exception of 'Littler's blue' which is very bright.
6. Lowestoft blue and white printed wares sometimes discreetly embellished with gliding on rims and finials.
7. New Hall exceptional with all-over patterns at a later date (c.1780–95) in competition with Spode patterns, but limited to tea ware, small sweetmeat and pickle dishes with hard paste body.
8. Glaze shows distinct signs of pooling and dappling in oblique light.

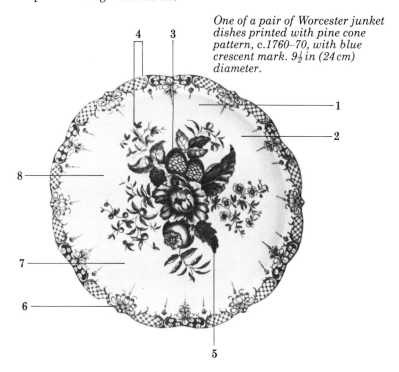

One of a pair of Worcester junket dishes printed with pine cone pattern, c.1760–70, with blue crescent mark. 9½ in (24 cm) diameter.

Materials and decoration

On soft paste, soapstone porcelain, hard paste and stoneware, fired once to biscuit stage, after which the print was prepared and fixed. The cobalt pigment was mixed with a flux to fix the colour to the biscuit body, and the copper plate of the engraving was inked and printed on to a specially prepared tissue paper which was dampened with soapy water. It was then pressed on to the biscuit surface and the copper plate reheated so that the colour softened slightly, allowing the paper to be eased off the engraved plate. The tissue was then rubbed to ensure that every line of engraving was clearly transferred to the biscuit and allowed to dry. After that, the tissue was washed off in cold water and the biscuit was fired to fix the decoration to the body. It was then dipped in glaze and fired a third time, usually stacked one above another in the kiln, separated by small 'thimbles' or 'spurs'. There is almost always a faint blurring where the colour has diffused into the glaze.

Principal producers and products

Worcester from c.1758; Caughley from c.1770; Lowestoft from c.1760; New Hall c.1780–95; Liverpool from c.1760; Spode from c.1785; Turner from c.1780.

Mugs, jugs, tea ware, small dishes, knife rests, tableware, sauce and butter boats, cabbage-leaf jugs, tea caddies, strainers.

A. *Two Worcester pickle dishes printed* (left) *with flowers, c.1775 and* (right) *in heavy under-glaze blue with deep blue border, c.1765–70. Both shaped like shells, c.5 in (12.5 cm) diameter.*

A

B

C

B. *Lowestoft jug and cover with painted decoration, with blurring and running under the glaze, second half of 18th century. 9¾ in (24.5 cm) high.*

Reproductions

From 1781, when Spode first went into commercial production with Staffordshire blue and white, there have been innumerable versions and copies of original Oriental and willow pattern transfer-printed wares. The early blue and white transfer-printed wares were not reproduced, since their short period of manufacture was superseded by such a mass of highly popular blue and white transfer-printed tableware and useful ware.

Variations

Early products of the Spode factory were of a particularly dense, dark blue, and patterns were less intricate, more closely derived from Oriental designs. The body is a hard, near-white earthenware with a creamy tinge, without the translucence of paste bodies, and heavier in weight than creamware.

Period of manufacture c.1760 to 1795.

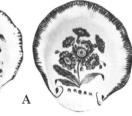

C. *Worcester cabbage-leaf mask jug with ring handle, c.1765, printed in blue with sprays of roses and vines. 9 in (22.5 cm) high.*

Price bands

Plates, dishes:
Caughley £250–£500;
Worcester £320–£600;
Lowestoft £100–£250;
Spode pearlware £80–£120.

Mugs (plain cylindrical):
Worcester from £175; Caughley from £145.

Lowestoft early wares expensive collectors' pieces.

Worcester porcelain

Historical background

It is possible to trace the whole decorative story of English porcelain through this one single factory, from its beginnings in 1752 when the Worcester company united with Lund's Bristol works, for it produced every fashionable shape, design and pattern of any importance. There are many people who collect only Worcester, either in small specialized sections, or from the whole period of its long history, and it is a subject which is extremely rewarding on its own. Perhaps because it has its own following of specialist collectors, it has developed a language of its own, which is sometimes confusing to the newcomer or to the 'outsider' whose interests range over a wider field.

Worcester porcelain starts with what is known as 'First Period', which covers a long span of styles and patterns from 1752 to 1783. Within this general category come the first blue and white series, the silver-shaped moulded wares and the first polychrome range. A major change occurred in 1768–9, when the Chelsea factory declined and closed, and a number of Chelsea artists and craftsmen moved to Worcester. After this date the range and quality of colours improved almost out of recognition, as Worcester gained all the expertise of the Chelsea soft paste porcelain range. Colours – which up to this date were more or less confined to pale enamelling, under-glaze blue in varying tones and a distinctive powder blue – now increased to a full range of mazarine blue, sky blue, pea green, French green (which was darker), sea green or turquoise, puce, purple and a vivid range of reds. At about the same time, around 1770,

James Giles was employed by the Worcester factory and his fabulous birds became the height of fashion, as well as landscapes, fruit, flowers and landscapes with figures.

The range of wares was at first confined mainly to tea ware, sauce and butter boats and other small items. It increased from 1763, after transfer-printing had been introduced in 1757, and was gradually extended to include all kinds of tableware and useful wares in all the latest and most fashionable designs, patterns and shapes. Japan patterns were also made from about this time, ranging from relatively simple patterns to elaborate versions of brocade designs, with dragons, chrysanthemums and fantastic phoenix-like birds. Special commissions for rich and famous people have given many Worcester designs the names of their patrons, such as

continued overleaf

Early Worcester teapot in lobed square shape with panels edged in brown, painted with pastoral scenes in enamel colours, c.1754–5. 4¾ in (12 cm) high.

Principal periods of manufacture

First Period 1752–83.
Blue and white c.1752–c.1760.
Moulded silver shapes from c.1752.
'Famille rose' and 'famille verte' enamels from c.1756.
Transfer-printed wares from c.1757 – Robert Hancock.
Fabulous birds and enamel painted decoration from c.1767 – James Giles.
Japan patterns from c.1767.
Full range of Sèvres colours from c.1769. Chelsea closure.
Death of Dr John Wall 1776.
Death of William Davis 1783.
Thomas Flight period 1783–93.

Royal Worcester Porcelain Co. 1788–1840.
Flight & Barr 1793–1807; bone china from c.1800.
Chamberlain's Worcester 1783–1840; 'Regent China' from c.1811.
Barr, Flight & Barr 1807–13.
Flight, Barr & Barr 1813–40.
Amalgamation of Chamberlain's with Worcester Porcelain Company 1840.
Kerr & Binns 1852–62.
Worcester Royal Porcelain Company Ltd 1862 to the present day.

Price bands

First Period Dr Wall blue and white from £320.

Silver shapes from £400.

'Famille rose' & 'famille verte' enamels from £600.

Black and white transfer-printed from £300.

Blue and white printed from £320.

Fabulous birds from £450.

Japan patterns from £320.

Chamberlain's Worcester from £40.

Flight, Barr & Barr from £150.

Kerr & Binns from £120.

Worcester Royal Porcelain from £120.

Prices increase steeply with rare patterns, shapes, commissioned pieces and collectors' items.

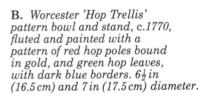

A. *Rare Worcester dessert basket with the rim pierced with interlaced circles, painted with flowers within gilded scrolled decoration on a deep blue ground. The outside is yellow and set with pink and green florets, c.1765. 10½ in (26.5 cm) diameter.*

D. *Worcester 'Dragons in Compartments' pattern c.1770 with a 'trio', a fluted dish and a heart-shaped dish. Dishes 7½ in (19 cm) and 10¼ in (26 cm) diameter.*

B. *Worcester 'Hop Trellis' pattern bowl and stand, c.1770, fluted and painted with a pattern of red hop poles bound in gold, and green hop leaves, with dark blue borders. 6½ in (16.5 cm) and 7 in (17.5 cm) diameter.*

C. *Worcester First Period tea service with barrel-shaped teapot and stand, with dark blue and gold leaf border and blue and gold decoration. Open crescent marks for 1755–70.*

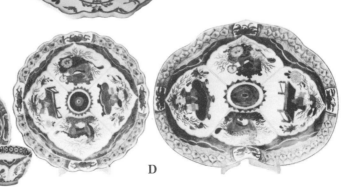

Worcester porcelain

the 'Joshua Reynolds' and the 'Lord Henry Thynne', among dozens of others.

The whole of this period is also known as the 'Dr Wall Period' or sometimes the 'Wall-Davis Period'. Dr John Wall in fact died in 1776, before his principal partner, William Davis – a Bristol scientist and technician – but the First Period continues until William Davis's death in 1783. Logically, one would expect there to be a 'second period', but Worcester is not so simple: the company was bought by Worcester's London agent and jeweller to the Royal family, Thomas Flight, and in 1778 Thomas Flight's company was granted the accolade of the title 'Royal Worcester Porcelain Company'. Thomas Flight died in 1791, but his son John continued to trade as Thomas Flight for a couple of years although he had taken Martin Barr into partnership in 1791. In 1793 the company was renamed Flight & Barr, under which title it was known for the next 14 years, until 1807. During this period, around 1800, bone china was made in addition to soapstone porcelain, and the formula for the latter was changed so that it became less translucent and slightly yellow when held to the light. After Martin Barr's son joined the firm in 1807, the formula was changed again to a far smoother, whiter porcelain, and the company was renamed Barr, Flight & Barr.

Robert Chamberlain, who had originally been employed by the Worcester factory as a decorator, broke away and set up on his own, also in Worcester, around 1786. For a while he bought wares from Caughley 'in the white', but in about 1791 he and his sons began to make porcelain of an unidentified hard paste-type body, which was greyish, hard and full of blemishes in the form of black spots. It was both illicit, since the New Hall restrictions on china clay and china stone did not run out until 1796, and not very satisfactory from all accounts. By the end of the century, however, Chamberlain had acquired some very important customers – among them Lord Nelson – and in 1814 and 1816 two showrooms were opened in Piccadilly and New Bond Street, where Chamberlain's Japan patterns were very popular. In about 1811, the factory had perfected a body known as 'Regent China', which was a version of soft paste, very white and translucent. In 1818 the company received a commission from the East India Company for 1,456 pieces with coats of arms, at a cost of £2,170 15s 0d.

In 1813, after further changes in the two families, the Worcester Porcelain Company was restyled Flight, Barr & Barr, and among the fashionable ranges produced by both rival companies were table services decorated with

Worcester Royal Porcelain Co. Ltd dessert plate with pierced panels round the rim, decorated with swans in flight on a pale blue ground, painted by Charles Baldwin with the date code for 1906. 8¾ in (22 cm) diameter.

landscapes. From 1820 to 1840 Chamberlain's Worcester included the words 'Royal Porcelain Manufactory', but all the Chamberlain marks always included his name as well as that of 'Worcester'.

In 1840 the two companies finally merged, though they continued to trade separately under the names of Flight, Barr & Barr and Chamberlain & Co. until 1852. At that date the whole business came under the management of Kerr & Binns and the next ten years saw a complete revitalization of the company, with a revival of Sèvres-style decoration with a rich royal-blue under-glaze ground and some of the finest enamelling ever produced by English porcelain factories. Many pieces at this period were marked with a shield and 'K & B Worcester'.

When Kerr retired in 1862, the company was renamed the Worcester Royal Porcelain Company Ltd and has remained so until the present day. It should be remembered that during the whole period that Thomas Flight was associated with the company, from 1788 to 1840, the crown of the 'Royal Worcester Porcelain Company' was included in all its marks.

E. *Worcester two-handled circular tureen and cover from the Flight, Barr & Barr period 1813–40. 7 in (17.5 cm) high.*

G. *Chamberlain's Worcester 'Regent China' covered bowl, c.1811–20.*

H. (Left and right) *Pair of Worcester plates painted with fantastic birds in landscapes with fluted rims in deep blue, hung with gilt swags. Centre 'Lord Henry Thynne' pattern plate printed with a landscape surrounded by fruit and birds on the wing, with a turquoise border to the central panel and a deep blue gilt-decorated rim. c.1775.*

F. *Worcester chamberstick from the Flight & Barr period, decorated with gilt, finely painted with feathers with an overlapping loop handle, 1793–1807.*

E

F

G

H

Landscapes: painted & printed

Historical background

Towards the end of the eighteenth century, a new fashion in decoration was introduced to the world of elegant chinaware, for which the Derby Porcelain Company was largely responsible. William Duesbury of Derby, who had bought out the Chelsea factory in 1769, died in 1786, and the factory was taken over by his son, also called William. One of his most talented artists at that time was William Billingsley, who left the Derby factory in 1796 to start the Pinxton porcelain works, also in Derbyshire, in partnership with John Coke. William Duesbury II was joined at Derby at the same time by Michael Kean, who was a miniature-painter. The series of landscape-decorated bone china from Derby began from about the same date. Both Thomas Flight's Worcester and Chamberlain's Worcester quickly followed suit, and a whole range of topographical scenes were used to decorate china from all the major factories.

William Billingsley did not stay long at Pinxton, but left in 1799 to start up a decorating workshop in Mansfield in Nottinghamshire, where he decorated quantities of unmarked porcelain and bone china. In 1813 Billingsley was in Wales, starting a small soft paste porcelain factory at Nantgarw with Samuel Walker; here again, among other wares, scenic and landscape painting of a very high quality was produced. In financial difficulties almost from the start, the factory was offered help by Lewis Weston Dillwyn of the Swansea factory in 1814, and both partners transferred to Swansea until 1817, when they returned to Nantgarw to make their wonderfully translucent soft paste porcelain. In 1820 Billingsley and Walker finally sold out to John Rose of Coalport. The height of this form of decoration was probably achieved by Rockingham.

*Two Derby cups and a saucer, fluted and bordered with gilt line and chain, with vines twisting round a dark blue line, finely painted with small figures by a shore in an English landscape. Late 18th century. Marked in puce script with crowned batons, **D** and **pattern No. 86.***

Signs of authenticity

1. On bone china and soft paste porcelain with translucent qualities.
2. On felspar porcelain and stoneware, either painted or printed.
3. Remarkable 'wash' effects similar to watercolour painting.
4. Painted over the glaze in enamelled colours until *c.*1828.
5. From *c.*1828 colour printing under the glaze, usually in limited palette of green, yellow, red and black.
6. Lithograph printing from *c.*1839 under the glaze, in the blue only until 1845, when multi-coloured lithographs in pink, green, purple, grey and black could be printed – at first in poor colouring, but in good palette from late 1850s.
7. Multi-coloured under-glaze transfer-printing with one firing only from 1848, limited to blue, red and yellow, with additional brown and green from 1852.
8. Descending value from full-coloured enamelled colours to more or less mass-produced wares using cheap printing techniques.
9. Correct marks for factories and period.

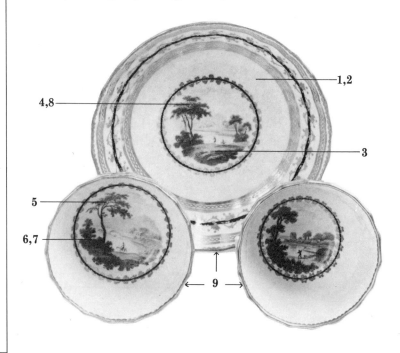

Materials and decoration

In soft paste porcelain by Derby, Pinxton, Nantgarw and Swansea-Nantgarw; in soapstone porcelain by Miles Mason, Worcester; in unidentified hard paste-type porcelain by Chamberlain's Worcester and Grainger's Worcester; in felspar and bone china by Spode; in stone china by Davenport and Turner of Lane End; in fine bone china by Rockingham; and in various stoneware bodies by unnamed Staffordshire potteries. The finest landscapes are painted in colours, at Derby, and by Billingsley. Some finely detailed landscapes are painted in sepia, such as those from Miles Mason, and there are some remarkably fine painted wares with topographical scenes from unnamed Staffordshire potteries, both for export and domestic markets.

Principal producers and products

Derby c.1796–1810; Pinxton 1796–9; Nantgarw 1813–20; Swansea 1815–17; Flight's Worcester from c.1790; Chamberlain's Worcester from c.1796; Monton from c.1800; Grainger's Worcester c.1801–12; Spode from c.1800; Miles Mason c. 1802–13; Davenport c.1805–15; Turner of Lane End c.1800–5; Rockingham c.1826–42; unmarked Staffordshire potteries.

Tea ware, coffee ware, dessert and table services, vases and ornamental ware.

A. *Staffordshire dessert plate painted with a mountainous landscape, probably the Alps, c.1860. 9½ in (24 cm) diameter.*

Price bands

Prices are for plates (mugs, coffee cans, tea ware more expensive).

Derby £200–£500 English named views. Worcester £280–£350.

Chamberlain's Worcester £250–£380 (heavy gilding from £400 upwards).

Pinxton, Billingsley £300 upwards (authenticated pieces).

Swansea £200–£400.

Coalport £120–£220.

Rockingham £800–£1,200 named views.

Rockingham copies £50–£80.

Printed ware: Davenport £80–£300 named views; Ridgway £100–£160; Spode £50–£180; unmarked £15–£40.

A

B

B. *Swansea dish with a romantic desert scene with Arab ponies and figures by an oasis, the rim intricately decorated with gilding. 8½ in (21.5 cm) diameter.*

Reproductions

The most luxurious and expensive of all these landscape themes is Rockingham, and inevitably reproductions of this fine ware have been made, both on the Continent and in England. Documentary evidence shows that Rockingham pattern numbers do not go above 2/100 and that no Rockingham ware ever carried a Patent Office registration mark. Some wares decorated after the Rockingham Works closed down are genuine, having been bought up by the one-time manager of the gilding department, decorated and sold between 1844 and 1851, but the best defence is a sound knowledge of Rockingham shapes, patterns and its unique brilliant body which is quite unlike any other.

Variations

Some of the early wares printed in new techniques such as printing in colours under the glaze and lithography are interesting for their historical significance, although the quality is poor, and monochrome transfer-printing of topographical views and themes from Staffordshire potteries is probably the real contemporary variation of these fine hand-painted landscape decorations.

Period of manufacture
c.1796 to 1825 and later.

C

C. *Swansea dessert dish with gilded handles and scrolled gilding with a scene of a Chinese junk in a harbour in the centre. 11 in (27.5 cm) diameter.*

Staffordshire blue and white

Signs of authenticity

1. Early wares from Spode and Minton more cream-coloured than true white.
2. Blues are rich, dark and soft for period up to c.1802.
3. Meticulous matching of joins in border patterns, centring of main design.
4. Quality of Spode's fine white pearlware body superior to products from unnamed Staffordshire potteries using less refined bodies.
5. From c.1794 bone china replaced earlier bodies at Spode.
6. From c.1796 Minton produced bone china, slightly flawed until c.1803.
7. Makers' impressed or printed mark signifies superior quality to unnamed makers.
8. Enoch Wood's products notably darker than other makers'.
9. J. & W. Ridgway paler, more defined transfer-prints with better detail, less smudgy appearance.
10. Nineteenth-century wares often distinguishable by use of 'flow blue' to produce deliberately hazy outlines, faintly reminiscent of early porcelains printed in blue.

Historical background

Some patterns had been printed in cobalt blue under the glaze by the Worcester porcelain factory and some other manufactories in about 1760, but the methods had been largely abandoned with the demand for richly decorated porcelain in the style of Sèvres. However, as soon as white-bodied earthenware was developed in the potteries, it was clear that such an inexpensive method of decoration was ideally suited for the large middle market of the late eighteenth century.

Obviously, transfer-printing threatened the livelihoods of all the artists and enamellers working in the potteries, who in due course appealed to Josiah Wedgwood, the most influential man in Staffordshire. He replied, 'I will given you my word, as a man, that I have not made, neither will I make, any Blue Printed Earthenware,' and he kept his promise: the Wedgwood factory did not make blue and white transfer-printed wares until after his death.

But Josiah Wedgwood could do nothing to stop his contemporary, Josiah Spode, from beginning the long run of popularity for mass-produced transfer-printed pottery, with a range of wares on a variation of a stoneware body. With the assistance of skilled craftsmen from the Caughley factory – one of whom was Thomas Minton, who joined Spode in 1783 – he produced an ever-widening range of Oriental patterns, including the willow pattern, the 'Two Temples', and the 'Mandarin and Rock', with a wonderful range of richly decorated printed borders. Thomas Minton started up his own manufactory in 1789, and in 1796 he began making bone china decorated with blue transfer-printed patterns, with enormous success.

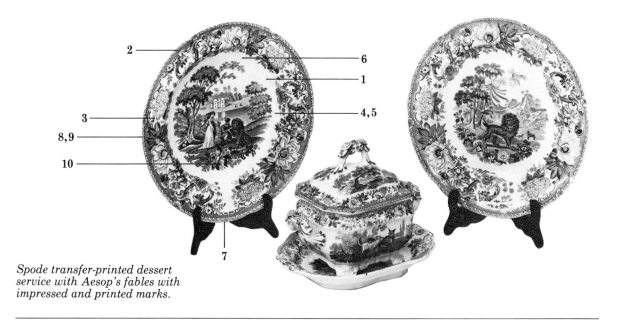

Spode transfer-printed dessert service with Aesop's fables with impressed and printed marks.

Materials and decoration

In hard paste (New Hall) and in soapstone porcelain (Caughley), but mainly in fine-bodied stone china, felspar porcelain, pearlware and bone china, as well as later ironstone chinas. There have been some seven hundred different patterns of transfer-printed wares documented over the main period of their manufacture, ranging from views to themes, portraits to the famous 'Doctor Syntax' series and, very desirable to today's collectors, Ridgway's series 'Beautiful America'. The height of popularity for Oriental designs was between 1780 and 1805 – some of the finest wares ever made came soon after, when Spode produced his Greek pattern in pearlware, derived from similar sources to Wedgwood's 'Etruscan' ware, with a different classical scene printed on each individual object. Other colours joined blue and white from c.1820, and dark green, sepia and puce in turn became the most popular colour for individual manufacturers.

Principal producers and products

Spode c.1784–1833; Minton c.1789–1830 and later; Don Pottery (green transfer) c.1790–1834; William Adams c.1804–19; Joshua Heath c.1770–1800; Herculaneum (Liverpool) 1793–1841; Clews & Adams c.1818–34; Elijah Mayer 1790–1804; E. Mayer & Son 1817–33; Joseph Mayer 1822–33; Enoch Wood c.1785–1840; Enoch Wood & Son 1818–46; Charles Meigh 1835–49; J. & J. Jackson 1831–5; Joseph Stubbs 1822–36; J. & W. Ridgway 1814–30; J. Rogers & Son 1815–42; Thos Godwin 1834–54; S. Tams & Co. 1820–30; Joseph Green & Co. 1809–42; Thomas Green 1847–59; James Edwards & Son 1842–82; J. & T. Edwards 1839–41; Mellor, Venables & Co. 1834–51; John & Richard Ritty 1802–28; A. Stevenson 1816–30; Ralph Stevenson 1810–35; Wedgwood from c.1805; and many other potteries and factories.

Full range of tableware, useful ware and domestic wares.

Period of manufacture
c.1780 to c.1825 and later.

Reproductions

It might be said that genuine transfer-printed wares extended only until the arrival of bone china, c.1810, although in many cases some of the finest printing was achieved after this date, particularly by the Spode factory.

Variations

The spate of transfer-printed wares has continued from their inception until the present day, with factories either reproducing their own designs and patterns, as in the case of Copeland (late Spode), or plagiarizing those which have been discontinued from factories that have closed down. The subject is so vast that proper study of specialist books, of which there are many, is well advised.

Price bands

Plates, dishes from £25.

Jugs from £45.

Mugs from early periods from £180.

Commemorative wares from £200.

Pearlware more expensive.

Named collectable potteries higher prices.

A. *Herculaneum blue and white transfer-printed jug, 7½ in (19 cm) high.*

B. *Middlesborough blue and white transfer-printed platter.*

C. *Spode blue and white transfer-printed 'Caramanian' series egg stand.*

D. *Spode blue and white transfer-printed oval dish with Indian sporting scene border.*

Lustreware

Historical background

It is said that Josiah Wedgwood experimented with gold lustre as early as 1776, with the intention of making mirror frames and picture frames – and it is certain that in 1805 the Wedgwood factory began to make pieces decorated at first with lustre bandings in a similar manner to gilding, and from about 1815 progressed to producing all-over silver lustre in imitation of sterling silver.

There are three main types of lustre: silver, gold or copper, and purple or manganese. Silver lustre was made from platinum oxide and was used to great effect on Staffordshire creamware from about 1810 onwards, in bands encircling transfer-printed scenes of idyllic country life and classical mythology. Some of the finest silver lustre was decorated with a 'resist' technique: the pattern to be coated with silver was blocked out with a solution – a mixture of china clay and honey or glycerine – which resisted the adherence of the metallic oxide so that, when washed before firing, the unsilvered part was left free of decoration. The reverse of this, stencilled lustre, developed in about 1806 at Davenport, produced the pattern in silver lustre and the rest of the piece in a plain glaze. The most typical decorations were flowers, song-birds, roses and purely English designs.

The best-known lustreware, from Staffordshire and Sunderland in particular, is the purple, made from a metallic compound, which varied in tone from pink to purple, and was used for banding, painted scenes, and in combination with commemorative motifs. A variation, much used in Sunderland, produced a splashed or mottled effect.

Copper lustre was scarce until about 1823, after which it was used in wide bands for a range of jugs and mugs.

All-over silver lustre was made in some quantities, particularly in Sunderland, in imitation of silver. Known as 'poor man's silver', it ceased to be made with the advent of electro-plating in 1840.

Sunderland jug in splashed purple lustre inscribed 'Francis & Betsy Taylor' above a verse, with a ship in full sail in panels on either side.

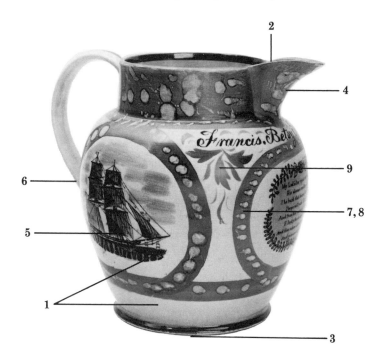

Materials and decoration

On creamware, red-brown stoneware or clay body, and on a wide variety of earthenware and stoneware bodies. Silver lustre, copper lustre, 'splashed' lustre – most typical of Sunderland – often used in association with black-printed or painted commemorative verses and inscriptions. Resist lustre is usually on a lightweight body, which today may look greyish with the effect of exposure to air and general ageing. Stencilled lustre is often on a fine ironstone-type body or white stoneware, and has fine detail. Most common, and typical of later wares, is the dull copper lustre on a red-brown stoneware body, often with purple lustre bands with rather blurred relief moulding, which has been made continuously through to the present day.

Principal producers and products

Wedgwood; Davenport; Herculaneum (Liverpool); Leeds; Sunderland; David Wilson, Hanley; Wood & Caldwell; Batkin & Bailey; Riddle & Bryan, Longton; J. & W. Ridgway; Ford & Patterson, Newcastle-upon-Tyne; Sewells; Dixon; Austin; Dixon Phillips & Co.; Dawson & Co.; Low Ford Pottery; Scott & Sons; many other unnamed Staffordshire and Sunderland potteries, often in association with commemorative wares.

Graduated sets and single jugs, tankards, tea and coffee services, cruets, writing and toilet accessories in 'poor man's silver', plaques, mugs, bowls, plates, dishes, vases, ornamental ware.

Period of manufacture
*c.*1805 to the end of the century.

Variations

In 1852 J. Ridgway & Co. invented a cheaper version of silver lustre, using electro-metallurgy processes, which were made in great quantities but which proved to be very impermanent, since the layer of platinum was extremely thin and quickly wore off. Lustre was used in conjunction with many cheap mass-produced commemorative wares from the mid-nineteenth century onwards, with transfer-printed designs surrounded by lustre frames, and with lustre neckbands, rims and foot-rims.

Reproductions

Since the best lustre is silver-resist, and some of the most collectable items are the Sunderland 'splash' lustre, reproductions of both of these have been made by modern makers with the imprint of the factory on the base. Sometimes these printed marks have been removed with acids, to deceive the unwary into believing they are genuinely old. The glaze is usually damaged where this has occurred, leaving a dull, non-shiny patch. Clear glaze should cover the whole base of genuine wares.

Price bands

A. *Set of four graduated Sunderland splashed lustre jugs transfer-printed in black with sailing ships, compasses and sailors' verses.*

B. *Silver ground lustre jug, early 19th century. 6½ in (16.5 cm) high.*

C. *Jug with moulded relief decoration in white on a silver lustre body. David Wilson, Hanley, c.1815. 5¾ in (14.5 cm) high.*

D. *Early 19th-century silver resist patterned jug with birds and flowers, from Leeds. 5¾ in (14.5 cm) high.*

E. *Elegant silver lustre stencilled jug with Greek key pattern round the collar.*

Commemorative ware

Historical background

Commemorative ware has been made ever since the first royal chargers marking the reigns of kings and queens were made in slipware and delftware, and in every paste and body down the long decades of invention and development of the eighteenth and nineteenth centuries. But in general this category is taken to begin with the wares made in the Staffordshire potteries from the last quarter of the eighteenth century, when cheaper methods of decoration were available, and a suitable cream-coloured or white body and glaze had evolved.

Commemorative wares usually mark a particular incident, celebration or tragedy: arrivals and sailings of ships (particularly from Liverpool and Sunderland), bridges, canals and railways opened, victories in war and – on a more domestic level – marriages and christenings, as well as the whole range of coronations, royal weddings and jubilees. The Worcester Porcelain Company's series of the 'King of Prussia' and the principal characters in the Seven Years' War are not usually included in this category, which is generaly confined to pieces from the potteries in various kinds of earthenware, stoneware, creamware and pearlware.

Many commemorative pieces were made as ornaments by Staffordshire potteries in the second half of the nineteenth century, ranging from grim houses where murders had been committed to famous greyhounds and racing events or coy portraits of the royal couple, famous admirals, generals and notable personalities. The stream of commemorative mugs, jugs and plates spans more than two hundred years, from the end of the eighteenth century to the present day.

Creamware jug from Liverpool of typical regional shape, with baluster body and high-set handle, printed and painted with 'An East View of Liverpool Light House and Signals on Bidston Hill' with a painted list below of the signals, inscribed 'Ruth Holden 1793'. On the reverse is a black transfer-print of 'Thoughts on Matrimony'. 7 in (17.5 cm) high.

Materials and decoration

In soft paste porcelain from Lowestoft, creamware – especially from Leeds, Liverpool, pearlware, stoneware and lustreware. Some fine early nautical ware in underglaze blue painted decoration came from Liverpool as early as c.1760s, as well as tin glazed punch bowls. In general, however, commemorative ware was in pearlware and light-bodied stonewares, transfer-printed in black, sepia, blue, lilac and red, sometimes with lettering painted over the glaze. Rarity value depends on unusual events, limited runs and local occasions. Much commemorative ware was neglected as a collectors' field until recently, when its value due to the ephemeral nature of wares was realized.

Reproductions

Recent fashions for Victoriana have revived many of the black and white printed domestic items – of the deliberate reproductions probably Sunderland and Liverpool wares are the most common, but they are made with the names of the factories printed or impressed on the bases and should not really deceive.

Price bands

Mugs and jugs:
Lowestoft from £380;
pearlware from £180; creamware from £350; Staffordshire (marked) £80–£320, (unmarked) £35–£280.

Railway, ballooning, royal, naval, nautical, military, and political all collectors' fields.

Coronation, jubilee mugs also specialist market.

A

A. *Pearlware mug c.1800 showing a 'View of La Guillotine or the beheading machine at Paris by which Louis XVI King of France was Beheaded Jan 21 1793' in black-printed engraved decoration.*

C

C. *Pearlware jug commemorating the Coronation of Queen Victoria printed in blue, probably Staffordshire, c.1837.*

Variations

Later wares printed with one of the polychrome printing processes deluged the market with each royal, loyal or national event, and have continued to do so until the present day. A sideline of this field has become popular in recent years: nineteenth-century domestic wares printed with advertising – names of companies associated with brands popular in their day. Among these, pot lids, on which a variety of new printing techniques were first used, have become a keen specialist collectors' field.

B

B. *Staffordshire pottery mug commemorating the 'Oaks Colliery Disaster' of 1866, transfer-printed in black with 'Cage blown into the Head Gear' and 'Oaks Colliery Second Explosion'. 4 in (10 cm) high.*

D

D. *White glazed earthenware pot lid with scene of an arctic expedition or a bear hunt, by T.J. & J. Mayer, c.1850, printed in several colours. These pots contained bear grease which was used as hair oil.*

Period of manufacture
c.1770 to the end of the nineteenth century and later.

Principal producers and products

Enoch Wood & Sons; Sewell & Donkin; Edge Malkin & Co.; Ellis, Unwin & Mountford; Jackson & Gosling; W. Smith & Co.; and many unnamed and named lesser Staffordshire potteries.

Graduated sets and single jugs, mugs, tankards, plaques, pin trays, pen trays, miniatures, writing accessories, toilet accessories, vases, ornamental ware, punch pots and bowls.

Porcelain figures and groups

Historical background

The beautiful, delicate figures and groups made by Dresden, Meissen and other major Continental porcelain factories were among the most coveted and precious possessions of the English at the beginning of the eighteenth century. It was natural that as soon as English porcelain factories could produce anything like a satisfactory paste, they should attempt to copy them. At first, the ornamental figures and small animals were left unpainted and simply glazed. These, like their Continental counterparts, are known as 'blanc de Chine' and they show clearly the varying qualities of soft paste, as well as the consistency and colour of the glaze.

Derby 'figars' were thickly glazed and not well modelled to begin with, though they began with quite ambitious series of dancers and figures representing the Seasons. By the 1750s Chelsea was making copies of Meissen figures with considerable success, with swirling rococo bases, though with much less gilding than Meissen figures. Derby in the main took Dresden as its model – Derby paste is much lighter in weight than either Chelsea or Bow. By the 1760s Chelsea figures were of such high quality and decorated in such glowingly brilliant coloured enamels that several Continental factories demanded that their importation should be banned. As fashions swung, subjects became more pastoral and romantic, inspired by the French painters Boucher and Fragonard, with shepherds and shepherdesses backed by leafy bocages, their bases scattered with flowers and blossoms, twining foliage and rococo swirls.

Derby group from classical mythology, of the great hunter Procris pulling an arrow from the breast of his wife, the beautiful Cephalus. Incised No. 75, c.1775–80. 7 in (18 cm) high.

Signs of authenticity

1. In soft paste porcelain, warmer to the touch than cold hard paste. Plymouth hard paste rare.
2. Early bases to c.1750s simple undecorated pad-shaped.
3. Rococo bases from c.1758.
4. Size seldom exceeds 11–12 in (28–30 cm). Individual figures smaller than Continental counterparts.
5. Derby figures from 1755 to c.1769 much whiter, more translucent paste, softer glaze and paler colour palette than Chelsea or Bow.
6. Derby figures with distinctive marks of pads on base on which models rested in the kiln, now discoloured.
7. Bow with more elaborate bases from c.1758, raised on small feet, a style copied by Chelsea and Derby soon after.
8. Bow typical bocages with hawthorn leaves, apple leaves with brightly coloured blossom.
9. Derby bocages more delicate and elaborate with very fragile thin leaves.
10. From c.1760, Chelsea bocages much heavier, with figures standing on heavily ornate rococo bases.
11. On Derby figures, glaze usually finishes just above the base where it has been neatly scraped off – known as 'dry edge'.
12. Many Bow figures show signs of modeller's tool or knife on the paste under the glaze where imperfections have been smoothed and details heightened before first firing.

Materials and decoration

Eighteenth-century English porcelain figures were made almost exclusively in soft paste porcelain. Hard paste is much colder to the touch, and is also a much more brilliant white than the slightly imperfect soft paste made by the three leading English makers, Chelsea, Derby and Bow. Of these three, Derby had the finest-quality modelling, Bow subjects tended to be more mundane and more robustly English, and Chelsea indubitably had the finest colour palette and enamelling.

B. *Pair of Bow figures of a Scotsman and his lass, after models by William Coffee, incised No. 370, c.1765–75. 9¼ in (24 cm) and 11 in (28 cm) high.*

Principal producers

Bow *c.*1749–75, limited palette of 'dry red', yellowish green, touches of blue, yellow and gold. From *c.*1758 palette includes puce, very typical of Bow, and a very pale blue. From *c.*1759 to 1764 further extended to include opaque purple, brick red and canary yellow.
Chelsea *c.*1749–53 'blanc de Chine' figures and birds. Many Meissen copies *c.*1753–6. Applied flowers on scrolled bases with very little gilding. *c.*1658–69, brilliant enamels in full palette, gilded scrolled bases, bocages blooming with flowers.
Derby *c.*1749–55 mainly in the white with thickish glaze, subjects mainly pastoral. Whiter, more translucent paste *c.*1755–69, with softer glaze, thinly painted

A. *Derby figures of* (left) *St Philip and* (right) *David Garrick in the role of Tancred. 9½ in (24 cm) high.*

C. *Meissen figures of Autumn and Winter, both on swirling rococo gilt bases, early 19th century, incised No. 2732 with under-glaze blue crossed swords.*

enamel colours in a pale palette, very fine, sharp modelling and detail. From *c.*1771 famous 'biscuit' models, mostly classical subjects. From *c.*1770 figures blossomed with brilliant colours, including clear apple green, canary yellow, orange, coral, rose pink, claret, crushed strawberry and semi-matt blue.
Longton Hall made some figures from *c.*1750 but much less sophisticated, with rather lumpy poor modelling.
Plymouth small output of hard paste porcelain figures *c.*1768–71, poorly modelled compared with soft paste porcelain but valuable for its rarity.

Period of manufacture
*c.*1749 to 1800 and later.

Variations

The Cookworthy factory at Plymouth made some rare figures, mostly in 'blanc de Chine' in imitation of Chinese figures. From *c.*1768–70 the Champion factory at Plymouth and Bristol also made a series of figures, both in the white and decorated. In the mid-nineteenth century 'statuary parian' was introduced by Copeland, and was then used extensively for figures and groups, but the subjects tend towards the mawkish, and they are generally larger in size than soft paste eighteenth-century figures.

Price bands

Bow single figures £350–£500.

Derby single figures £500–£650.

Chelsea single figures £900–£1,100.

Longton Hall £400–£600.

Plymouth hard paste single figures £680–£900.

Derby 'biscuit' single figures £500–£750.

Sets of four seasons (generally composite) £1,200 upwards.

Four continents £1,500 upwards.

Worcester figures 18th century (extremely rare) singles £1,300 upwards, pairs £3,000–£6,000.

Reproductions

Almost without exception, the reproductions which are intended to deceive are in hard paste porcelain, whether made on the Continent or in England. The most famous, or infamous, are those of Samson of Paris, who made deliberate copies of Chelsea, Derby, Bow, Meissen and Dresden, often marking the bases with the wrong period marks of the factories. The difference between hard and soft paste is easy to detect once one has held a piece of each and felt the difference in warmth and weight.

Lead glazed pottery figures

Historical background

This group of charmingly naive figures has been loosely classified as 'Wedgwood/Whieldon' type and it belongs to the same experimental period as agate and tortoiseshell ware. From the early 1740s, once Enoch Booth had developed a colourless lead glaze, many potteries in Staffordshire began to make small animals and trial figures using various combinations of mixed and marbled clays, two-coloured clays and coloured glazes which were applied after the clay had been fired once to a 'biscuit' state.

Some of these figures were almost certainly made by John Astbury, using white Devonshire pipeclay (which he had carried to Staffordshire on pack horses) and the local reddish-brown clay, sometimes glazed with an almost colourless lead glaze, sometimes with a tortoiseshell glaze. Lively figures of soldiers mounted on horses were certainly made in Staffordshire at this period, as well as some delightful models of men playing a variety of instruments, but the most common little ornaments are of sleeping cats, recumbent lions and – more rare – pairs of birds, and milkmaids under very basic bocages, milking their cows. In tortoiseshell glaze, the most famous and desirable figures are water buffaloes, modelled after Chinese originals with ox-herds sitting on their backs, and some of Staffordshire's attempts at figures from classical mythology, which date from c.1750–5, when English porcelain factories began to make their copies of Meissen and Dresden figures.

Figure of Ceres, the goddess of corn and harvests, with a symbolic ear of corn under one arm and a sickle in her right hand, with a small naked child at her knee. After a figure by Longton Hall. 5¾ in (14.5 cm) high.

Signs of authenticity

1. Earthenware body in reddish, buff or brownish clay.
2. Bases unglazed or clear glaze only.
3. On solid-agate-type figures, marbling or mingling of clays clearly seen on base, solid throughout figure.
4. Marbled clays usually in tones of blue, grey, cream and brown.
5. On tortoiseshell glazed figures, coloured glazes mainly in tones of brown and green on early examples.
6. Later additions to coloured glazes include yellowish green, near-black, slatey blue, and occasionally some touches of yellow.
7. Modelling unsophisticated but generous – knees, arms of figures well rounded, not simply bent into shape with consequent loss of thickness.
8. Characteristic running of glaze despite attempts to control colours to small areas.
9. Rudimentary modelling of small details – hands, paws, feet etc.

Materials and decoration

Earthenware in natural colours of reddish brown, brown, buff and light colours, fired once and then glazed, either with a colourless glaze or with glazes coloured with metallic oxides, generally in drab dark browns or a greenish non-opaque glaze. The figures were not moulded but made by hand in the early experimental years, and the marks of the modeller's tools can clearly be seen on the clay beneath the glaze. All the figures were small, and even the 'Arbour groups', which were forerunners of the many Staffordshire mantelpiece ornaments of lovers in leafy bowers, were not much more than 6 in (15 cm) high at most. Solid agate figures and ornaments are far more finely modelled, and include cow creamers, also made in tortoiseshell glazes, as well as seated and sleeping cats.

Many of the little animals are so blurred and smeared that it is difficult to realize what a great step forward they represented in terms of technical skill and knowledge at the time they were made.

A. Pottery cow creamer, with a spotted cow standing on a rectangular base with a translucent green wash. $7\frac{1}{2}$ in (19 cm) high.

B. A small, well-modelled recumbent lion of the Whieldon type, with experimental coloured glazes in browns and yellows, c.1750–60. 3 in ($7\frac{1}{2}$ cm) long.

C. Staffordshire solid agate figure of a cat, the eyes painted in chocolate-brown slip and the body streaked and splashed in brown and blue, c.1745–50. 5 in (13 cm) high.

Principal producers

Thomas Whieldon; Whieldon/Wedgwood; John Astbury and son; many unnamed Staffordshire potteries.

Period of manufacture
c.1470 to c.1780 and later.

Variations

In one form or another, the technique of applying coloured glazes continued to be used and experimented with by many Staffordshire potteries well into the nineteenth century, when it was known as 'smear glazing' and included other colours, such as a very acid green and a remarkably crude orange, as well as the slatey blues, brown and greys and greens of the early period.

Reproductions

It is inevitable that as soon as any piece of any age starts to fetch a good price, or becomes a collector's item, there are always those who are quick to take advantage of the rising market value. Many of these figures, not of any great aesthetic merit, have been convincingly copied since their historical significance was recognized in the 1920s, and some rare pieces that were collected at the beginning of this century, particularly those of the two-coloured clay variety attributed to John Astbury and his son, are now believed to be skilful copies. The commonest and most widely distributed are the seated cats, either in a pseudo-agate-type mingled clay body, or quite convincingly glazed with early coloured glazes. Since all surviving pieces fetch considerable sums today, it is advisable to handle and examine some genuine originals before even considering making a purchase.

Price bands

Astbury type and period £10,000–£13,500.

Small animals of Whieldon type: recumbent lions, seated cats £300–£1,200; rabbits, monkeys, dogs £800–£300.

Fierce collectors' market – prices have doubled in last five years.

Staffordshire figures

Historical background

Once the isolation of the Staffordshire potteries had ended, with the construction of the great network of canals that linked them to the rest of England and Wales, there was a hungry market for all manner of decorative objects as well as useful wares and plain, functional kitchen ware and tableware. Where the rich had porcelain figures and chimneypiece ornaments, the less well-heeled could brighten their parlours with cheaply printed cottons for curtains and tablecloths and proudly display all manner of gaily coloured plates on their dressers and ornaments on their mantelpieces.

From about 1780 onwards the potteries met this gratifying demand with their own versions of the Seasons, the Graces, some of the better-known gods and goddesses and many Biblical figures from the Old Testament. The people of the Midlands and the North were Nonconformist, Wesleyan and Chapel, as well as being fairly down-to-earth. There is an element of the fairground and folk art about the early series of Staffordshire figures, with which the name Felix Pratt is associated in particular. The most remarkable thing about these figures is their bold, bright use of high temperature colours applied under the glaze – though still limited to those metallic oxides that would stand up to the heat necessary to fuse the glaze to the 'biscuit' body: blue, of course, with yellows, browns, bright chestnut, a rather dirty green and black.

From the end of the eighteenth century the colours increased greatly as the technique of applying enamel colours over the glaze came into use – a process with which the names of Ralph Wood the younger and Enoch Wood, his cousin, are particularly associated.

Staffordshire figure of St George and the Dragon in colours applied under the glaze in typical dabs and bold areas of opaque pigment. A particularly well-modelled example, c.1790. 11 in (28 cm) high.

Signs of authenticity

1. In earthenware, usually a pale buff, pale cream or near-white colour.
2. Limited colour palette of blues, yellows, browns, bright chestnut, drabbish green and black.
3. Wider colour palette indicates over-glaze enamels.
4. c.1780–1800 colours applied under the glaze.
5. Moulded wares with varying degree of crispness of detail.
6. Typical of early period are colours applied in splashes or dabs.
7. No signs of colour running or colour in the glaze, except for a faint bluish tone to increase whiteness.
8. Sponged technique frequently used on bases, rockwork, and other suitable areas.
9. Robust modelling, sometimes fairly crude but lively.

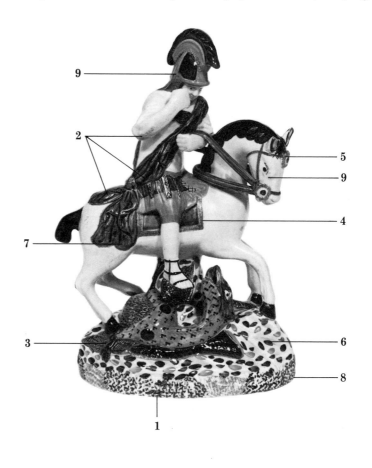

Materials and decoration

There are three distinct groups in this field. The first figures were in light-coloured earthenware with colours applied under the glaze in a limited palette; the second type used a far wider, brighter range of coloured enamels applied over the glaze, on creamware or pearlware as well as on coarser-bodied light-coloured clays; and the third group were modelled with far less care and taken repeatedly from the same moulds so that the detail became even more blurred. These later figures also used a distinctly different colour palette, which included a genuine royal blue, salmon pink, acid green, dark green, orange, glossy black, flesh pink and often quite a lavish use of gold. The colour range is quite similar in many respects to the colours used on ironstone china – which dates from the same era.

Variations

The last period of the three distinct divisions constitutes the widest range of subject-matter, and also includes the well-known 'Staffordshire flatbacks'. These are virtually without modelling on the back, and consist of groups, very often featuring the 'lover and his lass' theme as well as innumerable variations of Victoria and Albert in almost every stage of their lives and occupations. Particularly popular are those with the royal pair in Highland dress. Every national hero, politician, dignitary, leader, regiment and tableau of events was featured, infamous as well as famous.

Principal producers

Felix Pratt of Fenton; Ralph Wedgwood; Barker; Harley; Hawley; Dixon Austin & Co.; E. Bourne; W. Daniel; E. Wood; R. M. Astbury; Newcastle potteries; Leeds potteries; Ferrybridge; Jacob Marsh; many unnamed Staffordshire potteries.

Period of manufacture
c.1780 to 1890.

A. *Staffordshire flatback of lovers in an arbour, with gypsy child entertainers: a boy organ-grinder and a girl with a tambourine.*

B. *Four Staffordshire figures from the period c.1840 onwards: Napier and Garibaldi both wearing red shirts and obviously made as a pair, flanked by a portrait of a* *statesman, possibly Benjamin Franklin, and an actor in the role of Hamlet holding a skull with the inscription of 'Alas Poor Yorick' on the base.*

Reproductions

A great band of collectors has built up in this field, with specialists in every category: naval and military, church and state, political, theatrical, royal and regimental, as well as topical heroes and villains. Few names of makers are known, but those which are fetch premium prices, with Obadiah Sherratt heading the list. Inevitably, therefore, there are 'copies' as well as out-and-out fakes. These are nearly always much lighter in weight than the originals, and the glaze crazes uniformly over the whole piece, which is not at all typical of genuine period Staffordshire pieces. The pigments and colours, too, are often incorrect. Harder to detect are the later issues from original moulds from the Sampson Smith pottery, which made quantities of flatbacks between c.1847 and 1878 and continued to turn out figures from his moulds long after the death of the owner. After World War II some original moulds were unearthed and used again, but with a different colour palette which offers a clue to their late date – too many tones of one colour signals that something is wrong. The same applies to other, recent 'copies'.

Price bands

Late 18th-century figures and groups £500–£1,200.

Obadiah Sherratt figure groups from £1,200; single figures from £250.

Bull baiting, menagerie, circus £2,500 upwards.

Walton bocage groups £325 pairs.

Enoch, Ralph Wood single figures, small groups £260–£600.

Pratt £150–£500.

19th-century Staffordshire flatbacks: singles from £50, pairs £200 upwards.

Mantel dogs £100–£250.

Lions

Historical background

It may have been because the lions is one of England's symbolic heraldic animals that copies of the imposing marble lions which stood at the entrance to the Loggia dei Lanzi in Florence became such a popular subject for the Staffordshire potteries from about 1775. These lions, standing with their left paws on the globe of the world, may have been a reminder of England's might to her unruly American colonies, which had just begun their struggle for independence. Or maybe it was because of the fashion for menageries and circuses, which gathered momentum towards the end of the eighteenth century, or simply because the Staffordshire potteries wished to demonstrate that they had a passing knowledge of the Grand Tour of Italy. Whatever the reason, pairs of these lions were made in considerable numbers and with varying degrees of success – originating, it seems, in Scotland, where Thomas Rathbone of Portobello was among the first to make them.

In Staffordshire Enoch Wood, son of Aaron Wood, made some extremely finely modelled pairs of lions, but for collectors the more interesting versions were made with a splashed, almost tortoiseshell glaze technique by another member of the family, Ralph Wood. These are among the earliest of many copies of the famous lions. Many other potteries made them, using a variety of techniques, but the interest of these animals lies mainly in their fairground charm rather than their aesthetic beauty. Almost certainly the purist collector of fine porcelain will dismiss them as 'ugly lumps of clay daubed inexpertly with paint' but it is as well to remember that some of the early trial pieces from the famous porcelain factories can be just as charmingly naive.

One of a pair of finely modelled lions which closely follow the originals in Florence. These are copies of Ralph Wood lions, glazed with translucent brown glaze with a green-edged plinth. c.1840. $14\frac{1}{4}$ in (36 cm) long.

Signs of autheticity

1. In earthenware, usually light-coloured, buff or cream.
2. Finely modelled and decorated with coloured glazes indicates early versions from *c.*1775, possibly Ralph Wood.
3. Greyish-blue mottled colouring resembling marble in 'sponged technique' under the glaze originally made by Thomas Rathbone of Portobello.
4. Additional colours in dabs and dashes under the glaze should be limited to high-temperature colours – orange, blue, drab green and black.
5. Naive interpretations do not necessarily detract from value.
6. From *c.*1800 more commonly decorated in wider palette over the glaze.
7. Eyes painted like human eyes on naive versions very common and distinctive.
8. Correct copies should have left paw on ball representing globe, with head turned to the left.

Materials and decoration

In pale-coloured earthenware, usually buff or pale cream, with a similar development in techniques to Staffordshire figures, except that early versions may be covered in greenish glaze, splashed or smeared coloured glazes, or with sponged, mottled greyish blue resembling marble under a clear glaze. Bright under-glaze high temperature colours were irresistible to many potteries, however, and touches of strong blues, oranges, yellows, reds and black were added instead of well-modelled leaves on the base, in floral trails and on ears,

mane and tail. Black was often added to the lions' paws, giving the impression of shoes, or hoofed feet on more naive versions.

From roughly 1800 onwards, enamel colours applied over the glaze greatly increased the colourful appearance of these lions, many of which bore little resemblance to the grand original marble models. After about 1820, however, this model seems to have lost most of its identity and joined the Noah's Ark of brightly coloured mantelpiece ornaments in the shape of animals which proliferated in the Victorian era.

Variations

During the first few decades of the nineteenth century pairs of lions with more refined and elaborate modelling were made in terra cotta covered with a treacly, thick brown glaze, quite different from the translucent early coloured glazes used by Ralph Wood and his contemporaries. From about 1840 onwards, the standing lion was replaced by a recumbent

version, sometimes almost indistinguishable from some of the crudely modelled spaniels lying down.

A

A. Ferociously attractive lion from Staffordshire with reddish-brown coat, the base sponged in brown, yellow, black and blue. Early 19th century. $12\frac{1}{2}$ in (32 cm) long.

C

C. Rare Bow lioness 'in the white' in soft paste porcelain, dating probably from 1753–5. 9 in (23 cm) long.

B

B. Wonderfully naive model of a lion with his paw on the globe, probably Scottish, in marbled grey to simulate the original marble, on a blue base with red, blue, green and yellow decoration under glaze. $10\frac{1}{4}$ in (26 cm) long.

Reproductions

These pairs of lions reappeared during the second half of the nineteenth century, with their origin completely forgotten, often in company with a lamb in the Biblical context of the lion lying down with the lamb. They are also found as the base of Staffordshire spill vases, or by themselves, either without the globe at all or with a small, brightly coloured ball, like a lion in a circus.

Straightforward reproductions of the better-known Staffordshire models of animals and figures seem to have so far omitted these lions from their repertoire, but now that their prices have increased so enormously, it is inevitable that some skilful copies will have found their way on to the market, and great care should be taken in checking the authenticity of any piece that looks at all dubious.

Principal producers

Thomas Rathbone of Portobello; John Walton of Burslem; Wood & Caldwell; Ralph & Enoch Wood; Felix Pratt and other 'Pratt-type' Staffordshire potteries; Scottish, Yorkshire, Staffordshire potteries from *c*.1780.

Period of manufacture
c.1775 to 1820 and later.

Price bands

Enoch Wood £800–£1,000 singles.

Ralph Wood up to £2,300 singles; pairs more than double.

Pratt £1,000–£1,750.

Yorkshire and primitives up to *c*.1810 £800–£2,000; *c*.1810–1850 £200–£800.

Staffordshire animals

Signs of authenticity

1. In light-coloured earthenware, buff or light cream.

2. Colour palette bright and wider than colours applied under the glaze, including turquoise, salmon pink, apricot and yellow, as well as deep blue, black and glossy brown.

3. Many animal groups clearly taken from porcelain models, with bocages of very large leaves, bases often with rococo-type scrolling, gilding.

4. Free-standing or sitting animals are of later date, with the one exception of 'mantel dogs'.

5. Enamel colours with tendency to flake off if dated before c.1840.

6. Later production in white, chalky earthenware with enamels in thick blocks of colour.

7. On animals and figures after c.1840, lustre may replace gilding.

8. Early examples from 1780s to 1790s embellished with oil gilding, which has seldom endured except in patchy areas.

9. From late 1790s more brassy mercury gilding on finer pieces – from 1850s a gilding paste which required much less burnishing, known as 'brown gold'.

Historical background

In the experimental days of agate and tortoiseshell wares, while Staffordshire potteries were trying out new techniques of colour, glaze and body, the most common animals were cats, recumbent lions and rabbits. The latter were made in imitation of Meissen and Chelsea rabbits but, curiously, once the great flood of Staffordshire animals began to flow from the potteries, only the lions seem to have held on to their popularity. Delightful pastoral pieces of deer and fawns, ewes, rams and lambs appear to have been the first subjects chosen, mainly in imitation of porcelain figures. But soon the native ebullience of the potteries burst through the rather formal animal groups and, like other Staffordshire figures, animals became the subjects of topical interest, with winners of greyhound races and horse races, famous circus animals, sporting dogs, birds, and, of course, the obligatory pair of King Charles spaniels which stood on millions of mantelpieces on either side of a sturdily built clock. A somewhat similar dog with a flatter, more inane expression was also extremely popular. Today these are known as 'comforter' dogs, named after the lap dogs they portray, apparently no longer bred today. They were made in five standard sizes from 18 in (46 cm) to 6 in (15 cm), white with chestnut-red or golden spots and ears, with eyes and eyelashes like a human being. They had no collar, but a gilded chain with a padlock.

A bull-baiting group with the inscription 'Bull Beating' and 'Now Captin Lad' on the base, attributed to the famous Staffordshire potter Obadiah Sherratt of Burslem working from c.1822 to mid-19th century. 11 in (28 cm) wide.

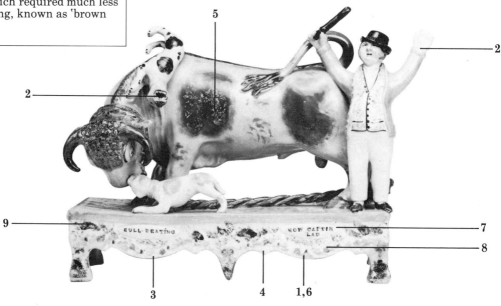

Materials and decoration

Light-coloured earthenware, fairly heavy in weight, usually buff or cream, with colour palette similar to that used on stone china of the same period – notably a rich, velvety blue, salmon pink, apricot or orange, and turquoise. These animal ornaments made at the end of the eighteenth century take their subjects to a large extent from porcelain figures of animals, with remarkably good modelling, and are decorated either in colours applied under the glaze or in a transitional mixture of colours blocked in or sponged under the glaze and enamels added after glazing.

From c.1840, in contrast, the body is almost white, with a more chalky consistency, and detail is sacrificed to mass-production.

Period of manufacture
c.1780 to c.1880 and later.

A. Pair of sheep and their offspring. A ram and a ewe with bocages of oak trees applied with large flowers on blue line bases from Staffordshire. Centre lambs in little nests under an exotic tree with blue flowers. Early 19th century. Ram and ewe 4¾in (12 cm), lambs 6¾in (17 cm) high.

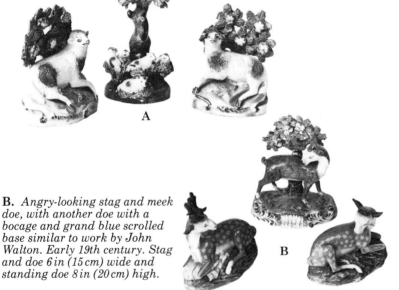

A

B. Angry-looking stag and meek doe, with another doe with a bocage and grand blue scrolled base similar to work by John Walton. Early 19th century. Stag and doe 6in (15 cm) wide and standing doe 8in (20 cm) high.

B

C. Pair of Staffordshire cats with brown patches and green bases and an angry rabbit with black patches. Early 19th century. 3¾in (9½ cm) and 3½in (9 cm) high.

C

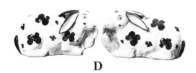

D

D. Rare pair of Staffordshire rabbits modelled after Meissen originals, also copied by Chelsea, with modelled lettuce leaves and four-leaf-clover markings. 3½in (9 cm) long.

Reproductions

Models taken from original moulds, particularly those of the Sampson Smith factory, are the most difficult to distinguish from genuine period pieces, except by their colouring and their relative lightness in weight. Two contemporary factories, at Lancaster and Sandlands, are making honest-to-goodness reproductions, but despite all their good intentions there is no guarantee that some of their products will not find their way on to the market as 'originals' after passing through the hands of the ignorant or intentional profit-makers.

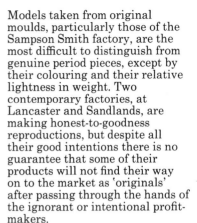

Variations

There was continuous production of Staffordshire mantel ornaments for almost two hundred years, and only those animal subjects made without bases which appeared towards the very end of the nineteenth century can be distinguished as being a distinct divergence from the traditional flatback or Staffordshire period models on bases.

Principal producers

Ralph Wood the younger; Enoch Wood; James Neale; Lakin & Poole; Wood & Caldwell; John Walton; Ralph Salt; Charles Tittensor; Obadiah Sherratt; Sampson Smith; many unnamed Staffordshire potteries.

Price bands

Bocage groups: deer, rams, lambs and ewes £260–£400; pairs £350–£500.

Enoch Wood, Walton, £475–£700; pairs £500–£850.

Cow and calf groups less.

Traditional, named groups considerably more.

Toby jugs

Signs of authenticity

1. On early Toby jugs, decoration in coloured glaze, from c.1770 to 1790.

2. Buff or light cream-coloured body moulded in several parts.

3. Palette limited to drab greens, browns, blues, manganese and greyish green – as with early tortoiseshell-coloured glazes.

4. Colours semi-transparent, not opaque.

5. Best examples and most valuable made by Ralph Wood the younger.

6. Impressed mark **Ra WOOD BURSLEM** enhances value.

7. Enamels painted over the glaze from c.1790 to 1810.

8. From c.1815 to 1840 glaze whiter, colours enamelled over the glaze more garish.

9. Surface of glaze less smooth than previous period.

10. Centre of tricorne hats are lids – damaged, chipped or missing diminishes value greatly.

11. Colours, glazes, modelling deteriorated from c.1820.

Historical background

All sorts of origins have been attributed to this enduringly popular gentleman jug, including Shakespeare's Sir Toby Belch, but the most credible seems to be that which commemorates a legendary toper nicknamed Toby Fillpot. His real name was Henry Elwes and he went down in history as a veritable king among drinkers when he logged a total of two thousand gallons of stingo, all drunk from his special silver beaker. Stingo is strong ale, but history does not record just how long this feat took to achieve. He was also commemorated in print: a short, fat, grim old man with lanky hair beneath a three-cornered hat, possibly a brewer's drayman by his clothes – and draymen were renowned for their consumption of ale. A long coat with large pockets, moleskin breeches, white stockings and buckled shoes complete Toby's original outfit, with a white stock round his energetic throat. His earliest appearance as a character was in a print dated 1761 but Toby jugs do not seem to have been made much before 1770.

By the end of the century the repertoire had begun to increase. The grim old face was considerably cheered up, particularly with the standing versions of 'the hearty good fellow' and a sailor, but – in whatever guise – the name Toby jug has stuck, even when the subject is Winston Churchill, and the Toby jug has become another Staffordshire commentary in clay of famous faces.

Left to right *'Thin man' Toby jug decorated in pale green and dappled grey glazes, c.1765–70. 9¼ in (24 cm) high. Ralph Wood Toby jug undecorated except for a brilliant blue-white glaze, c.1770–80. 10 in (25.5 cm) high. Late*

18th-century Toby jug with a slate-blue coat, brown waistcoat and ochre-coloured breeches. 10¾ in (27 cm) high. Ralph Wood Toby jug with a pale blue coat, green waistcoat and treacle-brown breeches, shoes and hat, on a deep

blue base, c.1770–80. 9¾ in (25 cm) high. Late 18th-century 'thin man' Toby jug of Pratt type decorated in colours under the glaze, coloured in ochre, yellow and brown. 9½ in (24 cm) high.

Materials and decoration

Principally in light-coloured earthenware, buff or light cream, although Toby jugs of various forms were made in brown stoneware, brown glazed earthenware, bone china and lustre. Three main types can be distinguished. Most sought-after are those made with typically drab, Whieldon-type coloured glazes, limited to greens, browns, blues, manganese and greyish green. The second group is in Pratt-type colouring under the glaze, in white or cream-coloured earthenware painted in blocks of blues, yellows, oranges, greens, browns and blacks. Some of these Toby jugs hold miniature Pratt jugs in their hands, and often their shoes are laced and not buckled. The third group comprises jugs with enamels painted over a brilliant clear glaze in a far wider colour palette, and includes those of Ralph Wood and Enoch Wood. All good early Toby jugs have the toes of the shoes protruding a little from the plinth.

Principal producers and products

Ralph Wood the younger; Enoch Wood; John Walton; Neale & Co.; Neale and Wilson; Felix Pratt; T. & J. Hollins; Davenport; Thomas Sharpe; Robert Garner; Lakin & Poole; Wood & Caldwell; John Turner; Ralph Salt; William Adams.

Brown stoneware *c.*1820–40.
Bone china *c.*1820–40 by Rockingham.
Brown glazed earthenware or Swinton *c.*1800–38.
Lustre rare but made *c.*1810–40.

Period of manufacture
*c.*1770 to the present day.

A. *Yorkshire Toby jug in raspberry-coloured coat and green breeches, c.1800. 10¼ in (26 cm) high.*

B. *Staffordshire Toby jug with mottled blue breeches and a brown coat. 9½ in (24 cm) high.*

C. *Late 18th-century Yorkshire Toby jug with flowered waistcoat and flowered inside turn-up to his hat. 8 in (20 cm) high.*

D. *Pratt-type Toby jug with grey-green coat and breeches, c.1800. 9¾ in (25 cm) high.*

E. *Toby jug of Winston Churchill designed by Clarice Cliff. Printed mark and facsimile signature. 12 in (30.5 cm) high.*

Reproductions

As Toby jugs have been made continuously from their first appearance to the present day it is difficult to say precisely where 'original' ends and 'reproduction' begins, except in the case of copies deliberately intended to deceive. These, like other Staffordshire reproductions, can usually be detected by the wrong colour palette, a certain stiffness in moulding, and a lighter weight of body than period versions.

Variations

Here is a rich field for the collector, with every nuance defined within each group. In addition to the original Toby, other grotesque figures joined the group, including a drunken parson, a night watchman, an English gentleman, a squire, a convict, a planter, a publican, a collier with a black face, a one-armed Toby, a snuff taker, a postillion and, standing, a 'hearty good fellow' and a sailor. Martha Gunn, a raddled old woman, was made by Davenport from about 1821. From the mid-nineteenth century the variety greatly increased, with regional variations as well as caricatures of famous figures.

Price bands

'Thin Man' £1,200–£2,000.

Whieldon type £450–£650.

Ralph Wood £550–£800.

Pratt £400–£600.

Yorkshire £300–£500.

Walton £300–£500.

Early Staffordshire £350–£500.

Martha Gunn £300–£700.

Specialist collectors' prices in excess of £1,000 have recently been paid for some Yorkshire examples. Rare Pratt Martha Gunn jugs can be as much as £1,200.

Candlesticks

Historical background

Candlesticks and chambersticks are among some of the earliest surviving examples of pottery from medieval times, and they form a continuous chain in the development of functional and decorative objects made in pottery and porcelain until the end of the nineteenth century and beyond.

The finest period in their long history in terms of delightfully decorative objects was during the eighteenth century. Combined with delicate and intricate bocages and swirling rococo stands, they were made by English porcelain factories – ornamental by day and fragile but functional after dark. Many were made for the suites of rooms frequented by the ladies of the house: in boudoirs, morning rooms, bedrooms and small drawing rooms, they matched the feminine atmosphere and decoration of the classical Adam-style interiors, gracing the fashionable blonde-coloured woods of *bonheurs du jour*, Pembroke tables, Sheraton toilet tables and elegant ladies' writing tables. Candlesticks with so much ornament were not entirely practical, considering the draughty rooms and guttering flames, although the invention of self-burning candle wicks in 1799 may have helped to stem the rivulets of melting wax.

In the nineteenth century, when ostentation and fashion crammed cabinets and display cases with flowery, heavily decorated porcelain, objets d'art and bijouterie, there was a revival of eighteenth-century rococo-style pieces, usually far more heavily encrusted with applied flowers and leaves than those of a century earlier.

A pair of Derby candlesticks depicting (left) *Venus, goddess of love, mother of Cupid – the child at her knee, and* (right) *Vulcan, whom she married. c.1785. 10½ in (27 cm) high.*

Materials and decoration

The production of porcelain candlesticks runs from the same period as that of porcelain figures and groups. They were made almost exclusively in soft paste porcelain, by Chelsea, Bow and Derby from c.1750 to c.1800. The effect of candlelight on these figures must have been an added inspiration to the modellers of the paste who excelled themselves in this particular field in intricacy, delicacy, colouring and decoration. Of the three major producers, Derby's colours are paler and applied more thinly than those of either Bow or Chelsea, between which there had been some exchange of craftsmen. From c.1770, however, when Chelsea was acquired by the Derby factory, the improvement in both the quality of the paste and the brightness and variation of colour palette is quite noticeable.

Variations

The great vogue for flower-encrusted bone china cabinet ware and ornaments began in the 1820s. Little bouquets of naturalistic flowers were made to hold scraps of sponge soaked in scented oils and fragrances – particularly by Derby (known as Bloor Derby from 1810). Rockingham, Coalport, Chamberlain of Worcester, Minton and many other leading and prestigious names were associated with these ornamental trinkets, which eventually became overblown and garish. By the end of the nineteenth century highly coloured table centrepieces and pot-pourri bowls displayed the same florid taste as many other ornamental objects made during the worst excesses of the Victorian period.

A. *Samson of Paris figures with bocages of a drummer boy and a girl, on rather too curvaceous rococo-style stands, slightly stiffly modelled with stilted, rather solid-looking bocages. Early 19th century. 9¾ in (25 cm) high.*

B. *Pair of Derby bocage candlesticks with cupids hiding among the flowers, on raised scrolled and gilt rococo bases decorated with turquoise, c.1770. 7½ in (19 cm) high.*

C. *Pair of Minton flower-encrusted candlesticks taken from an 18th-century rococo form, painted in vibrant coloured enamels with gilt and apple green swirling rococo bases.*

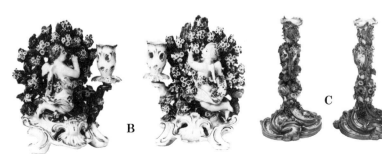

Reproductions

The work of Samson of Paris could be mentioned in a dozen different categories. This factory – which can be traced back to 1850 or earlier – made copies of thousands of pieces of English, Continental and Oriental porcelain. Many were produced at the request of customers during the nineteenth century, some of them as replacements when one of a set, a cup or a saucer had been broken, and sometimes marked with the marks of the factory whose wares they were copying – also at the customer's request. Samson's own mark is confusing, since it closely resembles the Meissen crossed swords mark – which, in turn, was not infrequently used by English factories in the eighteenth century. Many Samson pieces are made to their own designs, but they follow so closely the spirit of eighteenth-century English porcelain that they are extremely hard to distinguish. Samson's marks were always added over the glaze, and many of them have been removed by less scrupulous handlers of their wares, but the glaze should show a dull patch where it has been damaged. The factory remained in the family until 1964.

Principal producers

Bow c.1750–75; Chelsea c.1750–69; Derby c.1750–1810.
(See under Porcelain figures and groups.)

Period of manufacture
c.1750 to 1805 and later.

Price bands

Pairs: Bow bocage £1,000–£1,350; Derby £1,200–£1,500; Chelsea £1,200–£2,000; Longton Hall (rare) £2,000–£3,000.

Pairs more than double – condition of prime importance. Rare to find pairs without some repair, damage, chipping. Mint conditions adds considerably to price.

Garnitures and vases

Historical background

At the beginning of the eighteenth century the chimneypiece was lowered to elbow height and a chimney glass hung above the mantelpiece, both to give the illusion of a larger room and to allow the extremely foppish young men to admire themselves in the glass. By early Georgian times, fireplaces echoed the classical features of the outside of the house in marble or stone, with a wide ledge or mantelpiece above the fireplace, on which stood specially-designed sets of ornaments known as 'garnitures de cheminée'. These comprised five well-proportioned pieces of porcelain or pottery: two wide-mouthed barely waisted vases or spill-jars and three baluster-shaped vases with covers, the central one slightly taller than the two which flanked it.

By the 1770s, with the all-pervading influence of the Adam classical interiors, the focus shifted to the ceilings, whose designs were mirrored in the carpets beneath. Chimneypieces and mantel-pieces became part of the overall design, often flush with the walls and mouldings on either side. The mantelpiece did not return to favour until the nineteenth century, when once again it was laden with all manner of ornamental bric-a-brac and the term 'garniture de cheminée' came to denote not only sets of porcelain, ironstone and pottery, but also the French version of that period – a mantel clock flanked by ormolu candelabra. Delicate porcelain pieces were replaced by three massive ornamental vases – two spill-jars and a central vase, or combinations of shapes, all of which were purely ornamental and served no practical purpose.

Coalport vase and cover with deep blue ground, painted with realistic fruit, signed 'Budd', with gilt vines and tendrils decorating the ivory bands, and dark blue body, gilded ram's-head handles and pineapple finial. Printed crown mark. $9\frac{1}{4}$ in (23.5 cm) high.

Signs of authenticity

1. Made from *c.*1830 with revival of mantelpiece ornaments.
2. In bone china, or in ironstone or fine stoneware.
3. Ground colours under the glaze with reserves surrounded with elaborate gilding, framing remarkable hand-painted panels.
4. Finest-quality painted decoration by named artists.
5. Correct marks for factories, potteries.
6. Pattern numbers, date codes correct.
7. Diamond-shaped mark enclosing **Rd** indicates definite dating between 1842 and 1883 for introduction of design.
8. Registration marks and numbers, operating a similar system to hallmarking on silver, guaranteed protection from all copies for three years. Impressed or printed on bases.
9. If printed, should accord with potteries' mark for same period of manufacture.
10. On vases on pedestals, check for damage, restoration between body of vase and neck of base.
11. Inner flange to neck indicates that lid or cover is missing.
12. If rim of mouth is ungilded, also indicates absence of original lid or cover.
13. Brighter gilding, lack of signs of wear to handles, knop, base and cover may indicate damage recently repaired, regilded.

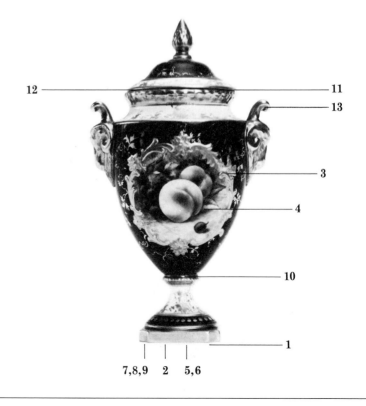

Materials and decoration

Garnitures are chiefly made in bone china or one of its allied pastes, although some excellent examples were also made in fine stonewares and in ironstone. Most of the finest pieces were individually thrown, then turned on a lathe to the correct thickness, and additional ornament such as handles and bases added before firing to the 'biscuit' state. Ground colours, notably the rich dark blue of many of these pieces, were applied at the biscuit stage, glazed and fired a second time. Artists then painted fruit, flowers, birds, landscapes, or whatever scene was demanded, in enamels over the glaze, after which the pieces were fired a third time at a lower temperature. Gilding, usually mercury gilding or solid gilding, was then applied, fired to fix it to the glaze, and then burnished with a bloodstone and polished.

Principal producers

Coalport (Coalbrookdale); Copeland; Copeland & Garrett; Davenport; Derby Crown Porcelain Co.; Royal Crown Derby; Doulton; Grainger, Lee & Co.; Grainger & Co.; Minton; Rockingham; Spode; Swansea; Wedgwood; Mason's Ironstone; Worcester, Flight, Barr & Barr; Worcester, Kerr & Binns; Royal Worcester Porcelain Company; Chamberlain's Worcester ('Regent China'); and lesser factories.

Period of manufacture
c.1830 to c.1920 and later.

Variations

It is not entirely true to say that those potteries which made garnitures, vases and ornamental wares in fine stoneware and ironstone were simply copying the major porcelain factories, since many of them produced designs which were unique to them. These were often less opulent and more restrained than the extremely grand porcelain pieces lavish with gilding and painted in a manner that more closely resembled oil paintings than decoration for ceramics or porcelain. It is perhaps more accurate to say that some of Coalport and Minton's garnitures were themselves variations on eighteenth-century porcelain.

A. *Elaborate pot pourri vase with three maidens supporting a vase, standing on a plinth, with applied flowers and garlands and a flowered finial to the scrolled pieced cover. Chelsea-Derby c.1779–84. 9 in (23 cm) high.*

B. *Rococo swirling pot pourri vase with pierced body and cover, smothered with flowers and painted with two song-birds. Late 18th century. 10½ in (26.5 cm) high.*

A   B

C. *Large Royal Worcester vase in apple green and gilt, painted with a scene of Highland cattle drinking by a loch by J. Stinton. Date code for 1917. 11¼ in (28.5 cm) high.*

C

Reproductions

Until recently there has been no reason for these grand, imposing objects to be reproduced: fashion for the last fifty years has been such that there has been no place for garnitures in modern interior design. With the revival of Victorian and Edwardian taste, however, prices have soared, and today a good signed piece by a named artist can fetch a great deal of money. Consequently it is possible that there may be some unscrupulous people attempting to add spurious signatures in order to increase the value. The existence of the Registration mark from 1842 to 1883 and of a date code for each year from 1885 to 1900 enables anyone to check with the Public Records Office for precise information if they harbour any suspicions and a large sum of money is involved.

Price bands

Mason's ironstone Japan pattern vases pairs £1,500–£1,800 up.

Coalbrookdale flower-encrusted wares £700–£900.

Worcester vases from £1,200 – more for animals, bird subjects.

Later periods considerably less except for bird, pairs £800–£1,000. 19th-century garnitures from Worcester factory currently as much as £1,200 and more for named artists.
Market very uneven.

D. *Bloor Derby garniture of three campana-shaped vases with deep royal blue ground. Marked **D** in red with crown, dots and crossed batons. 8 in (20 cm) and 6¾ in (17 cm) high.*

D

Cabinet ware

Signs of authenticity

1. On plates, cups, saucers, dishes, bowls, check rims and foot-rims for minute chips.

2. Condition of prime importance – any damage diminishes value considerably.

3. Single cups and saucers may originally have been part of boxed presentation sets of six – far more valuable than individual examples.

4. Check date codes, pattern numbers, registration marks where appropriate.

5. Signed pieces considerably more valuable than unsigned.

6. Subject matter of hand-painted pieces influences price: bird series usually more than fruit, flowers. Botanical, landscapes (particularly named topographical pieces), shells, butterflies are collectors' fields with consequent higher value.

7. Hairline cracks, restoration diminish value.

8. Mixed sets of different dates fetch lower prices than original matching sets. Check each piece if purchasing more than one of an original set.

9. Gilding should be mint-bright but with some sign of age – grinding off chipped edges and regilding them is not uncommon.

Historical backbround

Porcelain for display dates back to the early days of English pottery and porcelain making, when many wares were quite remarkably beautiful but so fragile that they could not be used. Early English delft plates, hand-painted with commemorative portraits and Biblical scenes, could probably be included in this category, and some of the extraordinary slip-moulded salt glazed stoneware pieces in intricate shapes could scarcely have been in everyday use. When English porcelain factories began to make soft paste porcelain, it was not for some time that it could satisfactorily be used, but nevertheless it was very decorative and highly prized.

Dessert services were among the first useful wares to be elaborately hand-painted and gilded. Seldom used for anything more punishing than peeling a hot-house peach, they were usually accompanied by glass liner-plates to ensure that no cutlery came into contact with the delicate surface. Even when durable glazes and decoration had been developed, the fashion for 'cabinet' pieces persisted – much of the Wedgwood jasper ware and basaltes was destined for fine display cabinets. In the 1820s the revival of flower-encrusted pieces lent new life to extravagant objects to fill the cabinets and display furniture that proliferated throughout the nineteenth century. The expansive Edwardian era, looking backwards with nostalgia to the last great days of Empire, was passionately attached to fading Victorian images, and many patterns and designs were revived on a smaller scale, in sets of coffee cups and richly painted plates and dishes.

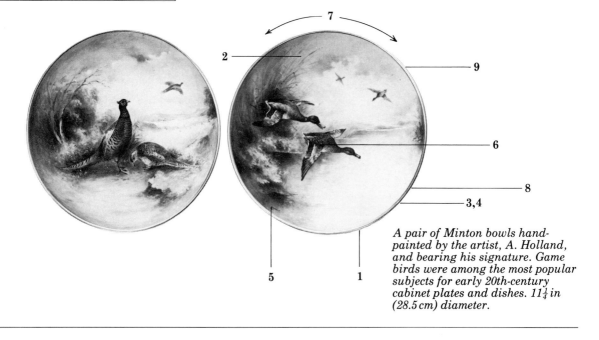

A pair of Minton bowls hand-painted by the artist, A. Holland, and bearing his signature. Game birds were among the most popular subjects for early 20th-century cabinet plates and dishes. 11¼ in (28.5 cm) diameter.

Materials and decoration

The sole common factor with all cabinet wares is that they should be eminently decorative and serve little or no purpose. This section deals specifically with nineteenth- and twentieth-century pieces since they are more likely to be within the reach of relative newcomers, though the recent escalation in prices has been such that items once despised by the broad sweep of antique collectors and dealers are now reaching small fortunes in salerooms and specialist shops. Of considerable interest in recent years has been the rise in value of Belleek, a curious hybrid which is neither pottery nor porcelain. This Irish company was established in 1857 and the following year began making ornately decorative cabinet wares in parian glazed with a smooth, iridescent substance resembling mother of pearl. To many people it has an unpleasant, almost slimy feel and appearance, and it has been largely neglected until the last few years when it, too, has gathered its own small and passionate band of collectors.

Principal producers

All major porcelain and pottery manufacturers, including makers of statuary parian and parian wares; the Irish factory of Belleek; Royal Crown Derby; Wedgwood; Copeland & Garrett; Grainger & Co.; Rockingham and Minton (floral encrusted wares); Swansea; Brownfield; and many small firms making copies of Meissen and Dresden figures. Firms such as Madeley of Shropshire were making much pseudo-Sèvres in the Regency, too, although seldom marked.

B. Royal Worcester coffee cup and saucer painted by L. Flexman. Date code for 1921. Cup 3¾ in (9.5 cm) high.

C. Two 'Chelsea Cheyne' figures: clown by Gwendolen Parnell (right) and romanticized West Country hobby horse dancer (left), c.1925–8. 6¼ in (16 cm) and 6¾ in (17 cm) high.

Period of manufacture
No time span – cabinet ware can be of any date from early eighteenth century to the recent past.

Reproductions

The most common reproductions of early cabinet wares are Continental copies in hard paste – among them the immense output of Samson of Paris – and the production from the New Chelsea Porcelain Company Ltd. This was established at Longton in about 1912 and was in operation until about 1951, making 'genuine reproductions' in bone china of early Chelsea, Bow, Lowestoft, Plymouth and Bristol pieces. Only the first seven years of production present a real problem, since they were largely unmarked, but from 1919 the printed mark was **New Chelsea**, **Chelsea** or **Royal Chelsea** together with an anchor.

Variations

Sets and series of miniatures by the Royal Crown Derby company in particular were made from just after World War II. Limited editions from the Royal Worcester factory were made from the 1950s onwards and the first series of birds, particularly the rarer ornithological species, has proved to be a good investment. Works by named artists such as Dorothy Doughty are quite sought-after, though some of her models have failed inexplicably while others have increased steadily in value.

A. Royal Worcester limited edition of blue tits and pussy willow after models by Dorothy Doughty, 1964. 10½ in (26.5 cm) high.

Price bands

Price determined by taste and budget: single 18th-century tea bowls and saucers, coffee cans, butter boats from £75, considerably less than currently fashionable 19th- and early 20th-century wares. Single finely painted dessert plates from £35 and upwards.

Doulton

Historical background

This workaday pottery, making salt glazed stoneware mainly for such mundane industrial purposes as water pipes and conduits, commercial bottles for inks and drinks, and cheap domestic wares, was destined to become one of the prime movers in the reaction against the florid taste and poor quality of mass-produced everyday items used in countless houses and homes in the nineteenth century. John Doulton founded the pottery, initially known as Doulton &

Watts, in about 1815, and began to reproduce early stoneware bellarmines, harvest jugs, pitchers, tankards and suchlike from about 1826, in time to catch the rising fashion for medieval romantic and Tudor revival of the first half of the nineteenth century.

In about 1862 Henry Doulton formed tentative links with the Lambeth School of Art, with the aim of producing some radical new designs using traditional methods and materials. Progress was slow, but gradually, as students from the Lambeth School of Art began to design for Doulton's Lambeth pottery, new forms began to be accepted. Among the names associated with the firm at this time are George Tinworth and

the Barlow family, to whom the factory owes much of its abiding fame. Henry Doulton was knighted in 1887 – a just reward for his seminal influence on many artist potters working in England.

The Doulton pottery managed to have its cake and eat it, as it were, for in 1882 a second factory was established at Burslem in Staffordshire, to make quantities of 'character jugs' and small figures, following the Staffordshire tradition of social comment in mugs, jugs and ornamental pottery.

One of a pair of Doulton Lambeth vases with pate-sur-pate borders by Eliza Simmance and a frieze of animals in a landscape decorated in sgraffito technique by Hannah Barlow, c.1890. 17¼ in (44 cm) high.

Signs of authenticity

1. From c.1858 all wares impressed **Doulton Lambeth**.
2. Experimental wares from c.1862 seldom marked with artist's name or mark.
3. 'Pate-sur-pate' embellishment introduced c.1871.
4. Hannah and Florence Barlow began working at Doulton c.1871.
5. From 1873 system of date marks introduced, continued until mid-1880s.
6. Artist's individual marks impressed on base.
7. From c.1878 division by mutual agreement with Florence keeping to bird subjects and Hannah to animals.
8. Lucy Barlow designing for Doulton c.1882–5 – extremely similar to both her sisters.
9. Sgraffito technique at first liable to be uneven, with cobalt pigment turning black with firing or vanishing from some incisions.
10. From c.1881 new stoneware body developed, called 'silicon': unglazed, using coloured clays as decoration.
11. Rarer animals – kangaroos, lions, deer – more sought-after than domestic animals.
12. Art Nouveau influence evident in scrolling, formalized foliage, decoration from 1890s.

Materials and decoration

Lambeth Doulton is principally known for its stoneware decorated with sgraffito incised scenes of birds and animals, and with pate-sur-pate, either separately or in combination. The technique of pate-sur-pate was originally developed at Minton in about 1870 – the unfired ground colour was washed with layers of semi-translucent slip, shaped and detailed with a sculptor's tool before firing, when it fused to the body in an almost marbled manner, allowing the ground colour to show through the thinner layers of slip or building to an intense white which was almost opaque.

The 'silicon' body was a form of vitrified stoneware coloured with pigments and unglazed, so that designs could be 'built in' to the body and sculpted into relief before firing. Doulton Faience was a tin glazed earthenware, similar to English delftware, but decorated more in the Italian manner with a maiolica-type palette of bright colours. Marqueterie takes its name from inlaid wood, and achieved a similar effect with marbled clays in chequerwork patterns.

Variations

The range of wares from the Doulton Burslem factory have a separate appeal and a vast following of collectors to whom series numbers are at once a code and a price-guide. Character jugs in particular, once an inexpensive hobby for pubs and working men's clubs as well as private collectors, have now reached prices which parallel some of the more rarified porcelain pieces. There is a large Doulton Collectors' Club, which issues its own newsletter and whose members are more concerned with transactions concerning a Red-Headed Clown than whether a highly prized vase was decorated by Hannah, Florence or Lucy.

A. *Two Doulton Lambeth ovoid vases moulded with fruit and flowers on a rich blue ground, the smaller inscribed on the base as follows: 'With best wishes from the Worshipful Master and Brethren of the Brentham Lodge. 22.10.32'. 13½in (34cm) and 7¼in (18.5cm) high.*

B. *Royal Doulton figure of 'Bluebeard' from the immense range of figures produced by the Burslem factory. 7½in (17cm) high.*

C. *Rare Doulton character jug of 'The Hatless Drake', date code for 1940, exceptional because it was never released for general sale and only a limited number were made as a trial. 6in (15cm) high.*

Reproductions

The Lambeth Doulton factory only ceased to make stoneware in 1956 and, since every piece has been registered, it is doubtful that the recent upswing in popularity has yet become the subject of reproduction. Nineteenth-century registration and trade protection should ensure that they are either unmarked, or marked by the potteries who made them at the time. Sadly for today's collectors, the Doulton system of date coding ceased in the 1880s and, although it was reintroduced in 1902, there is a possibility that mistakes may be made in attributions and dating during the gap.

Principal products

Salt glazed stoneware domestic and commerical c.1815–26; versions of sixteenth- and seventeenth-century pieces to c.1862; artists' or studio pottery from c.1871; silicon c.1881–1912; Doulton Faience from c.1872; Doulton Carrara ware c.1888–98; terra cotta from c.1851; marqueterie from c.1887.

Period of manufacture
c.1826 to c.1902, Doulton Lambeth; 1882–present day, Doulton Burslem. Royal Doulton mark found after 1902.

Price bands

Doulton Lambeth drab-coloured stoneware jugs, mugs, tankards £50–£350. Hannah, Florence Barlow vases £250–£400 with horses, cattle, sheep. Lions, wild beasts, rare subjects from £1,000 upwards.

Pate-sur-pate £250–£2,000 depending on shape, design and style.

Royal Doulton series figures £90–£1,200 and upwards for rare models.

Character jugs £50–£1,000 with as much as £3,000 for very rare examples.

Artist potters and studio potters

Historical background

While the students and graduates from the Lambeth School of Art were producing the first publicly accepted pottery as a genuine art form, around the 1870s others began to treat pottery as sculpture – a movement that culminated in what is called studio pottery. Among the earliest followers of Sir Henry Doulton's lead were the brothers Martin, known today for their famous grotesque bird jugs, but who also could be said to be among the first potters to treat the subject as sculpture. Wallace, Walter and Charles Martin worked from their studio, at first close to

Doulton where all three of them had been trained, Wallace at Lambeth School of art and the two younger brothers as apprentice designers for Doulton. Once well established, they moved to Southall, making a wide variety of pottery, almost entirely in rather drab colours but with new and interesting shapes.

Both William Morris and John Ruskin became involved in the artist potters movement, and their influence can be seen in the work of William de Morgan, which was brilliant with colour and sinuous shapes, many of them inspired by Persian tiles with their vivid blues, greens and lustre colours. By the turn of the century, pottery had become one of the leading influences in many areas of design, and

one person, who perhaps has been slightly eclipsed by the prolific output of Bernard Leach and his followers, was responsible for getting public recognition for pottery as a sculpture: Staite Murray, who began making pottery in 1912, acted as a bridge between the nineteenth-century artist potters and today's studio potters by persuading some art galleries to exhibit the work of young and talented potters together with work by young, serious artists of the modern movement. It is quite difficult to train the eye and mind to see and appreciate the many strange forms that pottery takes today, but it is a rewarding subject and, compared with a Warhol or a Hockney, still relatively inexpensive.

Signs of authenticity

This field is so wide and, to a certain extent, still untried in terms of definition that it is better to become acquainted with the shape and feel of pieces before considering starting a collection. Pieces made by artists for individual factories will be marked with the factory mark and a date code. Once one oversteps the production line and enters the territory of individually potted pieces by studios and named artists, the subject should be considered more in terms of fine art than commercially produced wares.

All successful artist potters have their imitators, and when a single artist reaches a high level of recognition, deliberate 'copies' appear to catch the fortunes of the rising market. Bernard Leach, collected avidly by the Japanese as well as having an international reputation, is a case in point – there were some unfortunate episodes connected with large sums of money paid for pieces which turned out never to have seen the inside of Leach's studio.

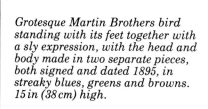

Grotesque Martin Brothers bird standing with its feet together with a sly expression, with the head and body made in two separate pieces, both signed and dated 1895, in streaky blues, greens and browns. 15 in (38 cm) high.

A. *Moorcroft oviform vase in 'Hazeldene' pattern painted in moonlight blue. Early work by Moorcroft/Macintyre dates from 1897. William Moorcroft established his own pottery in 1913 at Burslem. $15\frac{1}{2}$ in (39.5 cm) high.*

B. *Collection of the Martin Brothers' stoneware – gourds and vases. The centre gourd is coloured with green glaze and dated 1898 – other pieces date from the early 1900s. Range of sizes from 4 in (10 cm) to $2\frac{1}{2}$ in (6.5 cm), the tallest vase with tapered body $4\frac{1}{4}$ in (11 cm) high.*

B

A

D. *Bernard Leach stoneware bottle vase in mirror-black Japanese finish, dating from the late 1960s. Marked with St Ives seal. 15 in (38 cm) high.*

D

C

C. *Large decorative plate or plaque made by Wedgwood, painted by Alfred Powell in a manner which recalls William de Morgan. In blues, greens and purple lustre. Date code for 1925. $16\frac{3}{4}$ in (42.5 cm) diameter.*

E. *Left Lipped cream bowl in lustrous deep brown with ashen white interior in stoneware, 1960s. $5\frac{3}{4}$ in (14.5 cm) diameter. Right Stoneware vase with pitted texture, brown-speckled and pale turquoise-green surface. $7\frac{1}{2}$ in (19 cm) high. Both by Lucy Rie, 1960–70.*

Price bands

Martin Bros stoneware from £120 for small pieces.

Grotesque 'face' jugs £1,000 and upwards. Grotesque birds as much as £2,000–£5,000.

Moorcraft vases £100–£800. Moorcraft Macintyre from £80 up.

Bernard Leach commercial pieces from £120. Studio pieces variable collectors' market.

Cardew, Coper specialist field.

Lucy Rie from £320, escalating also into specialist market.

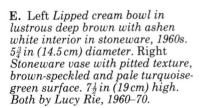

E

F

F. *Early Hans Coper stoneware vase with 'sharkskin texture' flaring neck, the interior dark brown, c.1955. $11\frac{3}{4}$ in (30 cm) high.*

151

A

C

B

A. *One of a set of three decorative plates designed by Laura Knight A.R.A. painted in brown, yellow, green and pink with a circus girl on a pony. Printed marks and* **Laura Knight** *facsimile signature. 9 in (23 cm) diameter.*

B. *Foley 'Pastello' earthenware vase with painted under-glaze decoration of a house with smoking chimney set in a purple landscape against a yellow sky. Printed mark* **The Foley 'Pastello' England***, c.1900. 6½ in (16.5 cm) high.*

C. *Oval serving dish designed by John Armstrong for Harrods painted with the 'Chaldane' design with a stylized horse in sepia and blue, and linear and criss-cross border in blue and black, 1934. Printed marks and* **John Armstrong** *facsimile signature. 12¾ in (32.5 cm) wide.*

D

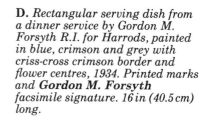

D. *Rectangular serving dish from a dinner service by Gordon M. Forsyth R.I. for Harrods, painted in blue, crimson and grey with criss-cross crimson border and flower centres, 1934. Printed marks and* **Gordon M. Forsyth** *facsimile signature. 16 in (40.5 cm) long.*

E. *'Gayday' vase painted with a wide border of colourful daisies on a cream ground with yellow rim and brown and green foot border. Printed marks and painted* **Gayday***, 1936. Clarice Cliff.*

F. *Large ewer painted in the 'Oriental' design with blue, green and pink stylized exotic fruits and foliage on a turquoise ground. Printed marks. Clarice Cliff. 10¾ in (27.5 cm) high.*

E   F

G. *Individual breakfast set designed by Eva Crofts painted with a robin, tall green trees and a brilliant yellow sun, with zig-zag yellow, black, green and red borders, 1934. Teapot 4½ in (11.5 cm) high.*

G

I

H. *Shelley three-piece pottery nursery tea set in bright colours on a white ground, designed by Mabel Lucie Atwell and painted, c.1925. Artist's signature on each piece. Teapot 7¾ in (19.5 cm) high.*

J. *Shelley tea set decorated with a painted scene of a sun rising over a country landscape in yellow and black on a white ground. Printed* **Shelley England** *and with registered No. 723404, c.1930. Teapot 5 in (13 cm) high.*

I. *'Fantasque' single-handled vase painted in the 'Summer House' design with tall trees in yellow, green, red, blue and black on a cream ground between orange borders, by Clarice Cliff. Printed marks, 1932. 11½ in (29 cm) high.*

H

Index of shapes

Teapots	Coffee pots	Bowls & cups

1700

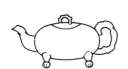

1750

Teapots	Coffee pots	Bowls & cups

1800

1850

Mugs	Sauce boats	Cream jugs

1700

 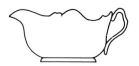

1750

Mugs	Sauce boats	Cream jugs

1800

 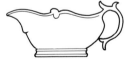

1850

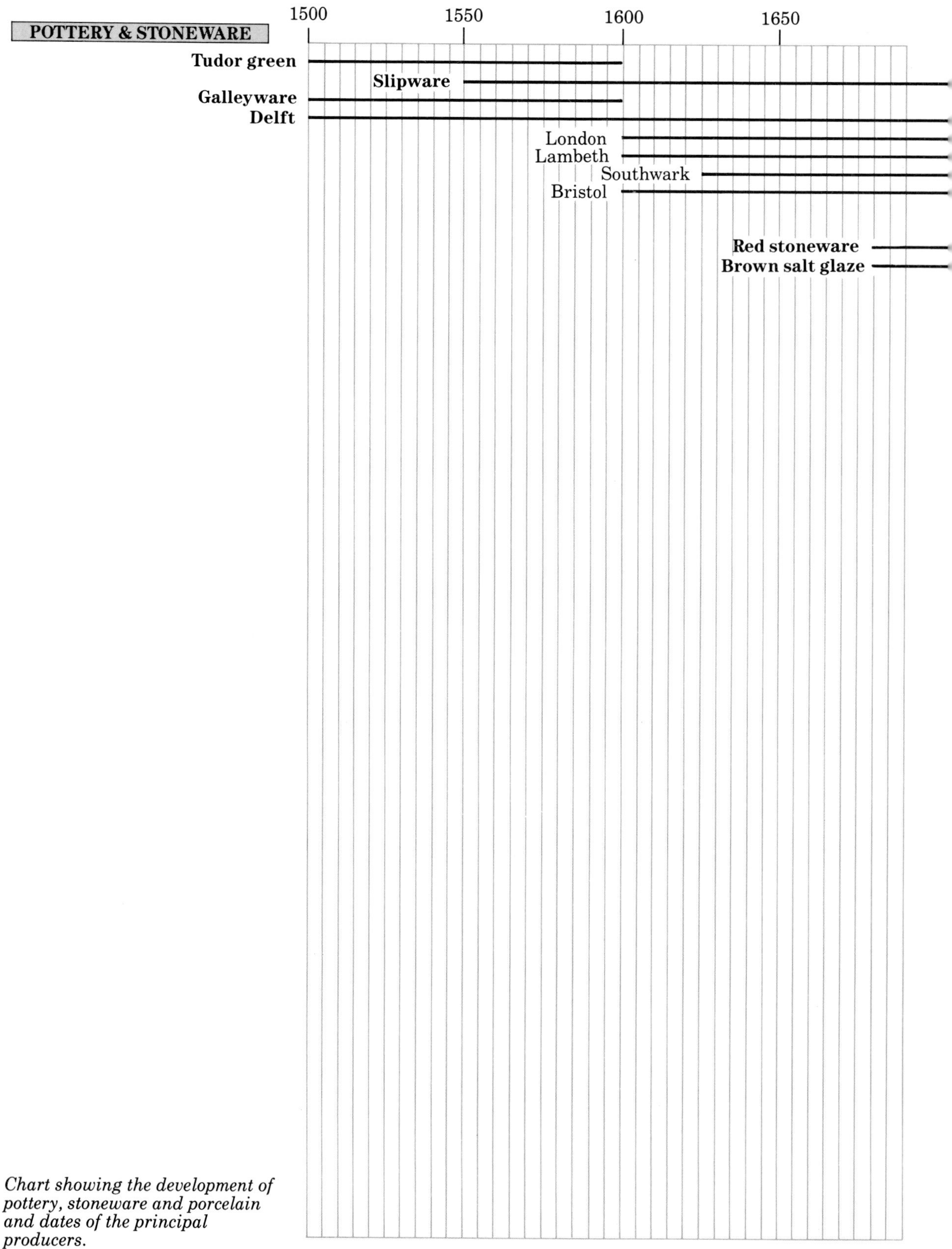
POTTERY & STONEWARE
1500
1550
1600
1650
Tudor green
Slipware
Galleyware
Delft
London
Lambeth
Southwark
Bristol
Red stoneware
Brown salt glaze

Chart showing the development of pottery, stoneware and porcelain and dates of the principal producers.

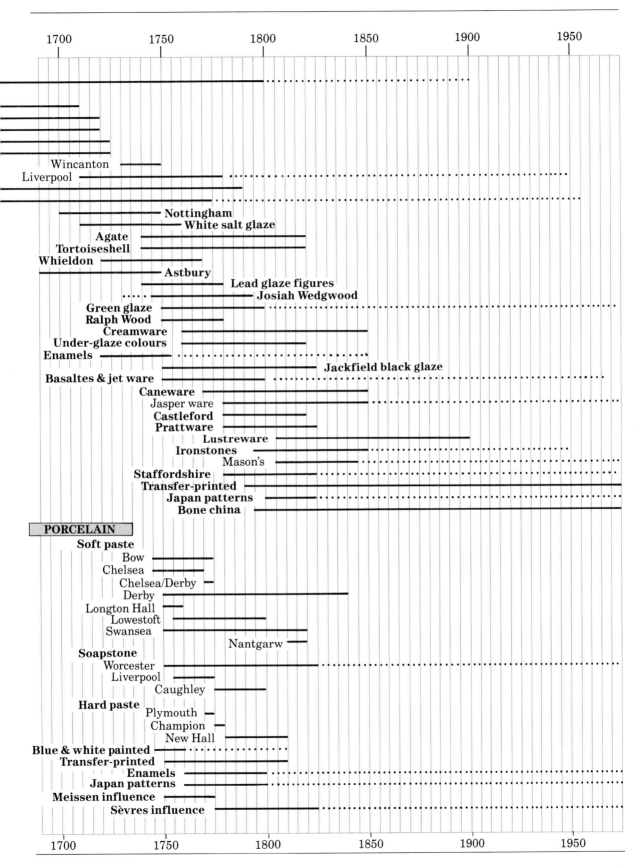

1700   1750   1800   1850   1900   1950

Wincanton
Liverpool

Nottingham
White salt glaze
Agate
Tortoiseshell
Whieldon
Astbury
Lead glaze figures
Josiah Wedgwood
Green glaze
Ralph Wood
Creamware
Under-glaze colours
Enamels
Jackfield black glaze
Basaltes & jet ware
Caneware
Jasper ware
Castleford
Prattware
Lustreware
Ironstones
Mason's
Staffordshire
Transfer-printed
Japan patterns
Bone china

PORCELAIN
Soft paste
Bow
Chelsea
Chelsea/Derby
Derby
Longton Hall
Lowestoft
Swansea
Nantgarw
Soapstone
Worcester
Liverpool
Caughley
Hard paste
Plymouth
Champion
New Hall
Blue & white painted
Transfer-printed
Enamels
Japan patterns
Meissen influence
Sèvres influence

1700   1750   1800   1850   1900   1950

Glossary

Bamboo ware.

Stoneware bellarmine.

Castleford teapot.

Acanthus leaf Classical leaf motif derived from Greek and Roman designs.

Agate ware Pottery in mixed and mingled clays (see *Bodies and Pastes*).

Antimony Metallic element used for making yellow colour pigment.

Applied Made separately and added.

Bamboo ware Fine cane-coloured stoneware modelled to resemble bamboo – fashionable in the Regency period.

Basaltes Fine stoneware stained black and fully vitreous (see *Bodies and Pastes*).

Bellarmine Drab-coloured vitreous stoneware flagon originating in Germany in the 16th century, with bearded mask decoration in relief.

Biscuit Once-fired unglazed earthenware, stoneware or paste.

Bisque Unglazed 'frit' porcelain figures with ivory-white velvety texture.

Black porcelain Stained or naturally coloured clay bodies which fire to black (see *Bodies and Pastes*).

Blanc de chine Glazed white porcelain, usually in the form of ornamental ware and figures.

Blue dash Pattern of Dutch origin on rims of plates, chargers and bowls, painted or sponged with diagonal lines suggesting ropework, much used on English delft in the 17th and 18th centuries.

Body Basic clay, earthenware or stoneware in its unfired state, the raw material from which pottery is made.

Bone china Paste developed *c.*1794 using china clay as an ingredient (see *Bodies and Pastes*).

Bone porcelain Soft paste with the additional element of bone ash for increased whiteness, translucence and strength.

Caneware Dry-bodied stoneware (see *Bodies and Pastes*).

Casting Technique of making articles by pouring liquid or molten materials or metals into a cast.

Castleford ware Porcellanous dry-bodied stoneware (see *Bodies and Pastes*).

Chasing Decoration in relief using blunt tools without cutting away any gilding or metal.

China Porcelain or pottery resembling imported Chinese wares (see *Bodies and Pastes*).

Chinese export Porcelain made by the Chinese specifically for the European market.

Clobbering The addition of coloured enamels and/or gilding over the glaze to early wares printed in blue under the glaze.

Crazing A web of very thin lines like fine cracks in the surface of glaze, sometimes penetrating through to the paste itself. The result of changes in temperature and atmospheric conditions over many years, causing paste and glaze to contract or expand at different rates.

Cream-coloured earthenware Light-coloured clays which, when fired at the right temperature, turn to a pale cream.

Creamware Cream-coloured earthenware coated with a clear or opaque, cream-coloured glaze (see *Bodies and Pastes*).

Crouch ware Drab-coloured stoneware imported from the Continent, its name probably deriving from the French word 'cruche' meaning pitcher.

Delftware Tin glazed earthenware. The name was confined to Dutch wares until Georgian times, when it became a generic description for tin glazed wares made in England as well as Holland.

Diaper A repetitive pattern consisting of diamonds, lozenges or trellis.

Dry bodies Fine-textured stoneware, fully vitreous and needing no glazing, sometimes with porcellanous qualities of translucence.

Earthenware Clay or pottery of any description which has been baked to make it hard and firm.

Egyptian black Stoneware stained black and fired at a temperature just sufficient to make it non-porous.

Embossed Surface decoration raised in relief.

Enamel Glassy opaque or coloured substance stained with colour pigments applied or painted over a glazed surface. When fired, the enamel fuses to the glaze.

Encaustic Method of decorating by burning in pigments to earthenware, usually in a brick red, often on a black stoneware body.

Engine turning Decoration consisting of incised line patterns, executed on a lathe.

Export ware Porcelain made specifically for the overseas market.

Faceted Decorated with shallow hollows forming a surface diamond pattern.

Faience Tin glazed earthenware, generally from France, but also from Germany and other European countries.

'Famille rose' Porcelain decorated with a rose-coloured opaque enamel developed by the Chinese from gold chloride and tin chloride, which produced a range of colours from pale rose to violet and purple, depending on the heat of the kiln. These rare rose colours are often present in very small areas of decoration, but are quite distinctive. The term was adopted by English porcelain manufacturers for their pinks, usually derived from manganese oxide, and in the 19th century the term came to denote any porcelain with a predominantly rose-coloured decoration.

'Famille verte' Chinese porcelain from the late 17th century K'ang Hsi period, decorated with a dominant vivid green, and including rust red, manganese purple and violet blue, enamelled over the glaze and enriched with gilding. English manufacturers used copper oxide to make green for enamels, but with considerable difficulty. A green pigment made from chromium was discovered in 1749 which was much more opaque and would take gilding, unlike copper oxide greens, but it was not used on English porcelain until the beginning of the 19th century.

Felspar porcelain A refined paste developed by Spode at the end of the 18th century for bone china (see *Bodies and Pastes*).

Felspathic ware Earthenware with the additional ingredient of powdered felspar (see *Bodies and Pastes*).

Diaper border.

Engine-turned mug.

Felspar porcelain vegetable dish.

Tin glazed earthenware flower brick.

Fuddling cup.

Galleyware claret jug.

Fine stoneware Refined stoneware bodies such as caneware, jasper ware and basaltes.

Finial Top ornament or decoration on lids of teapots, coffee pots, etc.

Flatware Plates and dishes in pottery or porcelain.

Flint ware Earthenware body with the addition of powdered calcined flint (see *Bodies and Pastes*).

Floret A small flowerhead.

Flower brick Tin glazed hollow ornamental brick from the late 17th and early 18th century with perforations in the top, generally supposed to have held flowers. Some have one or two large circular holes in the centre and can be presumed to have been used as ink wells, with the perforations for holding quill pens.

Fluted Decorated with parallel grooves.

Foot-rim The shaped rim under plates, dishes, saucers, and on hollow ware.

Frit A glassy substance composed of varying elements, molten, cooled and pulverized, which was added to porcelain pastes and to glazes.

Frit porcelain Porcelain containing frit.

Fuddling cup A drinking cup, generally made prior to the 18th century, composed of three or more interlinking cups. To empty one, the entire contents must be drunk.

Gadroon Repeating pattern of upright or slanting lobes, like a clenched fist.

Galleyware Tin glazed earthenware (see *Bodies and Pastes*).

Gallipot A small earthenware pot, often standing on three stumpy legs, used for cooking in the hearth and for storage.

Glaze The glassy coating on pottery and porcelain which renders it non-porous.

Glost oven A separate oven used for glazing.

'Gros bleu' The brilliant, rich, deep blue, applied under the glaze on Vincennes porcelain, later Sèvres.

Ground The main colour on a piece of pottery or porcelain, usually applied under the glaze.

Hard paste porcelain Immensely strong, translucent porcelain with the glaze fused to the paste so completely that it is an integral part.

High temperature colours The only colour pigments which would withstand the high temperatures of the kiln: cobalt blue, iron red, manganese purple, green from copper, and orange and yellow from iron or antimony. Applied at the biscuit stage with the exception of tin glazed earthenware, where colour pigments were painted on to the dry, powdery surface before firing.

Ho ho bird A distinctly Oriental bird with long trailing tail feathers, resembling a bird of paradise.

Honey gilding In use from *c.*1755 on English porcelain, made from powdered gold, oil of lavender and honey (see *Techniques and Terms*).

Imari Patterns derived from Japanese brocaded silks in predominant colours of scarlet, deep blue and gilt. First used on English porcelain, in imitation of Japanese export wares, from *c.*1770.

'Improving' The latter addition of coloured enamels over the glaze on early wares.

Incised Decoration scored, scratched or cut into the surface.

Iron red Colour pigment extracted from iron oxide.

Ironstone china Felspathic earthenware with slight translucency (see *Bodies and Pastes*).

Ivory porcelain Glazed parian – a translucent porcelain paste containing felspar developed in the 19th century.

Jackfield Brownish-red earthenware covered with thick black glaze, named for one pottery known to have made it from *c.*1751 (see *Bodies and Pastes*).

Japanese export ware Porcelain made in Japan specifically for the European market.

Japanning A method of hardening-on lacquers and enamels to woods, metals and ceramics.

Jasper dip Fine-bodied stoneware dipped in coloured slip.

Jasper ware Also known as solid jasper, when fine-bodied stoneware was stained right through with colour pigments.

Jet ware Loose term including earthenwares glazed with a rich black glaze, or stained and fired to black.

Kakiemon Delicate patterns of rocks, roots, peony and prunus derived from Japanese paintings on paper or silk.

Kaolin China clay – a vital ingredient of porcelain.

Kiku mon Stylized flowerhead – an element of Kakiemon patterns.

Lambeth Faience Revival of early tin glazed wares by Doulton from 1872.

Littler's blue A particularly strident cobalt blue named after the manager of Longton Hall pottery, William Littler.

Long Elizas, Long Lizzies Tall, thin figures of women, featuring in early blue and white chinoiserie designs, taken from Chinese originals.

Lustre ware Earthenware or bone china coated with a metallic finish (see *Bodies and Pastes*).

Maiolica Italian tin glazed earthenware, some of the earliest to be made in Europe.

Majolica The name Minton gave to a range of wares decorated very approximately in colours of the maiolica palette.

Manganese Metallic element from which colour pigment was made producing a range of tones from light purple, puce, purple, brown to black.

Mazarine blue Deep blue ground colour of English porcelain applied under the glaze in imitation of Vincennes and Sèvres 'gros bleu'.

Metallic oxides Metallic elements which have been burned off to remove impurities – the base of most early colour pigments and glazes.

Mercury gilding Powdered gold in a flux of mercury, used on English porcelain from *c.*1790 (see *Techniques and Terms*).

Chinese ho-ho bird.

Dishevelled bird.

Long Eliza.

Nottingham double-walled stoneware 'carved jug'.

Pate-sur-pate.

Piecrust ware.

Moons Characteristic blemishes in the shape of a nail-paring or a moon, caused by grease spots – found particularly in Chelsea soft paste porcelain.

Moulded Shaped in a mould from a solid malleable substance. In some cases known as casting, but technically casting implies liquid poured into a mould.

Nottingham stoneware Drab-coloured salt glazed stoneware made from the 1680s onwards (see *Bodies and Pastes*).

Oil gilding Thick gold leaf applied to an adhesive substance on ceramics and then fired at low temperatures (see *Techniques and Terms*).

Opaque Not transparent.

Palette The range of colours used in any type of decoration.

Parian Translucent porcelain paste containing felspar, developed in the 19th century (see *Bodies and Pastes*).

Paste The raw material from which porcelain is made.

Pate-sur-pate A technique used in the 19th century by Doulton and other leading manufacturers. Thin white slip was applied in varying thicknesses over a ground colour to achieve a semi-transparent milky decoration.

Pearlware Near-white earthenware body containing calcined flint and china clay (see *Bodies and Pastes*).

Petuntse China stone – a vital ingredient for hard paste and its glaze.

Piecrust ware Fine cane-coloured stoneware (see *Bodies and Pastes*).

Pigment Colouring matter extracted from various substances.

Pill slab Small tin glazed tiles of specific shape used by apothecaries for rolling medicaments into pills.

Pipe clay Very fine-bodied clay occurring naturally in Devon and other geologically suitable sites. Used for making clay pipes.

Porcelain Pure, translucent, white substance, originally made in China (see *Bodies and Pastes*).

Porcellanous Having some of the translucent qualities of porcelain.

Pottery Earthenware, stoneware – bodies without the translucence and whiteness of porcelain.

'Queen's China' Registered name for bone china made by the Queen's pottery, Longton, Staffs.

'Queen's Ware' Courtesy name give by Wedgwood to his range of creamware after a royal commission.

Red china Contemporary name for a particular red stoneware (see *Bodies and Pastes*).

Red porcelain Grand name used for early wares in red stoneware.

Red stoneware Vitreous reddish-coloured earthenware.

Reeded Parallel lines of convex moulding.

'Regent China' Registered name for luxury range of bone china made by Chamberlain's of Worcester.

Relief Standing out from the surface in high or low relief. This form of decoration may be moulded or applied.

Rocaille One of the main motifs in rococo decoration based on shapes of rocks and shells.

Rococo 18th-century design originating in France based on asymmetric shapes characterized by elaborate, graceful ornamentation.

Rosso antico A fine rose-coloured version of red stoneware (see *Bodies and Pastes*).

Salt glaze Method of glazing stoneware. Salt thrown into the kiln at high temperatures vaporized and was deposited as a glassy film (see *Techniques and Terms*).

Scratch blue Incised decoration into which cobalt pigment was rubbed before firing and glazing.

Sgraffito Incised decoration filled with coloured slip or colour pigment before firing and glazing.

Slip Clay diluted to a creamy consistency with water.

Slip casting Slip poured into an earthenware or plaster of Paris mould and left until a layer of solid clay built up on the inside of the mould (see *Techniques and Terms*).

Slipware Earthenware decorated with naturally coloured slip (see *Bodies and Pastes*).

Smalt Cobalt pigment mixed with molten glass, ground to a fine powder and used as an enamel (see *Techniques and Terms*).

Smear glaze Technically a form of semi-matt glaze used on parian ware. The term has also come to include later variations of 'tortoiseshell' ware, where the glaze is smeared and streaked with colour.

Soapstone porcelain A variation of English soft paste porcelain.

Soft paste porcelain An English formula using frit and other substances mixed with fine-bodied clay which produced a reasonable imitation of true Chinese porcelain (see *Bodies and Pastes*).

Solid agate Earthenware body made of mixed and mingled clays (see *Bodies and Pastes*).

Solid jasper Extremely fine-bodied stoneware stained with colour pigments.

Sparrow-beak A rather sharply shaped lip to 18th-century jugs.

Sprigged Applied ornament in the shape of small sprigs of flowers and leaves.

Stamped Relief decoration stamped out of malleable clay. Later whole items were stamped out by machine and impressed with surface decoration, known as moulded in relief.

Stone china Earthenware body mixed with powdered felspathic stone to produce an opaque, finely textured body (see *Bodies and Pastes*).

Stoneware Earthenware body with added vitreous substances, or with vitreous elements occurring naturally.

Tazza A shallow bowl or cup on a footed stem – used for fruit and sweetmeats and as a centrepiece.

Teapoy 18th-century word for a tea caddy.

Terra cotta Once-fired earthenware with a rich red colour.

Thrown Hollow ware made on a potter's wheel.

Sparrow-beak jug.

Sprigged decoration applied on stoneware.

Slip-cast white salt glazed stoneware tureen.

18th-century Worcester teapoy or tea vase.

Transfer-printed willow pattern – Spode's earliest version.

Welsh ware pie plate – 19th century.

Tin glaze Liquid lead-based glaze with tin oxide added to produce an opaque, brilliant white glassy surface.

Tin oxide Tin which has been burned off to remove impurities.

Tortoiseshell ware Cream-coloured earthenware stained with metallic oxides which were absorbed into the glaze (see *Bodies and Pastes*).

Transfer-printing A print taken from a copper plate and transferred to the glazed surface of porcelain *c.*1754–70 or printed in cobalt under the glaze from *c.*1760 on porcelain and from *c.*1784 on earthenwares (see *Techniques and Terms*).

Translucent Opaque but with transparent qualities when held up to the light. Literally means letting light through.

Trio A matching set of tea bowl, cup and saucer.

'True' porcelain Porcelain made in China and the Orient from china clay and china stone (kaolin and petuntse) with pulverized china stone in the glaze. When fired at very high temperatures the glaze fused completely to the body, which acquired a great degree of translucency.

Tudor green Earthenware with a streaky green glaze (see *Techniques and Terms*).

Turned, turning Spun on a lathe to trim and decorate, and to reduce the thickness of an object.

Tyg A drinking cup with more than one handle, passed from hand to hand so that people could drink hygienically from different parts of the rim. Made mainly before the 18th century.

Under-glaze Colour pigments applied after a single firing at the biscuit stage, before glazing.

Under-glaze blue Small amounts of cobalt pigment added to a glaze like a 'blue whitener' to improve the whiteness of the finished object. Although this technique was used by potteries while earthenware bodies were still an unsatisfactory off-white colour, the term is usually applied to ornamental figures glazed with a brilliant white glaze.

Useful ware Defined by Wedgwood as 'everything used at the table'.

Vitreous stoneware Clays and earthenware bodies containing sand, calcined flints or other mineral stones which, when fired at high temperatures, fused with the body to produce a crystalline non-porous substance.

Vitrified Bodies containing vitreous substances which have been fired.

Welsh ware Later production of slipware, which was made in rural potteries long after more advanced earthenwares had been developed (see *Bodies and pastes*).

Whieldon ware A loose term to describe some solid agate and tortoiseshell ware, after Thomas Whieldon.

Marks on pottery & porcelain

Marks on pottery and porcelain are like silver hallmarks – often difficult to decipher, frequently duplicated with very small variations by other manufacturers, and changing with periods of manufacture and management of the pottery or porcelain factory. Stoneware and earthenwares were seldom marked until the late eighteenth century, and even some genuine pieces of eighteenth-century porcelain are found without marks.

Authentication therefore is seldom simply a question of identifying the maker and the period from a sign or symbol.

However, scattered through the pages of this book are references to some of the more important marks and periods of certain famous potteries and porcelain factories, and in order to clarify these references, a very brief guide is given below.

Porcelain

Bow China Works London
*c.*1747–76.
1, 2. Early incised marks.
3. Anchor and dagger mark, painted, *c.*1760–76.
4. In under-glaze blue *c.*1760–76.

 1   2   3   4

Bristol hard paste. Founded by William Cookworthy *c.*1770, later Cookworthy & Richard Champion, closed 1781.
1.–5. Painted marks.

 1   B 2   B6 3   4   5

Chelsea Porcelain Works London *c.*1745–69.
1, 2. Incised mark *c.*1745–50.
3. Raised anchor mark *c.*1749–52.
4. Red anchor mark from Red Anchor period *c.*1752–6.
5. Rare mark in under-glaze blue *c.*1748–50.
6, 7. Gold anchor mark of Gold Anchor period *c.*1756–9. Also found on some Derby porcelain painted at Chelsea *c.*1769–75. Occasionally a large anchor is founded in under-glaze blue on blue and white wares.

 1   2   3   4

 5   6   7

Chelsea-Derby
On porcelains decorated at Chelsea after William Duesbury of Derby purchased the Chelsea factory, 1769–*c.*1784.
1. In gold, and infrequently, red.
2, 3. In gold.

 1   2   3

Derby Porcelain Works *c.*1750 – the present day. Founded *c.*1750. Original factory closed 1848. Marks only until this period ends shown below.
1. Incised *c.*1770–80. Occasionally also in blue.
2. Painted *c.* 1770–82.
3. Standard painted mark in puce, blue or black *c.*1782–1800 and in red *c.*1800–25.
4.–6. Printed mark of Bloor Derby *c.*1825–40, *c.*1820–40 and *c.*1830–48.

 1   2   3

 4   5   6

Lowestoft Porcelain Works
Suffolk c.1757–1802.
1, 2. Copies of Worcester crescent
and Meissen crossed swords
marks, in under-glaze blue, on
blue and white wares c.1775–90.
3.–5. Artists' marks on blue and
white wares c.1760–75, usually
painted near or inside foot-rim.

1   2   3   4   5

Minton Stoke-on-Trent 1793–the
present day. Only main marks
shown.
1. Painted mark on porcelains
c.1800–30 often with pattern
number below.
2. Incised or impressed on early
Parian figures c.1845–50.
3. The 'ermine' mark painted,
from c.1850 onwards, with or
without letter 'M'.
4, 5. Printed marks of the 1860s.
6. Standard printed 'globe' mark
c.1863–72.

1   2   3   4   5

6

Plymouth Porcelain Works
Devon. William Cookworthy
1768–70. See also *Bristol*.
1, 2. Chemical symbol for tin in
under-glaze blue or enamels
c.1768–70.

1   2

Worcester Porcelain Factory
c.1751–the present day. First
Period marks to 1793 only given
below.
1.–4. Crescent marks, painted or
printed in under-glaze blue
c.1755–90.
5. Fretted square painted in
under-glaze blue c.1755–70.
6.–9. Letter 'W' painted or
printed in under-glaze blue same
period.

1   2   3   4   5

6   7   8   9

10, 11. Pseudo-Chinese marks
painted in under-glaze blue
c.1753–70.

10   11

12.–14. Meissen crossed swords
usually on wares in Meissen style,
painted in under-glaze blue
c.1760–70.

12   13   14

15.–17. Letters 'RH' for engraver
Robert Hancock and anchor rebus
of Richard Holdship found on
pieces printed in over-glaze
enamel.

15   16   17

18. Crescent painted in blue
c.1783–8, alone or with 'Flight'.

18

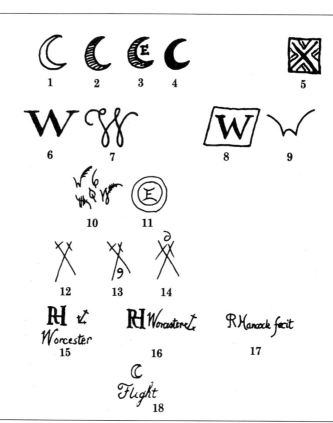

Earthenware and Stoneware

Davenport Longport c.1793–1887.
1,2. Name impressed, sometimes with an anchor. Lower case letters 1793–1810, upper case after 1805.
3. Printed on stone china c.1805–20.
4. Printed, c.1795, sometimes with 'Longport' instead of 'Davenport'.
5. Impressed on wares of all periods.

Doulton & Co. Ltd Lambeth c.1858–1956 and Burslem c.1858–present day.
1. Impressed c.1858 onwards.
2, 3. Painted or impressed c.1882–1902, 'England' added from 1891.
4. Printed or impressed c.1887–1900.
5. Impressed c.1881–1912. 'England' added after 1891.
6. Impressed or printed c.1872 onwards.
7. Impressed c.1888–98.
8. Standard impressed Doulton mark from 1902 onwards. 'Made in England' on all wares from 1891.

Charles James Mason & Co. Lane Delph.
1,2. Standard Patent Ironstone mark 1813–29 used by G. M. and C. J. Mason with 'Improved' added c.1840 and with 'Ashworth' from 1862.
3. Basic mark without the scroll c.1845.

Minton Stoke on Trent 1793 onwards.
1. Moulded mark on moulded wares c.1830–40.
2. Printed mark c.1900–8.

Spode Stoke-on-Trent c.1784–1833. Later management marks not shown.
1,2. Impressed on blue-printed wares c.1784–1800.
3. Impressed on New Stone body c.1805–20.
4. Printed in black c.1804–15 and in blue c.1815–30.
5.–7. Printed c.1805–33.

Josiah Wedgwood & Sons Ltd
Burslem *c.*1759, Etruria *c.*1769.
Later marks not shown.
1,2. Impressed marks *c.*1759–69
3. Standard impressed mark
*c.*1759 onwards. 'England' added
from 1891. 'Made in England'
denotes 20th century.
4. Impressed on ornamental wares
*c.*1768–80 (Wedgwood & Bentley).

5. Impressed or in relief on
garnitures, vases *c.*1768–80.
6, 7. Misleading marks:
Wedgwood & Co. Ltd *c.*1860
onwards and John Wedge Wood of
Burslem *c.*1845–60.

Wedgwood

1

WEDGWOOD

2

WEDGWOOD

3

WEDGWOOD
& BENTLEY

4

5

J.WEDGWOOD

6

WEDGWOOD & CO.

7

Patent Office registration marks and numbers

Diamond-shaped marks, printed or impressed on the base, are
official marks of the Patent Office's Registry of Designs, set up in
1842 to protect manufacturers from plagiarism and piracy. In 1868
the positions of the code letters and numbers were changed, but the
registration mark continued until December 1883, when it was replaced by a serial number. Registration of a design gave three years'
protection, during which time there could be continuous or spor-
adic production of the design or pattern.

Right *Registration mark 1842–67.*
Far right *Registration mark 1868–83.*

a = category IV – ceramics
b = year
c = month
d = day
e = batch number

Date letters:

1842	X	1856	L	1870	Q	January	C
43	H	57	K	71	A	February	G
44	C	58	B	72	I	March	W
45	A	59	M	73	F	April	H
46	I	60	Z	74	U	May	E
47	F	61	R	75	S	June	M
48	U	62	O	76	V	July	I
49	S	63	G	77	P	August	R
50	V	64	N	78	D	September	D
51	P	65	W	79	Y	October	B
52	D	66	Q	80	J	November	K
53	Y	67	T	81	E	December	A
54	J	68	X	82	L		
55	E	69	H	83	K		

Bibliography

General reading
British Porcelain 1745–1840 R. J. Charleston (ed.). 1965.
Collectors' Encyclopaedia of English Ceramics Bernard and Therle Hughes.
  Abbey Library.
A Collector's History of English Pottery Griselda Lewis. Barrie & Jenkins, 2nd
  Edition, 1977.
Encyclopaedia of British Pottery and Porcelain Marks G. A. Godden. 1964.
English Porcelain and Bone China 1743–1850 Bernard and Therle Hughes.
  Abbey Library, 1956.
English Pottery and Porcelain – an Historical Survey Paul Atterbury (ed.).
  Peter Owen.
An Illustrated Encyclopaedia of British Pottery and Porcelain Barrie &
  Jenkins.
Pottery and Porcelain Tablewares J.P. Cushion. Studio Vista.
Nineteenth-Century English Pottery and Porcelain Geoffrey Bemrose. Faber.
Victorian Porcelain Geoffrey Godden. 1961.
Victorian Pottery and Porcelain G. Bernard Hughes. 1959.

Specialized subjects
Blue and White Transferware 1780–1840 A. W. Coysh and R. K. Henry Wood.
  London, 1974.
Caughley and Coalport F. A. Barrett. Faber.
Caughley and Worcester Porcelains 1775–1800 Herbert Jenkins. 1969.
Coalport and Coalbrookdale Porcelains Geoffrey Godden.
Creamware and other English Pottery at Temple Newsam House Peter Walton.
  1976.
Crown Derby Porcelain and Derby Porcelain F. B. Gilhespy. 1961.
English Blue and White Porcelains of the Eighteenth Century Dr Bernard
  Watney.
Davenport Pottery and Porcelain 1794–1887 T. A. Lockett. David & Charles,
  1972.
English Cream-Coloured Earthenware Donald C. Towner. Faber, 1978.
English Delftware F. H. Garner. Faber.
English Porcelain Figures of the Eighteenth Century A. Lane. 1965.
English Transfer-Printed Pottery and Porcelain Cyril Williams-Woods. 1981.
The Leeds Pottery Donald Towner. Faber, 1963.
Longton Hall Porcelain Dr Bernard Watney. Faber, 1957.
Lowestoft Wares Geoffrey Godden. Antique Collectors' Club.
The Illustrated Guide to Lowestoft Porcelain Geoffrey Godden. Barrie &
  Jenkins, London, 1969.
Mason Porcelain and Ironstone 1796–1853 R. G. Haggar and E. Adam.
The Masons of Lane Delph R. Haggar. Lund Humphries, 1952.
Minton Porcelain of the First Period Geoffrey Godden. Barrie & Jenkins,
  London, reprinted 1979.
New Hall and its Imitators D. Holgate. Faber, 1971.
The Pictorial Pot Lid Book H. G. Clarke. 1970.
The Price Guide to Pot Lids and other Underglaze Colour Prints on Pottery
  A. Ball. 1970.
Ornamental Rockingham Porcelain Dr D. G. Rice.
The Rockingham Works Dr Alwyn and Angela Cox. Sheffield City Museum,
  1974.

The Illustrated Guide to Ridgway Porcelains Geoffrey A. Godden. Barrie & Jenkins, London, 1972.

Royal Doulton 1815–1965 Desmond Eyles.

Spode – a History of the Family, Factory and Wares 1733–1833 Leonard Whiter. Barrie & Jenkins, revised edition 1978.

Spode's Willow Pattern and other Designs after the Chinese Robert Copeland. Studio Vista/Christie's, 1980.

Swansea Porcelain W. D. John. 1958.

Staffordshire Pottery A. Oliver. 1982.

The Turners of Lane End Bevis Hillier. 1965.

Underglaze Color Picture Prints on Staffordshire Pottery H. G. Clarke.

Wedgwood Jasper R. Reilly. 1972.

Wedgwood Ware W. B. Honey. Faber, 1947.

The Story of Wedgwood A. Kelly. 1962.

Victorian Parian Ware C. D. Shinn.

Worcester Porcelain Franklin A. Barrett. Faber.

The Illustrated Guide to Worcester Porcelain Henry Sandon. Barrie & Jenkins, 1969.

Royal Worcester Porcelain Henry Sandon. 1978.

Index